INTERNATIONAL BUSINESS PARTNERSHIP

Also by Monir H. Tayeb

INTERNATIONAL BUSINESS
GLOBAL BUSINESS ENVIRONMENT
ORGANIZATIONS AND NATIONAL CULTURE
THE MANAGEMENT OF A MULTICULTURAL WORKFORCE
THE MANAGEMENT OF INTERNATIONAL ENTERPRISES

International Business Partnership

Issues and Concerns

Edited by
Monir H. Tayeb
Heriot-Watt University
Edinburgh

Foreword by
Farok J. Contractor
Rutgers University

First published 2001 by
PALGRAVE
Houndmills, Basingstoke, Hampshire RG21 6XS and
175 Fifth Avenue, New York, N.Y. 10010
Companies and representatives throughout the world

PALGRAVE is the new global academic imprint of
St. Martin's Press LLC Scholarly and Reference Division and
Palgrave Publishers Ltd (formerly Macmillan Press Ltd).

ISBN 0–333–77301–2

This book is printed on paper suitable for recycling and
made from fully managed and sustained forest sources.

A catalogue record for this book is available
from the British Library.

Library of Congress Cataloging-in-Publication Data

International business partnership : issues and concerns / edited by
Monir H. Tayeb ; with a preface by Farok J. Contractor.
        p. cm.
    Includes bibliographical references and index.
    ISBN 0–333–77301–2
    1. International business enterprises. 2. Partnership. 3. Strategic
alliances (Business). 4. International economic relations. I. Tayeb, Monir H.

    HD2755.5 .I53676 2000
    658'.044—dc21   00-048346

10   9   8   7   6   5   4   3   2   1
10   09 08 07 06 05 04 03 02 01

Printed and bound in Great Britain by
Antony Rowe Ltd, Chippenham, Wiltshire

Contents

List of Tables	x
List of Figures	xi
Foreword	xiii
Acknowledgements	xv
Notes on the Contributors	xvi

Introduction | **1**

PART I BUSINESS PARTNERSHIP ACROSS THE FENCE: CONTEXTUAL AND SETTING-UP ISSUES

1 Cross-Border Partnership: The Context | **9**
Monir H. Tayeb

Introduction	9
Home country	9
Host country	10
government political economic ideology and policies	10
legal requirements	14
pressure groups	15
trade unions	15
cultural characteristics	17
global and regional agreements	18
level of economic advancement	19

2 Partner Selection: Motivation and Objectives | **22**
Janine Stiles

Introduction	22
Definition	23
The cooperative/competitive dichotomy	24
Aims of the research	25
Theoretical basis for the study	26
strategic choice – or strategic behaviour – theory	26
international business theory	27
transaction-cost theory	27
game theory	27
the resource-based view	28
Research questions	28
Focus for the study	32

The research method 33
The research findings 34
  underlying forces driving service-sector partnerships 34
  the level of mobility 35
  the level of imitability 36
  the level of uniqueness 37
  the level of value 39
  the level of transparency 40
  the level of complexity 42
  the level of cultural compatibility 43
  the level of experience 45
Final discussion and conclusions 46
Areas for future research 48

**PART II ISSUES OF CONCERN FOR INTERNATIONAL
COLLABORATION: INTERNAL MATTERS**

**3 Autonomy and Effectiveness of Equity International
Joint Ventures (EIJVs)** **55**
William Newburry, Yoram Zeira and Orly Yeheskel

Introduction 55
Hypotheses development 56
  business strategy development 56
  business policy implementation 57
  local-based HRM practices 58
  top executive participation in parent company
  policy-making meetings 58
  resource dependence 59
  dominant parent 60
Methods 61
  questionnaires 61
  independent, dependent and control variables 61
  test procedures 63
Findings 63
  summary statistics 63
  regression analyses 64
Discussion and directions for future research 66

4 Learning in International Joint Ventures **72**
David Pollard

Introduction 72

Learning and knowledge development 73
Internationalization and learning 75
International joint ventures – the learning context 75
Learning and knowledge development in international
   joint ventures 77
    individual level 78
    group level 79
    organizational level 79
Learning in international joint ventures – cross-cultural issues 82
Expatriate deployment and learning 83
Technology transfer and learning 85
The importance of trust in learning within IJVs 86
Learning and the evolution of the international joint venture 86
Learning and networks 87
Cases 89
   case 1 89
   case 2 90
   case 3 91
   case 4 91
Implications for managers in IJVs 92
Concluding remarks 94

**PART III ISSUES OF CONCERN FOR INTERNATIONAL
COLLABORATION: THE CULTURAL CHALLENGE**

**5 Merging Organizational Cultures: Lessons for
International Joint Ventures 101**
Thora Thorsdottir

Introduction 101
Differing views and paradigms 101
Levels of culture 102
Acculturation – theories in anthropology 103
The Social Science Research Council's view of acculturation 105
Acculturation and acquisitions 107
A study of acquisitions from a cultural perspective 108
   cultural analysis of acquisition 1 – consumer wholesale 109
   cultural analysis of acquisition 2 – production 111
   cultural analysis of acquisition 3 – manufacturing 113
   cultural analysis of acquisition 4 – service industry 114
   comparison of group acculturation across cases 116
   cultural compatibility and level at which discrepancy occurs 118

discrepancies between desired modes of acculturation | 120
group acculturative process | 121
Conclusions | 124

6 National Culture and Cross-Border Partnerships | **128**
Monir H. Tayeb

Introduction | 128
National culture and negotiations | 128
communication with others | 129
other people's language | 130
building relationships | 132
attitudes to time | 134
adapting to the partner's negotiation style | 136
National culture and human resource management (HRM) | 138
HRM issues specific to cross-border partnerships | 139
HRM issues and national culture | 140
management style and organizational hierarchy | 143
company language | 144

**PART IV   ISSUES OF CONCERN FOR
INTERNATIONAL COLLABORATION: SIZE MATTERS**

7 Interorganizational Relationships and Firm Size | **153**
Sarah Cooper

Introduction | 153
Economic change | 153
Small firms and new technologies | 154
The small technology-based firm and alliances | 157
Conceptualizing alliances: their appropriateness
  for the small firm | 159
Small technology-based firms and the pressure towards
  alliance formation | 163
technological change | 164
research and development cycles | 164
increasing technological complexity | 165
global competition | 166
barriers to entry | 166
'government' encouragement | 166
market factors | 167
the 'price' of organizational restructuring | 168
Making alliances work | 168

Alliances in biotechnology   172
A twenty-first century view   173

**PART V   BUSINESS PARTNERSHIP ACROSS
THE FENCE IN EUROPE**

8   Interfirm Linkages: The European Experience   179
Sabine Urban, Ulrike Mayrhofer and Philippe Nanopoulos

Introduction   179
Section 1   Primary characteristics of interfirm linkages   183
    geographic layout: going global   184
    distribution among sectors: constant reconfigurations   185
    legal classification: risk-management strategies   187
    underlying strategic and operational schemes: from
      congeniality to force   191
    logical foundations   191
    strategic expression   192
Section 2   The dynamics of linkages: strategy for
  adapting or anticipating?   193
    the evolution of linkages, 1993–98   193
    towards a reconfiguration of actors in interfirm linkages? 194
    strategic alliances and value migration   196
Towards 'co-opetition': trust or treachery?   197
Conclusions   199

PART VI   THE FATE OF THE OFFSPRING

9   The Endgame   205
Monir H. Tayeb

Introduction   205
Failure and success – definitions and criteria   205
Factors contributing to success or failure   207
Culture and performance   211

Index   219

List of Tables

3.1	Summary statistics for independent, dependent and control variables	63
3.2	Pearson correlations of dependent, independent and control variables	65
3.3	Results of hierarchical regression analysis of autonomy variables on IJV effectiveness as measured by GOALS and INDEX 5	66
5.1	Dichotomous answers to questions of acculturation	104
5.2	Varieties of acculturation as determined by group response	105
5.3	Four types of acculturating groups due to variations in freedom of contact and mobility	106
5.4	Acquired firm's modes of acculturation	108
5.5	Levels of culture observed in the present study	109
5.6	Native's views of acquirer and target	110
5.7	Native's views of acquirer and target	112
5.8	Native's views of acquirer and target	114
5.9	Native's views of acquirer and target	115
5.10	Group acculturative states initially, on contact and today	117
5.11	Nature of cultural discrepancy and the levels at which they occur across the cases	119
5.12	Discrepancy in desired mode of group acculturation between acquirers and targets	121
5.13	Variations in group adaptive states depending on physical integration, the group's longing for a relationship and the group's right to choose	123
7.1	Innovation management in small firms	156
8.1	Contents of the CESAG database	183
8.2	Geographic dynamics of linkages undertaken by European companies, 1993–98	195
8.3	Dynamics by sector of linkages undertaken by European companies, 1993–98	196

List of Figures

1.1 Host-country institutions influencing IJVs and ISAs   11

2.1 Classification of sub-groups within service-related industries   33

2.2 Strategic-alliance drivers   35

2.3 The cooperative/competitive matrix   47

3.1 Two dimensions of EIJV autonomy   69

8.1 Range of interfirm links   182

8.2 Geographic distribution of linkages developed by European enterprises, 1993–98   184

8.3 The ten most active sectors for interfirm linkages, 1993–98   185

8.4 Legal forms of linkages undertaken by European enterprises, 1993–98   187

8.5 Legal configuration by activity sector   189

8.6 The distribution of capital in joint ventures by geographical zone (% of total), 1993–98   190

8.7 Axes of a development policy coordinated among several actors   192

8.8 The evolution in number of interfirm linkages undertaken by European companies, 1993–98   193

8.9 The evolution of agreements undertaken by European companies by form of integration in % of total per year, 1993–98   194

8.10 Geographic dynamics of linkages undertaken by European companies, 1993–98   195

8.11 The triangle of corporate strategy   199

Foreword

Man is a cooperative being. Puny and insignificant in physical attributes, even while venturing tentatively out of the putative African homeland they cooperated in bringing down prey and reaping the first harvests. Later, in Adam Smith's pin-making workshop, they demonstrated that division of labour and specialization are but the obverse of collaboration, albeit under one corporate ownership. The era of mass production in the twentieth century carried this idea to its limits, the zenith of vertical integration, where the entire value chain from research or extraction to retail delivery came under the aegis of a single corporation. Just fifteen years ago firms such as IBM or GE prided themselves on 'going-it-alone'. It was the era of internalized ownership, and hierarchical control. Corporate partnerships and alliances hardly figured in OECD economies, but were regarded as curiosities such as licensing contracts or joint ventures mandated by socialist governments as a precondition for market entry.

In the twenty-first century, alliances (a rubric for a wide variety of inter-firm collaboration) are ubiquitous in the major economies of Europe, North America and Japan. According to a recent Arthur Andersen report (Kalmbach, C. and Roussel, C., *Dispelling the Myths of Alliances*, New York: Arthur Andersen, 2000), alliances already account for 6 to 16 per cent of the market value of US companies. They expect this percentage to grow significantly in the next five years. What explains this growth? One explanation lies in the transition mankind is making from an economy based on matter, to one based on knowledge or ideas. In the OECD nations, services displaced manufacturing as the larger component of the economy sometime in the latter half of the twentieth century, and emerging nations are following the same evolutionary path where ideas and services collectively become more valuable than tangible objects. An economy of objects favours mass production, vertical integration and hierarchical control under one corporate ownership. An economy of ideas favours customization, flexibility and rapid response which is often helped by a deconstruction of the value chain, into pieces under different ownership which cooperate with each other.

This is not to suggest that alliances will take over the world, or even be the dominant mode of organization. The prescriptions of transaction cost, internalization and other economic theories remain valid. I simply assert that a fundamental shift has occurred at the margin, in the composition and organization of economic activity, to make alliances act more frequently as useful and superior substitutes to internalized control. Several environmental factors in the twenty-first century are fostering this shift towards greater interorganizational cooperation. Harmonization of standards, reciprocal acceptance of data, and codification of knowledge make the transfer and pooling of knowledge across cooperating organizations easier. The triumph of the Anglo-American concept of intellectual property protection and its global spread under the aegis of WTO and multilateral bodies mitigates the fear of misappropriation of knowledge assets, reduces the problem of valuation of ideas, provides a means of leverage over alliance partners, and provides a framework for licensing and knowledge-based alliances. Acceleration in technical change, the proliferation of multi-disciplinary knowledge sources and escalating costs and risks in R&D, are promoting interfirm cooperation in development. At the same time, there has been a proliferation in the end-applications of new technologies in the final product marketplace. Few companies feel they can handle it all alone. The former arch-exemplars of internalized control, IBM or GE, each have well over a thousand alliances and cooperations with firms all over the planet. Entire departments are devoted to merely track and monitor such arrangements. Information technology is providing the lubricant, and a medium, for rapid logistical and design cooperation by spatially-separated companies. It fosters communication and coordination of allies over the value chain. The end result in some firms is customized designs for end-users who pick and choose their own configurations. The logistical implication of each order is then seamlessly and instantaneously transmitted to each supplier upwards in the value chain, with each alliance partner coming together symphonically to deliver their part, at the right time and place. Other aspects of information technology that foster alliances include codification of knowledge, artificial intelligence systems that partners can tap into, and enabling spot markets to substitute for oligopolies in formerly regulated sectors such as utilities.

This book is itself a testament to cooperation across borders and institutions. Dr Tayeb simply provided an attractive nexus for cooperation which, with a growing reputation for organizing and editing ideas, elicited significant contributions from noted authors. These collected papers, which cover the life-cycle of corporate partnerships from formation to eventual termination, will make a significant addition to our understanding of this still elusive phenomenon. Mankind is still learning the arts of cooperation.

New Jersey   FAROK J. CONTRACTOR

Acknowledgements

This book is the outcome of a cross-border partnership between a group of academics from several countries and a number of members of staff at the UK offices of the publisher.

All the chapters have been specifically written for the book by authors who have a wide range of teaching, research and other professional experience in different parts of the world. I am immensely grateful to all of them for their invaluable contributions, support and encouragement, which made this international joint venture a success story, from inception to completion.

I would also like to take this opportunity to thank the past and present staff of the publisher, especially Samantha Whittaker and Zelah Pengilley, who oversaw the book's editorial and technical work at different times and stages of its life-cycle.

My special thanks go to Keith Povey and Paul Dennison of Keith Povey Editorial Services for their professionalism and impeccable copy-editing.

Heriot-Watt University   MONIR H. TAYEB
Edinburgh

Notes on the Contributors

Sarah Cooper is a Lecturer in the School of Management at Heriot-Watt University, Edinburgh. Her teaching and research interests are in the fields of business strategy, entrepreneurship and the establishment and growth of small, innovative technology-based firms. She has participated in research programmes focusing on technology-based sectors in the UK and North America, the results of which have been published in a range of books and journals. (Contact address: School of Management, Heriot-Watt University, Edinburgh, EH14 4AS. E-mail: S.Y.Cooper@hw.ac.uk)

Ulrike Mayrhofer is a Lecturer in Marketing and International Business at IECS Graduate School of Management and a research fellow at the Centre for Applied and Theoretical Research in Business Administration (CESAG), Robert Schuman University, Strasbourg. She holds a PhD in Business Administration. Her research and publications focus on the management of interfirm linkages.

Philippe Nanopoulos is a Lecturer in Marketing and Quantitative Methods at IECS Graduate School of Management and a research fellow at CESAG, Robert Schuman University, Strasbourg. His research and publications focus on interfirm linkages and media marketing.

William Newburry joined Rutgers University as an Assistant Professor in the International Business/Business Environment Department in September 1999, having previously worked six years at McDonnell Douglas Corporation as a contract administrator. He obtained his PhD in International Business and Management from New York University, and also earned an MA in International Affairs (Washington University) and a BS in Business/Finance (Truman State University). In addition, he attended the University of Tasmania on a Rotary Scholarship. His research interests include autonomy and control issues in multinational corporations, communication and shared perceptions within multinationals, and collaboration in international environmental management. He has published in the *Journal of Management Studies*, *Management International Review*, the *Journal of World Business*, *International Business Review*, the *Journal of Third World Studies*, and the *Academy of Management Best Paper Proceedings*. (Contact address: Rutgers University, Graduate School of Management, 111 Washington Street, Newark, New Jersey 07102 USA. E-mail: newburry@business.rutgers.edu)

David Pollard is currently a Senior Lecturer in Management and manages the international MBA programmes at the Dundee Graduate School of Management, University of Abertay Dundee. Until 1990 he was employed in various multinational companies, in the fields of management services and computer systems management. His current research interests are the management of international joint ventures and business development in transformation economies and in China. His published work includes journal articles, contributions to edited books and he regularly reviews books for various journals. He was a European Union Visiting Professor at Zhejiang University, Hangzhou, China, in 1998. (Contact address Dundee Graduate School of Management, University of Abertay Dundee, Dudhope Castle, Dundee DD3 6HF, Scotland. E-mail: D.Pollard@mail1.tay.ac.uk)

Janine Stiles is Head of Strategic Management at Henley Management College. Her research interests since the early 1990s have been in strategic alliances and value-added partnerships, developing more recently into issues associated with public/private sector partnerships. Janine's publications include a number of articles and book reviews in business journals, co-authorship of a book on finance for the general manager alongside contributions to a number of edited business texts.

Monir H. Tayeb is a Reader at Heriot-Watt University. She has been conducting research in cross-cultural studies of organization since 1976. Her current interest is in the human resource management policies and practices of foreign multinational companies located in Scotland. Her publications include several articles in academic journals, books and contributions to edited books. (Contact address: School of Management, Heriot-Watt University, Edinburgh EH14 4AS, Scotland. E-mail: m.h.tayeb@hw.ac.uk)

Thora Thorsdottir has for the past three years worked as an account manager for a software company specializing in social, market and media research. Previously, she has worked for survey design and survey research companies specializing in human resources. She has also worked in banking, recruitment and the public health sector. Born in Norway, she has lived in Iceland, Canada and Scotland, before settling in Surrey, England. She holds a BA in Psychology and a PhD in Business Organization. (E-mail: Thorat@compuserve.com)

Sabine Urban is a Professor at Strasburg's Robert Schuman University and heads the CESAG/IECS which is affiliated to it. She teaches international economics and corporate strategies in several universities both in France and abroad. She sits on the board of several industrial and financial firms. Her main research fields are international business and the European economy. Her publications include several books on strategic alliances, European economy and business, and similar topics.

Orly Yeheskel is a Lecturer in the Faculty of Management at Tel-Aviv University, in both MBA and Executives programmes. Her fields of interest are international management, strategic alliances and organizational behaviour. Her current research interests include management of international strategic alliances (especially international joint ventures and acquisitions), and human resource management issues in multinational companies. She also serves as a consultant and is involved with executive training and development processes in a number of Israeli companies. (Contact address: Faculty of Management, Tel Aviv University, Ramat Aviv, Tel Aviv, Israel. E-mail: orlyy@post.tau.ac.il)

Yoram Zeira is a Professor of Management and International Business at Tel Aviv University. He has been conducting research on international human resource management and on international strategic alliances since 1975. His current research and consulting interests focus on developing new approaches to improve the pre- and post-incorporation stages of international joint ventures and international acquisitions. He has published widely in most major management academic journals, as well as edited special issues of academic journals dealing with a variety of international management topics.

Introduction

Monir H. Tayeb

Multinational firms play a significant role in our lives, at both national and individual levels. They shift around the globe natural resources, products and services; they recruit people in different countries and introduce 'alien' management styles and 'ways of doing things' into host countries; they create as well as serve various markets, all the while influencing people's tastes and lifestyles as well as accommodating them.

These firms, operating as they do in a highly complex, volatile and competitive world, are extending their presence all over the globe for a multitude of purposes and through a multitude of forms, from simple export and import activities to foreign direct investment and wholly-owned subsidiaries.

International partnerships have been growing in importance in recent years as a choice vehicle for companies to expand their product, geographic or customer reach (Contractor and Lorange, 1988; Gugler, 1992). Between 1990 and 1995 the number of domestic and cross-border alliances grew by more than 25 per cent annually (Bleeke and Ernst, 1995). Such alliances permit multinational firms to spread their limited resources more widely than wholly-owned investments, place less capital investment at risk in any individual transaction, and provide access to complementary resources and skills to enhance the potential to gain competitive advantage in unique local markets (Beamish and Killing, 1996). These arrangements include joint ventures, strategic alliances, R&D partnerships and consortia, and involve technology transfers, licensing agreements, management service and franchising agreements, cross-manufacturing agreements and other strategically innovative business transactions.

Alongside the expansion of cross-border partnerships and strategic alliances, there has been an impressive amount of research into the extent and nature of such strategies and the conduct, operations and mandate of the companies that pursue them. However, most of the research and publications to date have concentrated on international joint ventures and, even then, as Beamish and Killing (1996) point out, full understanding of IJVs is still far away.

The present book is an attempt to contribute to the understanding of major forms of international partnership, including joint ventures. This

1

book, although it is written by a number of authors, is not intended to be a collection of papers as many multi-authored books are (see for instance, Beamish and Killing, 1997a,b,c). Rather, it covers the life-cycle of such partnerships and follows a coherent sequence of steps, from strategic decisions to enter into a partnership, to partner selection, to formation of the partnership, to management issues, and to the final outcome – a prosperous partnership or disengagement. Moreover, the book contains a section in which partnerships between large and small firms are discussed, a strategy whose implications and dynamics are qualitatively different from partnerships between firms of roughly similar size and status.

Although international joint ventures are a form of international strategic alliance and partnership, there is a fundamental difference in terms of depth of involvement of partners between joint ventures and all other forms of international partnerships. And this difference is reflected in the topics covered by the book. As the terminology implies, the companies involved in a strategic alliance join together in an exercise of shared strategies and vision, usually in order to be able to handle their environment and markets more effectively, but not of shared financial and managerial activities. These companies may own a certain proportion of each other's shares, but they do not become a jointly-owned entity and do not lose their independence. They may even exchange senior executives on a reciprocal short-term 'visit' basis, and develop common career management learning and development policies, but they do not merge their employees. Joint ventures move a few steps further than strategic alliances, to shared assets and ownership, pooled skills and knowledge, mixed employees, and joint management.

Some of the issues discussed in the book, such as partner selection and negotiations, are of relevance to all forms of international alliances. Some topics, such as people management and acculturation processes, are relevant only when partnerships deepen into joint ventures. This book itself is a living example of an international partnership and joint venture. The authors live and work in the United States, Israel, the United Kingdom and France. They have conducted research in Asia, Europe and the United States, and form a truly multicultural team, bringing their varied work experiences and cultural heritage into the partnership.

PLAN OF THE BOOK

Chapter 1 sets the scene and context within which cross-border partnerships take place. International alliances between two or more partners, especially those which lead to the formation of a third entity such as a joint venture, are subject to various super-organizational influences which have implications for their ultimate form, operations and internal organization. National political and economic institutions of the partners' home country influence greatly the form a partnership/venture may take. In addition, the institutions of the country which hosts the venture influence the way in which it is set up and run. Moreover, the partnership is subject to rules and regulations of regional and global agreements and institutions to which host and home countries of the partners and their venture subscribe. Chapter 1 will discuss in detail these and other related issues.

Chapter 2 is based on both an in-depth study of previous literature, and on subsequent interview research data which examined 101 alliance partnerships from selected service sector industries. Data were collected and analysed to investigate how the intent with which respective partners in this sector enter an alliance can influence the success of the relationship.

The chapter considers the different objectives and drivers for strategic partnering. It then looks at the implications of these drivers and how they can influence the intent of a particular partner, and the partner choice. Aspects considered from this perspective include the perceived value and individuality of each partner's contributions, the level of mobility with which skills and competencies can be moved from one partner to the other, and/or the extent to which these may be copied.

Once the relationship is established additional factors can influence the realization of the defined intent of a particular partner. The chapter therefore considers this aspect by looking at the level of transparency and the extent to which interlinkages have been created between the partners, national and corporate similarities or difference in culture, and the extent to which a partner has prior experience or partnering, and is therefore prepared or organized in a way which allows it to learn from past experiences. The chapter finishes with a cooperative/competitive matrix of partner intent developed by the author which pulls the above aspects together and considers its practical applicability in enhancing partnership success.

Chapter 3 focuses on the issue of managerial autonomy in cross-border partnerships. A central debate in the international business literature revolves around the issue of how much to coordinate international operations versus how much to adapt to the local environment. There has been a discussion of the forces for global coordination and integration of efforts within a transnational corporation and how these forces play out against forces for national responsiveness and differentiation. A central concept in achieving national responsiveness is that of managerial autonomy. According to the literature, there appears to be a general assumption that equity international joint ventures (EIJVs) should not be given complete autonomy in their actions, concluding that 'instead of accepting the premise that JVs should be controlled to the same extent as wholly-owned subsidiaries or the assumption that control should be divided among parent firms, more fruitful research may begin with the notion that significant autonomy should rest with the JV management' (Lyles and Reger, 1993: 399).

The chapter builds upon this assumption as well as the work of two of its authors (Newburry and Zeira, 1999) concerning equity international joint ventures in Britain and Hungary, by examining when autonomy (evaluated using multiple measures) is correlated with EIJV effectiveness. In the current study, a sample of EIJVs from China, the USA, Britain, Hungary and Israel are examined in order to determine when autonomy is most likely to be correlated with EIJV effectiveness. In general, the model proposes that certain EIJV autonomy measures correlate with EIJV effectiveness no matter where and under what circumstances an EIJV operates, while other autonomy measures are only important in certain situations. By operationalizing autonomy as a continuum of managerial activities, we are able to clarify why some previous authors have found support for granting EIJV autonomy, while others support the opposite viewpoint.

Chapter 4 deals with the question of exchange of information, knowledge and skills. Alliances provide a platform for organizational learning and the firms involved give and get access to one another's knowledge. The significance of the flow of knowledge between partners has been emphasized by many researchers to the extent that it has been argued to be a major motive behind some alliances. This chapter takes a life-cycle view of the learning process in alliances and discusses major relevant issues from various angles.

Differences in corporate cultures of the partners involved play a significant part in the management of alliances especially joint ventures. Corporate culture embodies ways of doing things, such as power structures and control systems, management and leadership styles, and attitudes to investment and risks. Variations in organizational cultures across the parent companies and within the venture might constitute a major impediment to effective implementation and subsequent operations.

In Chapter 5 the concepts of organizational culture, acculturation, at both group and individual levels, and the adoption of anthropological models of acculturation to a new entity formed by partners will be analysed. The chapter will further discuss the change process in terms of how and when culture should be assessed and how culture can be changed and managed (emphasizing that changes cannot be forced). Examples taken from case studies conduced by the author will illustrate and clarify the arguments. The study, although it concerns the merging of organizational cultures in domestic acquisitions, has obvious lessons for international joint ventures which bring together people from two or more different organizations with their distinctive cultures.

The issue of national culture is of great significance in general to all cross-border businesses, especially at the negotiation stage, and to international joint ventures in particular with respect to HRM and other people-management issues. Chapter 6 will accordingly focus on, first, the issues surrounding the process of negotiations and conclusions of alliance agreements with special emphasis on cultural issues, and, second, the ways in which national cultural differences might be reflected in HRM and management styles. It will be argued that these stages of cross-border cooperation require sensitivity to the cultural backgrounds of the partners involved and that cultural insensitivity is a prescription for failure.

Chapter 7 will focus on the issue of international partnerships and alliances from the perspective of small-sized enterprises. The chapter examines the appropriateness of such alliances for small firms and discusses the pressure on them towards alliance formation, with special emphasis on such factors as technological change, research and development cycles, increasing technological complexity, global competition, barriers to entry, government encouragement and market factors.

Chapter 8 provides a window to the trials and tribulations of international strategic alliances as experiences in Europe, especially the EU member states. The chapter draws on an extensive database regarding the EU firms which entered into strategic alliances with major economies, notably the 'Triad' countries, in the period between 1993 and 1998.

Chapter 9 concludes the book by focusing on the last stage of alliances: a prosperous new entity or a parting of the ways and failures. Success and failure will be discussed within the context of international alliances and major contributing factors and arguments will be presented and explored.

References

Beamish, P. W. and Killing, J. P. (1996) 'Introduction to the Special Issue', *Journal of International Business Studies*, vol. 27(5): iv–xxxi.

Beamish, P. W. and Killing, J. P. (1997a) *Cooperative Strategies: North American Perspective* (San Francisco: New Lexington Press).

Beamish, P. W. and Killing, J. P. (1997b) *Cooperative Strategies: European Perspective* (San Francisco: New Lexington Press).

Beamish, P. W. and Killing, J. P. (1997c) *Cooperative Strategies: Asian-Pacific Perspective* (San Francisco: New Lexington Press).

Bleeke, J. and Ernst, D. (1995) 'Is your Strategic Alliance Really a Sale', *Harvard Business Review*, January–February: 97–105.

Contractor F. J. and Lorange, P. (1988) *Co-operative Strategies in International Business* (Lexington: Lexington Books).

Gugler, P. (1992) 'Building Transnational Alliances to Create Competitive Advantage', *Long Range Planning*, vol. 25: 90–99.

Lyles, M. A. and Reger, R. K. (1993) 'Managing for Autonomy in Joint Ventures: a Longitudinal Study of Upward Influence', *Journal of Management Studies*, vol. 30(3): 383–404.

Newburry, W. and Zeira, Y. (1999) 'Autonomy and Effectiveness of Equity International Joint Ventures (EIJVs): An Analysis Based Upon EIJVs in Hungary and Britain', *Journal of Management Studies*, vol. 36(2): 263–85.

Part I
Business Partnership Across the Fence: Contextual and Setting-up Issues

1 Cross-Border Partnership: The Context

Monir H. Tayeb

INTRODUCTION

Business transactions, like so many interactions between people, take place within the sociopolitical context where the actors involved live and work. In the case of international strategic alliances (ISAs), including international joint ventures (IJVs), this context spans more than one set of the sociopolitical domain and is therefore eminently more complex.

International alliances between two or more partners, especially those which lead to the formation of a third entity such as a joint venture, are subject to various super-organizational influences which have implications for their ultimate form, operations and internal organization. National political and economic institutions of the partners' home country greatly influence the form a partnership/venture may take. In addition, the institutions of the country which hosts the venture influence the way in which it is set up and run. Moreover, the partnership is subject to rules and regulations of regional and global agreements and institutions to which host and home countries of the partners and their venture subscribe. The following sections discuss these and other related issues in some detail.

HOME COUNTRY

Freedom of movement of capital across borders and offshore share ownership is a major influencing factor regarding the decision to enter into alliances with foreign firms operating outside one's own country. In most liberal-trade nations, portfolio investment and other forms of share-ownership in foreign firms operating abroad are not hindered by the state, but in protectionist economies the flow of capital from the domestic market to foreign lands are either severely restricted or not permissible at all. For example, the Indian government until recently did not allow, and still continues to control somewhat, the movement of capital overseas to acquire foreign assets. As a result of such policies, the involvement of firms from

India and other fellow protectionist countries in IJVs tend to be in the form of local partners of an incoming foreign investor.

Sometimes, because of home-country taxation policies, companies might prefer to engage in joint ventures, especially with minority equity ownership, rather than set up wholly-owned subsidiaries abroad. As Beamish (1993) points out, tax advantages in the home-country result because in some countries minority ownership is treated as an investment whereas wholly-owned subsidiaries and majority-owned joint ventures are not.

HOST COUNTRY

National culture and other institutions of the country in which an IJV is situated play a significant part in the actual form that the organization and management style of the joint venture will take. In other words, the host country forms the immediate external environment of the IJV with which it has to interact and to whose pressures and expectations it has to respond. Companies undertaking expansion through IJVs need to understand the significant elements of local country culture, especially in terms of initial negotiations and partner selection (see also Chapters 2 and 6).

Major institutions which serve as the channels of influence on an IJV, or any other form of ISA for that matter, generally fall within six broad categories: legal system, political culture, industrial relations culture, level of economic advancement, membership of global and regional agreements and the national culture as a whole. In most countries influences of these institutions on a venture's activities are incorporated in the rules and regulations governing businesses in general, some more explicitly than others. In some countries, there are further rules and regulations which apply specifically to foreign companies, including joint ventures with local partners, operating within their territories, over and above those which apply to all firms. Figure 1.1 summarizes the relationship between ISAs/IJVs and their host country.

Government Political Economic Ideology and Policies

The host country's policies regarding foreign direct investment and the forms it should take within its domain play the determining role. In but a handful of western economies with strong liberal trade traditions governments are usually involved in the decision to allow foreign companies to set up 'shop' on their land. This involvement is either directly through negotiations or indirectly through putting in place the necessary licence

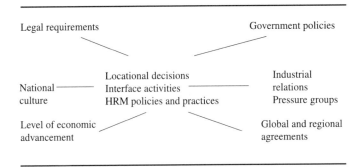

Figure 1.1   Host-country institutions influencing IJVs and ISAs

and permission regulations and requirements. In many of these nations, joint ventures with either the state itself or local private partners are usually preferred to wholly-foreign-owned subsidiaries. The reasons could be anything from purely economic to political and even to cultural or some combinations of all these.

In addition, in the vast majority of these countries the amount of shares allowed to be owned by the foreign partner is determined by the host government and is usually less than 50 per cent to ensure, in theory at least, the domination of the local interest in the venture.

The standing of the host country in the international marketplace as a favourable location for foreign direct investment might also put them in a position to dictate entry terms to foreign suitors. In this connection Gomes-Casseres (1990) also argues that the more attractive a host country market, the more foreign firms will be willing to trade away their ownership preferences for access to the market (see also Ruber, 1973; Lecraw, 1984; Korbin, 1987). China, for example, is considered by multinational companies as one of the major emerging markets, and that in order to do business with her these companies must ideally have manufacturing or other forms of operation presence there. As a British manager once told the present author, 'the Chinese like to have joint ventures for a certain line of product, they do not like one big company coming in saying they can manufacture anything. They [also] like one line of product, and so that is what [many foreign companies currently do]' (Tayeb, 1998: 352). In addition, the local companies which will be their partners are owned and managed by the government.

Sometimes IJVs are not permitted at all in certain industries or sectors of the economy. Until recently, for example, it was widely assumed that the Japanese government would not allow a foreign company to purchase a large part of a Japanese financial group, although it has since changed its policies for, perhaps, practical reasons. In June 1998 the Japanese government threw its weight behind a new alliance between Travelers Group, a US financial services group, and Nikko Securities, Japan's third largest broker. According to a report in the *Financial Times* (2 June 1998: 19), a senior finance ministry official had said: 'We support this because it is in line with our big bang reforms and the liberalization of capital markets. We expect more alliances to emerge'. Nikko's president also emphasized the practical reasons behind the deal: '... The Japanese big bang is a reality and we are witnessing the global consolidation of the financial industry; ... we need partners to be a global winner'. The new venture makes Travelers the largest shareholder in Nikko and represents the biggest equity stake taken by a non-Japanese group in a Japanese bank or broker.

Policies towards foreign investment are of course only a small part of the government's overall political economic policies. The extent to which the state controls trade and other economic and business activities varies from one country to another, with extreme cases at either end of a capitalist–socialist continuum. But a whole series of variations exist in-between, whether or not these countries have declared themselves as capitalist or socialist. Under capitalism the type of activities performed by the government is of necessity limited, whereas this is not the case under socialism. In socialist economies, the formal political apparatus is responsible to a much wider extent in determining who gets 'what, when and how': the political process decides the distribution of resources between various social groups and interests (Lane, 1977).

Beamish's (1993) analysis of a number of studies shows there are clear differences between China, the world's major centrally-planned economy in the 1990s, developed and developing market economies in many policies and practices regarding IJVs. For example the government pressure as the major reason for creating joint ventures and the overall use of IJVs as distinct from other forms of foreign investment are much higher in China compared with market economies.

In most developing countries the government plays an all-pervasive and crucial role in the management of the economy as well as in politics. Almost all of them pursue protectionist industrial and economic policies. And a vast majority of them have centralized non-democratic governments. There are however some variations here. For instance, India, for long a protectionist centralized economy, has recently opened up its market and allowed some degree of trade liberalization. A few years ago, Mexico and Chile, having suffered from the consequences of their debt crises, adopted a decentralized and liberal economic and trade policy, largely as a condition to receive loans from the IMF and the World Bank.

Developing nations can use IJVs as a means to help them acquire new technology, capital and managerial know-how and gain competitive advantage in international markets, yet at the same time maintain a measure of control over the ownership of foreign firms operating within their territories. Moreover, as Beamish (1993: 36) points out, in the majority of these nations 'the requirement to use the joint venture form is more closely linked to particular sectors of the economy. For example, the desire to acquire experience with a new technology can serve as an impetus to a government to require joint venture in that sector'.

In advanced industrialized countries the picture is patchy too. In the United States and the United Kingdom, especially when conservative parties are in power, governments usually adopt a relatively hands-off policy, certainly with regard to the manufacturing sector, compared to their liberal/socialist counterparts. In Japan, France and the newly-industrialized countries of Southeast Asia governments play a more active role in the management of the economy.

The ex-socialist countries of Europe, for instance, are currently in the process of moving from a centrally-planned economy to a more decentralized one, with varying degrees of success. Poland, Hungary and the Czech Republic have gone much further down the road, in both political and economic spheres, than their other fellow central and eastern European countries. In China, from time to time, signs of decentralization of economic policies can be seen. Also, there are regions which are practically run on a capitalistic model; but the political economic system of the country as a whole is still highly centralized and the government is in full control.

The restrictions that some nations impose on foreign direct investment and its form are partly rooted in their history, especially with regard to their political economic relationships with other nations. Recent or distant past conflicts and exploitative relationships with others tend to linger on in a nation's collective memory (Tayeb, 2000). The Opium War (China), East India Company (India) and the 1953 coup d'état staged in Iran by some foreign powers are examples of historical roots of mistrust and suspicion towards foreign investors. Joint ventures with minority foreign shareholdings is perceived, rightly or wrongly, to be a guarantee against such exploitations.

IJVs should not however be seen as a second-best choice and an option that multinationals only reluctantly choose. There are certain advantages in setting up joint ventures with local businesses, such as the partner's knowledge of the local scene and, in some cases, its political connections and ability to work with the bureaucracy and handle myriad other issues. In Russia for instance, as Tallman *et al.* (1997: 185) point out, 'IJVs ... combine the capabilities of foreign companies with local knowledge and contacts, as well as a certain amount of legal protection, thereby reducing uncertainty and potentially providing decreased costs and increased revenues.' In addition, in some 'risk-prone' countries entering into joint ventures with local partners reduces the risk of nationalization without compensation or other politically and economically motivated threats to the foreign partners' investment. These and similar considerations inform multinational firms' proactive strategic decisions leading to engagement in IJVs as opposed to other forms of foreign investment (Porter and Fuller, 1986; Harrigan, 1988; Hébert and Beamish, 1997; see also Chapter 2 in this book).

The foreign partner of an IJV, having scaled the entry hurdles, could be subject to further rules and regulations specifically targeted at such investors. Their managerial prerogative might, for instance, be restricted not only with regard to strategic aspects of the IJV, but also the internal organizational aspects. In China, for instance, the government requires that joint ventures with foreign partners house and feed their workers. Some-times the foreign partners in IJVs voluntarily give up some of their managerial prerogative, especially in the HRM area, because of local complications (see for example Namazi, 2000, on IJVs in Iran).

Legal Requirements

Legal considerations are a major issue addressed by managers in firms of all kinds. Included in these are factors like the substantive laws which have evolved and the societal propensities for their enforcement. In fact legal constraints may be among the strongest environmental pressures for structural and procedural changes facing firms (Rosensweig and Singh, 1991).

Foreign companies operating in a host country, regardless of their ownership and managerial configurations, are subject to that country's laws. Business laws governing foreign firms are quite elaborate in some nations, prescribing procedures which cover all of their activities from registration to the choice of operating sites and human resource management styles. Other laws regarding health and safety, environment, social responsibility and the like could also impinge on the managers' prerogatives. In France, for instance, companies larger than a certain size must provide training for their employees and organize social events and facilitate access to sport and leisure activities and opportunities (Tayeb and Thory, 2000).

It is worth noting that international laws may alter the domestic laws of nation-states over time, prompting their inclusion as a moderator variable. This amalgamation of laws in turn defines not only a range of labour-related issues (see also Chapter 6) but also government–firm relations as a whole. In the case of IJVs and subsidiaries of multinational companies existing restrictions may sometimes be bypassed if alternative arrangements are secured from the host countries through negotiations and proactive strategic initiatives, such as lobbying government ministers and officials and parliament to repeal laws, and to get exemptions. Otherwise the firms are expected to change their policies to achieve compliance throughout the organization; failure to adapt to the prevailing laws can have serious financial and operational repercussions for companies (Florkowski and Nath, 1993).

Pressure Groups

Pressure groups are more successful in some countries than in others, both in terms of their numbers and their influence on government policies, which in turn have implications for business organizations. Pressure groups can aim their activities at various levels: national, regional, local, industry and firm.

Some groups such as anti-pollution and other environmental organizations try to influence government policies through changes in legislation, or even direct action (for example Greenpeace). Some may focus their attention on increasing the general public's awareness about certain issues, such as the harmful effects of some food additives, potential risks involved in genetically-modified foods and the dangers associated with the nuclear power industry. Provisions of child-care facilities for working single parents is another example of the issues that some pressure groups in some countries have fought for and managed to put on governments' and business firms' agendas. The changes thus caused in legislation and consumers' awareness force companies to adopt new policies and take appropriate actions.

Trade Unions

Another way in which nations vary from one another is in their use of trade unions, which are a form of pressure groups. Free and independent trade unions are institutions which are encouraged and flourish in many democratic nations (for example Germany). In some societies, however, unions are rubber-stamping puppets of the regime (for example the pre-1989 eastern and central European countries, China). In yet others they are either non-existent or heavily circumscribed (for example some countries in the Middle East).

The nature of the ideology and activities that unions might adopt also differs from one society to another. For instance, in France unions are highly political and tend to engage in class struggles. The Polish trade union, *Solidarity*, and the Siberian miners of the Republic of Russia in the former Soviet Union are another example of highly politicized labour movements. In Britain, trade unions are more pragmatic and have no intention of overthrowing or challenging the authority of the management or the government. They only fight for their jobs and for better working conditions. Trade unions in the United States are even less militant and more pragmatic than those in Britain.

There are differences, too, in the nature of industrial relations in different countries. In Britain, for instance, the management–workers relationship in many companies is hostile and is characterized by a 'them and us' division. In Japan the unions recruit both management and workers. The character of unions and management is moulded by the company culture, and the relationship between the two sides, if they can be described as such, is based on cooperation and harmony.

Forms of unionization are also different among nations. Trade unions in Japan, for instance, are company-based – Toyota has its own union, as has Nissan and Hitachi. Compare this with Britain where unions are craft-based; that is, transport workers have their own union (Transport & General Workers Union), coal miners theirs (National Union of Mineworkers), teachers theirs (National Union of Teachers) and so on. In a Japanese company there is only one union. Again compare this with the situation in many British companies, especially in the manufacturing sector, whose workers are represented by a number of unions depending on the number of crafts or jobs that the workers and employees perform.

Unions enjoy differing degrees of power depending on where they are situated and under what economic and political conditions they function at any given point in time. As mentioned earlier, free and independent trade unions did not exist in most of the European socialist/communist countries before the 1989 revolutions, and still do not exist in China and other communist countries. The workers who organized themselves as such were quickly suppressed and dispersed by the ruling Party (for example *Solidarity* under Poland's former communist government).

In some countries, such as India, which has traditionally had socialist-oriented policies, the organized sector is relatively very small compared to the total workforce, but industrial relations laws are 'pro' workers and the unions have more power compared to their counterparts elsewhere. However, there are sometimes political motives behind pro-workers legislation. In the pre-1979 revolution Iran, the Shah's regime would attempt to secure workers' loyalty by measures such as compulsory employee profit-sharing schemes and share ownership of medium- and large-sized firms.

Cultural Characteristics

There is little doubt that national culture, of both home and host countries, has a profound bearing on many activities of the firms, foreign or domestic. Within the context of the present book, the host national culture can have implications for what IJVs do but also how they do it. The implications of these for cross-border negotiations and HRM will be discussed in Chapter 6. Here the implications of national culture for other major aspects of IJV activities are examined.

The host country cultural values and attitudes are relevant to IJV interface activities with their customers such as product specifications, sales and marketing. In addition, these same values and attitudes influence the expectations of the public at large from the companies which are located in their community. The ingredients of products and services normally comply with customers' tastes, preferences and taboos or at least should not violate them. The role of religion, traditions, age-old customs and prejudices is significant here, but there is also room for companies to influence and change some of these, at the superficial level at least. The French establishment considers, for instance, certain US-originated soft drinks and fast-food chains as a threat to their way of life and the 'exception française', but the same companies have won over the younger generation and somewhat changed their eating and drinking habits.

Within the same national culture, there also exist subcultures and social strata with their own specific preferences and tastes. In the United Kingdom, for instance, where the vast majority of people are said to be class-conscious, the stereotype might be that working-class people might go to a pub for a drink, usually beer, to spend an evening out, while their middle-class compatriots may frequent wine bars and drink champagne; the former's favourite team sport is soccer football and the latter's rugby football. Whilst this is clearly a stereotype, it may not be too far from the actual situation.

Foreign companies which target specific countries as their export market or location for their investment as an IJV, or a wholly-owned subsidiary for that matter, do well to take these subtle differences into consideration when making products for these markets. A few years ago a Japanese manufacturer of hi-fi systems introduced two different models of one if its amplifiers to the British market, one had a number of flashy features and buttons and was aimed at under-30s pop-music fans, the other had a sombre and graceful look aimed at the over-30s classical-music listeners.

Sales and marketing strategies are also usually adapted to take into account local sensitivities – what works for a secular society could be totally rejected in a deeply religious country. In many nations, the use of a woman's body or racially prejudicial language in commercials is politically incorrect if not a legally punishable offence, in other societies people may not even notice the 'bad taste' in them.

Global and Regional Agreements

As mentioned earlier, international laws could substantially alter the domestic laws that historically structure employment relationships. This generally occurs when a country accepts a new international standard which covers an aspect of work that was previously unregulated or less rigorously regulated by the country. Foreign and local firms alike inevitably become covered by the new standards when the host government signs up to them.

International laws can emerge from global, regional or bilateral sources. The International Labour Organization (ILO), for instance, facilitates the growth of 'universal' labour law through the passage of conventions and recommendations. Conventions articulate legal principles that should be present in the indigenous laws of member-nations, and must be separately ratified by each affiliated sovereignty. Recommendations act as guidelines for government action on issues that are not ripe for a convention or as supplements to existing conventions. Both instruments are designed to furnish minimum standards that do not supplant any law, custom or agreement which already is more favourable to workers (see Tsogas, 2000, for a detailed discussion on the ILO and its influences on business firms). There are of course other global institutions, notably the World Trade Organization, whose member-states are more or less equally covered by its rules and standards of practice. Bilateral treaties may also authorize special arrangements among countries, as exemplified by the Friendship, Commerce and Navigation treaties between the United States and many other nations.

Similarly, regional trade and economic agreements may have profound effects on what foreign and domestic firms can or cannot do within the jurisdiction of member-states. The European Union, with its Single Market which came into force in 1992, is the most prominent example of influence of regional rules and regulations on business firms. A vast amount of directives and laws have been passed since the inception of the Single Market which cover almost all aspects of business activities, harmonizing some, standardizing others, as well as enabling the free movement of capital, services, goods and people within the Union.

With the number of enterprises operating in more than one member-state increasing, managers are having to develop a European approach to their business especially with regard to environmental issues and employee relations. With regard to human resource management, for instance, as Teague (1993) foresaw many years ago, more firms are now operating across national boundaries and greater number of employees are travelling and working in other member-states. As a result of increased contact between employees in different countries, enterprises are having to take on board various pan-EU personnel policies, particularly in relation to wages and working conditions. Moreover, changing expectations within the labour market have also pushed companies in similar directions. For instance, many of the better graduates will only join a company which gives them the prospect of working and living in another European country. In recent years, many of Britain's leading transnational companies have devised programmes in this mould to satisfy such a demand.

Other regional agreements, such as NAFTA (North American Free Trade Agreement), ASEAN (Association of South East Asian Nations) and (AFTA) Arab Free-Trade Area, also have some influences on the business environment of member-states, but not so extensive as those exerted by the EU on its signatories. The last two have in fact a very minimal impact on trade between member-nations let alone common regulations covering activities of companies operating within them (see also Tayeb, 2000, chapter 2).

Level of Economic Advancement

The level of economic advancement and industrialization of a country also has profound implications for companies located there. The availability of a highly-trained and skilled workforce, access to the latest technology, modern information and physical infrastructure such as reliable economic statistics and data, telecommunications, and extensive and properly maintained road and rail networks could make a significant difference to how companies can carry out their day-to-day operational activities and set their future strategic plans and goals.

The world in which international joint ventures and other firms with international business interests work is of course a patchwork as far as the level of economic advancement is concerned. The countries situated nearer the lower end of an advancement continuum will not only have less chance of attracting IJV partners, they also pose challenges that only well-seasoned companies are able to meet. It is not, therefore, perhaps surprising that the bulk of foreign direct investment, both in the form of wholly-owned subsidiaries and joint ventures, takes place between industrialized nations.

In summary, the collaboration of firms across borders brings together many political, economic and sociocultural differences which lead to a very complex and at times volatile business context within which IJVs and ISAs have to operate. Chapter 2 will discuss partner selection and other related issues with such a context as the backdrop.

References

Beamish, P. W. (1993) 'The Characteristics of Joint Ventures in the People's Republic of China', *Journal of International Marketing*, vol. 1(2): 29–48.

Florkowski, G. W. and Nath, R. (1993) 'MNC Responses to the Legal Environment of International Human Resource Management', *The International Journal of Human Resource Management*, vol. 4: 305–24.

Gomes-Casseres, B. (1990) 'Firm Ownership Preferences and Host Government Restrictions: An Integrated Approach', *Journal of International Business Studies*, First Quarter: 1–22.

Harrigan, K. R. (1988) 'Joint Ventures and Competitive Strategy', *Strategic Management Journal*, vol. 9(2): 141–58.

Hébert, L. and Beamish, P. W. (1997) 'Characteristics of Canada-based International Joint Ventures', in P. W. Beamish and J. P. Killing (eds), *Cooperative Strategies: North American Perspective* (San Francisco: New Lexington Press).

Korbin, S. J. (1987) 'Testing the Bargaining Hypothesis in the Manufacturing Sector in Developing Countries', *International Organization*, Autumn: 609–38.

Lane, D. (1977) 'Marxist Class Conflict Analyses of State Socialism', in R. Scase (ed.), *Industrial Society: Class, Cleavage and Control* (London: George Allen & Unwin).

Lecraw, D. J. (1984) 'Bargaining Power, Ownership and Profitability of Transnational Corporations in Developing Countries', *Journal of International Business Studies*, spring–summer: 27–43.

Namazie, P. (2000) 'A Preliminary Review of Factors Affecting International Joint Ventures in Iran', paper presented at the 27th Annual Conference of Academy of International Business (UK Chapter) Strathclyde University, April.

Porter, M. E. and Fuller, M. B. (1986) 'Coalitions and Global Strategy', in M. E. Porter (ed.), *Competition in Global Industries* (Boston: Harvard Business School Press): 315–44.

Rosensweig, P. M. and Singh, J. V. (1991) 'Organizational Environments and the Multinational Enterprise', *Academy of Management Review*, vol. 16: 340–61.

Ruber, G. L. (1973) *Private Foreign Investment in Development* (Oxford: Clarendon Press).

Tallman, S., Sutcliffe, A. G. and Antonian, B. A. (1997) 'Strategic and Organizational Issues in International Joint Ventures in Moscow', in P. W. Beamish and J. P. Killing (eds), *Cooperative Strategies: European Perspective* (San Francisco: New Lexington Press), chapter 8.

Tayeb, M. H. (1998) 'Transfer of HRM Polices and Practices Across Cultures: An American company in Scotland', *International Journal of Human Resource Management*, vol. 9(2): 332–58.

Tayeb, M. H. (2000) *The Management of International Enterprises: A Socio-Political View* (Basingstoke: Macmillan).

Tayeb, M. H. and Thory, K. (2000) 'Human Resource Management Within the Context of Parent–Subsidiary Relationships: A Scottish Experience', paper presented at the 27th Annual Conference of Academy of International Business (UK Chapter) Strathclyde University, April.

Teague, P. (1993) 'Towards Social Europe?', *International Journal of Human Resource Management*, vol. 4(2): 349–76.

Tsogas, G. (2000) 'Labour Standards, Corporate Codes of Conduct and Labour Regulation in International Trade', in M. H. Tayeb (ed.), *International Business: Theories, Policies and Practices* (London Pearson Education), chapter 4.

2 Partner Selection: Motivation and Objectives

Janine Stiles

INTRODUCTION

Strategic alliance management has become a vital part of the toolkit for many businesses trying to compete effectively in today's turbulent and increasingly unpredictable environment. Over the past 25 years the phenomenon has continued to sustain a rapid growth in popularity. It has been embraced throughout the developed world from the United States across Europe to the Far East and is increasingly seen as the key to achieving competitive success when dealing with today's fast-changing global markets.

This continuing trend has helped companies enter otherwise inaccessible markets, brought together sometimes surprising bedfellows, and facilitated the development of new ideas and product offerings, all in the crusade towards achieving customer satisfaction, and competitive advantage. It has also contributed towards change in the industry structure, challenging traditional definitions. The metamorphosis of some business sector structures, and the generation of new ones where, for example, the transformation of the multimedia industry is bringing together firms from traditionally diverse areas, can partly be attributed to the strategic alliance. It can also be seen as the fundamental 'glue' bringing together large networks of firms in many industries – the consolidation and resultant creation of alliance networks in the airlines and telecommunications industries are well-known and frequently reported in the news. Given the dynamics and uncertainty in today's business environment the strategic alliance offers a flexible, responsive and transformational key allowing the holder the possibility of gaining access to a new world of networks, coalitions and opportunities (Doz and Hamel, 1998).

Good alliance management does not, however, happen easily. The history of collaboration is riddled with examples of failed or struggling partnerships where the anticipated value-added benefits of the relationship have been, instead, replaced by unexpected costs and difficulties. Even those alliances which appear to plod along avoiding the major disasters that have befallen others often fail to achieve the full benefits a good strategic partnership can provide, or are commuted by one partner or the other before the true value has been identified or built upon. The statistics consistently reflect a poor picture, regardless of the criteria for evaluation. A survey on the success rate of strategic alliances undertaken by Bleeke and Ernst (1991) found that 66 per cent of cross-border alliances ran into serious managerial problems within the first two years, with a further 19 per cent reporting mixed results. On average over the first four years of the relationship approximately 50 per cent of the alliance population surveyed were recorded as failures. Yet the trend towards alliance management continues to grow undeterred, fuelled by the need to collaborate. The challenge to companies is therefore not if, but how, they should manage a strategic partnership.

Many of the factors contributing to the traditionally high levels of failure for strategic collaboration can be related back to the selection of the partner firm, and the intent with which the partners enter the relationship. This chapter reports on a research project undertaken in this area to understand the key motivational drivers underpinning the objectives of a firm entering an alliance relationship. It also considers the implications of these drivers and how they can influence the partner choice, the intent and expectations of a particular partner firm, and the ultimate development – or destruction – of the relationship.

DEFINITION

Various terms have been used to describe the many different forms of strategic partnering which may be seen to fit within the umbrella term of 'strategic alliance'. These have included 'international coalitions' (Porter and Fuller, 1986), 'strategic networks' (Jarillo, 1988) in addition to the more common 'strategic alliance'. Definitions are just as varied. Some simply reflect different combinations of alliance drivers. Others suggest a highly competitive aspect to the relationship which can unfairly bias the interpretation away from the more cooperative spirit of the approach. A further failure of some of the many definitions that abound is the failure to incorporate the strategic aspect which, it may be argued, is a fundamental distinguishing characteristic of modern-day alliances and therefore needs to be reflected within the definition (Doz and Hamel, 1998). In response to this the definition of the strategic alliance developed for this research was:

> *Coalitions between two or more firms, either formal or informal, who share compatible goals, acknowledge a level of mutual interdependence, and are formed for strategic reasons.*

THE COOPERATIVE/COMPETITIVE DICHOTOMY

As the alliance concept has developed over time, growing in complexity and dimension, partner-objectives of the alliance have also become more sophisticated. Traditionally this form of business operation has been viewed simply as a cooperative arrangement. From this perspective partner firms can be seen to collaborate in order to combine resources and share information, thus gaining from the value-added synergies that such ventures could offer (Berg *et al.*, 1982; Bleeke and Ernst, 1991; Mohr and Spekman, 1994). Cooperative drivers therefore focus upon such aspects as:

• The pooling of resources or capabilities, and the consequent synergies which can be gained within the partnership and used for mutual strategic advantage (Lynch, 1990; Mohr and Nevin, 1990; Lorange and Roos, 1992; Mohr and Spekman, 1994).
• A means of counteracting the depreciation of resources and capabilities over time through imitation by rivals which can result in an individual firm's competitive advantage, and its consequent returns, becoming eroded. Cooperation therefore can potentially provide the opportunity to upgrade both firms' positions comparatively quickly via, for example, new product development and innovation (Grant, 1991; Mahoney and Pandian, 1992).
• Inter-organizational cooperation can potentially assist in the reduction of transaction costs, and therefore promote competitive advantage through increased efficiency[1] (Williamson, 1975; Kogut, 1988; Hennart, 1988).
• Aiding replication of experiential knowledge such as complex organizational routines which may not, otherwise, be easily transferred through the traditional marketplace.

However, in more recent years an increasing amount of research has also revealed a more competitive aspect within this form of relationship. Some firms have been found to deliberately enter alliances in order to appropriate value from the partner firm, potentially allowing the entrant partner to develop a new set of core competencies at a relatively more rapid rate (Kogut, 1988; Hamel, 1990; Lei and Slocum, 1992; Lei, 1993). Thus, where cooperation in the past was viewed as the key driver for the relationship, a new type of alliance driver has been recognized that is aimed at value appropriation. The key focus from this perspective includes:

• The transfer of core competencies or capabilities from one partner to another with the intent that one partner gains at the advantage of the other. Ultimately, termination of the partnership with a resultant skewing of relative power and position of the now competing firms can then occur.

- Induction of a level of dependency in the weaker partner. This can skew influence and control within the relationship and is often a precursor to an aggressive merger or acquisition by the dominant player (Devlin and Bleackley, 1988; Hamel, 1991; Lyons, 1991).
- Effective 'de-skilling' of competencies or processes crucial to the overall process may be encouraged. This can generate a dependence by one partner on the other for such things as components, supplies, design, skills and technologies. This again may speed the possibility of takeover of the weaker partner and/or improve the dominant partners' relative competitive strength in the marketplace once the partnership is curtailed (Hamel, 1990, 1991; Lynch, 1991; Lei and Slocum, 1992; Lorange and Roos, 1992; Lorange, Roos and Bronn, 1992).
- Deliberate calibration of a partner's strengths and weaknesses than would otherwise be possible. As a consequence, the competitive risk in future collisions with that partner may be significantly altered (Hamel, 1990, 1991).

Thus it may be seen that the cooperative and competitive aspects of the strategic alliance appear to have major implications both for the individual partners involved and for the future of the alliance relationship. From the cooperative perspective they can facilitate rapid upgrade of resources and create synergistic benefits associated with economies of scale and efficiency. Competitive drivers will focus, instead, upon skill and competence acquisition, control and market positioning.

Although categorized here, for simplicity, into cooperative and competitive intents, these intents are not necessarily mutually-exclusive. Firms entering partnerships are often faced with a complex mix of intentions towards the alliance that may frequently reflect varying combinations of both cooperative and competitive drivers. How these combine to generate the overall intent of a particular partner, and whether this can be realized, is the objective of the current research into strategic alliance partnerships outlined below.

AIMS OF THE RESEARCH

Most of the prior research undertaken in the strategic alliance field has favoured evaluation of the partnership from either a purely cooperative or a competitive perspective. However, as the above consideration illustrates, competitive and cooperative intents may each be driven by different objectives. It is therefore argued here that it is the combination of both cooperative and competitive characteristics that will tend ultimately to shape the overall intent of an individual partner within the relationship. Thus the emphasis of a firm towards an overall cooperative or a competitive approach to the partnership will be due to the particular combination of both cooperative and competitive drivers of intent to which the firm is responding, and how effectively these are realized within the relationship.

It can logically be deduced from this initial valuation that where two partner firms entering an alliance are responding to different drivers, or experience differing levels of realization, this may in turn result in different objectives for each partner towards the relationship. These may still prove to be complementary. However where they are to some extent opposing, or where one partners' objectives appear more aggressive, this can then create divergence within the partnership and may ultimately result in the destruction of the alliance. In response to this, the aims of the research were to investigate the factors influencing firms in respect of their cooperative/competitive intent in order to gain a better understanding of how to manage strategic alliances successfully.

THEORETICAL BASIS FOR THE STUDY

Six major theoretical streams were identified from previous research into strategic partnering.

Strategic Choice – or Strategic Behaviour – Theory

This theory focuses on the concept of profit maximization through competitive advantage in the marketplace (Harrigan, 1988). The approach builds upon the concept of competitive positioning and how this influences the asset value of the firm (Kogut, 1988). In this respect it would help to explain moves to alter the competitive balance within an industry, or attempts to establish 'strategic symmetry' (Vickers, 1985; Gray and Yan, 1992; McGee, Dowling and Megginson, 1995). However, the application of the theory fundamentally focuses the researcher upon value-creation whilst subordinating any internally competitive considerations. It is therefore argued that the use of this theoretical approach in terms of the current research would impose a bias within the study.

International Business Theory

This theory considers the strategic alliance in terms of its transitionary role in achieving global competitive advantage. It therefore provides a basis within which to consider both cooperative and competitive aspects of the relationship in a relatively less-biased way than strategic behaviour theory allows. It also introduces a dynamic element into the interpretation through its ability to recognize change (Gray and Yan, 1992). However, it may be argued that its transitionary focus could omit relevant consideration of the cross-equity, more stable alliance partnerships that currently exist. Further, it assumes bargaining power as a key variable in creating change in alliance behaviour. As such it may be argued that there is still an element of competitive bias which could necessitate compensatory measures in the analysis.

Transaction-Cost Theory

Theorists from this perspective focus upon the improvement in economic efficiency through inter-organizational cooperation (Williamson, 1975). Thus the choice between open-market operations and collaboration is based on minimizing production and transaction costs – either financial or non-financial – between firms (Kogut, 1988). This theoretical stance allows recognition between the various entry modes into international markets. It also takes into account competitive and collaborative aspects whilst allowing consideration of both tangible and intangible resource contributions. As such the theory allows a good explanation of why alliances are established. However it is less useful when considering their continued development and thus de-limits the investigation.

Game Theory

Game theory considers the firms' movements in terms of a zero sum, sum-positive or sum-negative result. It is therefore applicable in terms of anticipating competitors' reactions to movements of a firm in the marketplace (Hay and Williamson, 1991) and creates an initial framework for analysis relating to both competitive and cooperative issues. It can also be seen to highlight the interdependency aspect of the alliance relationship. However, although providing a useful starting point for the analysis it has often been criticized for being too simplistic and restrictive as a key theoretical structure.

The Resource-based View

Like transaction-cost theory, the resource-based view has its roots in organizational theory (Mahoney and Pandian, 1992). However, it allows recognition of both the tangible and the intangible resources and capabilities of the firm. It considers the alliance from the perspective of a permeable membrane through which access to resources, skills and information is traded through a process of collaborative exchange (Badaracco, 1991; Grant, 1991; Hamel, 1990, 1991). The resource-based view also incorporates the insights of transaction-cost theory by considering the alliance as an alternative to market-based transactions, whilst bringing the competence aspects of the firm into play. Equally the view fits comfortably within the context of organizational economics and may be seen as complementary to industrial organization theory (Mahoney and Pandian, 1992). As such, it was considered that the resource-based view allowed a dynamic, unifying and strong basis for consideration of the alliance concept without imposing bias on the research from the cooperative/competitive perspective.

RESEARCH QUESTIONS

As the above discussion outlined, game theory provides an appropriate starting point for the initial basis for consideration of the cooperative/competitive question. The resource-based school, however, provides the key contribution and overall underpinning for the research. From this perspective a number of key issues were identified from the existing literature.

The level of transferability of resources from one firm to another can vary. At one extreme the mobility of such things as customer lists and process knowledge may be extremely high. At the other extreme tacit knowledge such as politics or experience of operations may not be easily transferable in codified form (Hennart, 1988; Kogut, 1988; Grant, 1991; Peteraf, 1993). Thus, although a strategic alliance between two parties may provide access skills and/or capabilities, the ease with which these may be captured by the other partner firm may vary. Where the immobility factor can be reduced significantly over time via a level of experiential learning, the continuation of an alliance partnership may actually be prolonged until this can be achieved. Where a very high level of organizational specificity exists, it may be argued that this would, then, encourage a continuing cooperative approach to the partnership from the other partner. In contrast, where transferability is relatively straightforward and no prohibitive costs to this approach exist, a competitive or acquisitive intent may be adopted. This leads to:

Proposition 1   To what extent does the mobility of the resources or competencies of a partner firm key to the relationship influence the cooperative or competitive emphasis within the entrant firm?[2]

Where the mobility of the resources or competencies of a partner firm is not feasible, entrant firms may, instead, attempt to imitate or replicate these via internal investment where competitively viable (Grant, 1991). In this case the partnership may simply act as a short-term vehicle to provide sufficient familiarization of the resource or capability to allow effective imitation to occur. However, if the key resources or competencies targeted are based upon highly complex organizational routines, are fused into the firm's corporate culture, or would incur excessive financial costs in relation to the projected benefits, a more cooperative approach to the relationship would be expected to result (Hamel, 1990; Grant, 1991). This leads to a second proposition:

Proposition 2   To what extent does the ease of imitability of key resources or capabilities of a partner firm influence the cooperative/ competitive intent of an entrant firm?

The basic characteristic that underlies the productive value of resources and capabilities is their heterogeneity (Penrose, 1985; Barney, 1991; Peteraf, 1993). This heterogeneity provides the basis of market competition as it results in differing levels of efficiency, utility or superiority within the industry. Thus it may be argued that, to varying extents, all resources and capabilities are unique. This uniqueness may be viewed as an influencing factor of intent in that the more unique – or superior – a particular capability or resource, the fewer alternatives an entrant partner has. Where one partner had control over this type of resource within a partnership, the contribution it represents may eventually be converted into a level of control or power within the partnership and can impose a threat of eventual take-over. In order to redress this dominance it may be argued that the partner is likely to seek, where possible, to acquire and apply it within their own organization. Thus a further research proposition can be formulated to consider:

Proposition 3   To what extent does the level of uniqueness of key resources or capabilities of a partner firm influence the intent with which the entrant firm enters and operates within the alliance partnership?

Although it can be argued that all resources and capabilities have value, variances may occur as the synergistic context of particular resources and capabilities when applied against different variables, or combination of variables, within each firm may differ. Contrasting values may, therefore, exist between similar capabilities and resources when applied to different firms (Peteraf, 1988). If the perceived value[3] to be gained from the acquisition of a particular resource or capability is relatively high, it is likely the partner will consider efforts to internalize it, thus encouraging a competitive approach to the relationship (Hennart, 1988). Conversely, where the perceived value is low a firm is unlikely to make efforts to introduce the resource or capability into their own organization and a cooperative approach is more likely to be favoured. This generates a fourth proposition:

Proposition 4　　To what extent does the perceived value of a partner firm's key resources and capabilities induce a cooperative or competitive intent on the part of the entrant firm?

The four areas outlined above identify the main factors which literature on strategic alliances suggests will influence the cooperative/competitive intent of an entrant firm. However, it is argued here that this intent can only be realized through consideration of an additional four factors. These are discussed below.

It may be argued that the level of openness to, or transparency of, access one partner grants to another to its key resources or capabilities, will have a direct influence upon the success of an entrant firm in pursuing a particular intent (Hamel, 1990, 1991; Grant, 1991). Each firm entering an alliance does so with the intention of either sharing, or combining, some skills or capabilities of its partner. Even those who are characteristically protective will need to offer sufficient contribution to provide an 'entry fee' to the relationship (Hamel, 1990). Where the level of openness remains low a competitive approach to even highly-valued or imitable skills or competencies by its partner is likely to be disappointed. From this the following proposition can be suggested:

Proposition 5　　To what extent does the level of transparency of a partner firm enable/disable the competitive or cooperative intent of an entrant partner?

Alliances can now be used to generate highly complex multiple systems between numerous partners, encouraging a level of interdependence within the relationships (Harrigan, 1986). This multi-partner interdependency can have the effect of dissuading a firm from pursuing a competitive approach towards a particular partner, as the costs of leaving the partnership network may be higher than the direct benefit of skill or competency acquisition from a particular partner. This suggests a further proposition:

Proposition 6 To what extent does the level of complexity of the alliance arrangement support the pursuit of a cooperative or competitive intent by the entrant firm?

Cultural differences have long been recognized as a key cause of partnership disintegration. Different approaches, ways of operating, systems and perspectives can all create tensions between the different players (Harrigan, 1988; Mohr and Spekman, 1994; Mowery, Oxley and Silverman, 1996). Where cultural dissimilarities persist, either in a corporate or national context, it may be argued that partner firms will be less committed to a longer-term, cooperative view of the relationship. They may, therefore, be encouraged to pursue a more aggressive and short-term approach to a partner firm. This suggests:

Proposition 7 To what extent does the level of cultural compatibility of the partners enable/disable a cooperative or a competitive view of the relationship to be pursued?

Previous research in this field has identified a positive link between the level of experience of working in partnerships, and the success rate of the venture (Pekar and Allio, 1994). Thus firms with significant experience appear more able to manage complex and diverse strategic partnerships relatively more satisfactorily than their less-experienced counterparts. It is argued from this that the level of experience can therefore influence the extent to which firms are able to drive through a defined competitive intent in a relationship. This suggests:

Proposition 8 To what extent does the level of experience of partnering relationships enable/disable the ability of an entrant firm to exercise a cooperative or competitive intent?

The propositions above provided the key focus for the research in establishing a theoretical framework for the investigation based on the concepts of intent drivers and realizability drivers within strategic partnerships.

FOCUS FOR THE STUDY

In order to provide a suitable focus for the research the service sector was identified as the basis for the study. Previous research in this field has been strongly biased towards manufacturing-sector studies, suggesting in itself a need to spread investigation into other areas. This argument is further fuelled by strong evidence that the service sector continues to show significant growth in importance amongst industrial economies, and currently constitutes the fastest growing part of international trade (Jones, 1989; Akehurst, 1989). Strategic partnerships within this sector have also been increasing, a trend that is projected to continue into the foreseeable future (Segal-Horn, 1989; Goodman, 1990).

The service sector can be defined in a number of ways. Arguably the most appropriate definition is provided by Akehurst (1989: 6) who specifies inclusion of: 'retail and wholesale distribution, banking, finance and insurance, other business services (legal, advertising, marketing, etc.) hotels, catering, tourism, health, education and welfare services, transport and communication services, other personal services (e.g., laundry, repairs).' Although clearly outlining the parameters of the term 'service sector', Akehurst's definition does, however, highlight the difficulties of focusing on a sector which includes such a wide variety of diverse industries. This posed a potential issue in terms of comparability amongst the population data and therefore required a further refinement.

In determining a relevant sub-group for the study, an initial distinction was made between services which are naturally 'networked' and those which remained as proximity-based.[4] In this context, networked meant those service-sector firms which could rely upon the use of a network to provide their service regardless of their geographical proximity to the point of sale. For firms in this category, separability between the service and consumption of that service had become flexible through the partnering option. In contrast, proximity-based firms were those for which a network may provide some secondary benefit; however, the primary need for the service remained at the 'point of sale'. Here, inseparability between the product and consumption remained fixed. This latter category was excluded from the survey population as it was considered this did not provide an unbiased basis for the research.

The above distinction provided an initial identification of a sub-group for the study; however, a further categorization became evident from the literature. This related to industries which provided part of an integrated solution and were therefore reliant on others within a particular process, and those which reflected sole or complete capability of a particular

	PART OF INTEGRATED SOLUTION	SOLE CAPABILITY
NETWORKED	Advertising, marketing	Transportation, telecommunications, banking, finance and insurance, distance-learning education
PROXIMITY-BASED	Hospital cleaning, laundry, catering, personal services	Retail, medical services, local education and welfare, hotels, legal services

Figure 2.1   Classification of sub-groups within service-related industries

process independent of those around it. Service organizations which were simply the equivalent of outplacements of a parent firm's activity and could therefore be viewed as part of its integrated solution were excluded from the selected sample for the research. It was considered that this forced integration would otherwise impose a bias upon the partner decision-making process.

The above matrix (Figure 2.1) depicts these four factors and the types of service organizations that were considered to relate to the different categories. As can be seen from the matrix, the organizations that complied with both networked and sole-capability characteristics were represented in the top right-hand box. It was argued that focus on this group would offer the least bias in terms of the study, and would also allow a level of comparability between the organizations. The organizations therefore selected for the research-base included those from the airline, telecommunications and insurance industries.

THE RESEARCH METHOD

An initial literature review allowed an evaluation of the existing theories and data on strategic alliances. From this theoretical base the key variables associated with alliance management were identified and used to construct a conceptual framework for the research. This framework then provided an initial level of guidance and structure for the development of the subsequent interview questions. These were piloted and reviewed prior to their application to the main population. A process of interviews rather than questionnaires was selected as this was considered the most appropriate method to use to gain more depth and understanding of the identified issues from the literature. It was also seen to allow potential benefits to be gained by incorporating exploration of the softer core concepts of the research area through inclusion of a qualitative, inductive emphasis within the research process (Parkhe, 1993; Baker, 1994).

Thirty in-depth semi-structured interviews were completed in total, encompassing information on 101 strategic alliances within the telecommunications, airlines and insurance industries. A mix of national, regional and international, small, medium and large, and different-nationality-owned organizations were selected in order to provide a 'fair and true' picture of alliance operation in this sector. Interviewees were key alliance managers and were selected by key informant technique. Each interview lasted for between 2 and 4.5 hours. Where relevant, two managers from the same company involved in a particular alliance attended the interview. Subsequent analysis and evaluation of the data generated from the interviews then allowed a reevaluation and development of the initial theoretical argument and conceptual framework first identified. Extracts from these interviews are used in the following.

THE RESEARCH FINDINGS

Underlying Forces Driving Service-Sector Partnerships

Previous literature has identified some key driving forces for alliance partnerships. These have included globalization, market access, risk and uncertainty, access to technological skills, response to increasing competition and the need to consolidate market position. Data collected in the survey confirmed that a number of objectives for alliance entry existed in line with those noted from the literature. These objectives[5] were categorized into:

- *Product-focused drivers* – encompassing those objectives associated with the need to develop new, or broaden current, product/service offerings and bring them to market ahead of the competition.
- *Market-focused drivers* – which included those objectives relating to the need to establish, or be part of, a large global presence, to gain market knowledge and size, ensure competitive defence and/or to deal with regulatory and political barriers to new market entry.

Market focus

Financial focus   Product focus

Figure 2.2   Strategic-alliance drivers

- *Financially-focused drivers* – referring to objectives associated with a means of maintaining, or improving, the individual firm's financial position under given competitive circumstances (see Figure 2.2).

Examination of the data further showed that the overriding aim for many respondents was the need to retain position and profit margins by entering and operating within one of the growing networks of 'blocks' created within the respective industries:

> We cannot compete with everyone. We end up having megablocks as others ally resulting in block competition of big systems. We need to be in these systems.

Thus the partnership response within service-sector industries demonstrated a direct link with the increasing competitiveness and dynamics of the business environment in which these firms operate. However, it was found that for some there was a reactive aspect overriding their approach to the alliance. For others the alliance strategy was used as a more positive and driven opportunity to move forwards. Further, the majority of evidence collected showed that financial objectives, alongside market-focused objectives, took priority as key drivers for entry into an alliance partnership. Once established, however, product-focused objectives were then pursued by the more productive relationships, but were rarely a sole driving force for the partnership at the beginning.

The Level of Mobility

It has been assumed in previous literature that certain aspects of the firm such as complex operational experience or processes might be viewed as immobile by partner firms, and that the approach to the partnership would, therefore, be influenced by this. Analysis of the data identified a number of characteristics of mobility relative to the competitive/cooperative intent of a partner firm. Where a resource or competence considered key to a relationship was viewed as transferable to the entrant firm without undue cost or difficulty, there was evidence that this engendered a competitive intent within some relationships. Of the responses, 6.9 per cent cited it as a direct intent of entry into the alliance either on their own part, or as a reflective observation of their partner:

> Success is measured in increased number of passenger seats sold ... We may move away from the partnership if we can pull over a massive demand for seats to the US.

The end result was either a termination of the partnership, or acquisition of the weaker partner. A further 6.9 per cent of responses stated that they openly agreed to progress towards an acquisition of the partner at a set date in the future with the assumption of skills/knowledge transfer between the two parties up to that date. In this context the transfer of capabilities simply acted as a means of integrating and developing a staged acquisition. In contrast, where key skills or competencies were viewed to be largely immobile by the partner, a cooperative emphasis was evident (27.7 per cent of responses), with little evidence of transfer of even lower-level operational or technical skills during the lifetime of the relationship. It was notable, however, that such factors as relative differentials in size or reputation between partners could act as a barrier to acquisition intentions from an entrant firm even where mobility was possible. Additionally, where the industry was experiencing a high level of uncertainty, technological change or environmental dynamism, mobility was reduced. In these cases a more stable relationship often developed, with some lower level transfer of skills or competencies occurring.

With reference to the research question on mobility it was therefore deduced from the data that mobility of the resources or competencies of a partner firm key to the relationship does significantly influence the cooperative/competitive intent of an entrant firm. However, the extent to which this occurs will be influenced by the level of complexity and rate of development of the technological environment and the particular dynamics and characteristics of the industry.

The Level of Imitability

The literature-based research suggested that where imitability occurs it may be viewed as an alternative to the transference – or mobility – of key skills or competencies within a partnership (Grant, 1991). However, key factors influencing imitability were found to have a strong focus on influences external to the partnership. These included such things as cost, speed and time required, and pace of the external environmental dynamics. In contrast, those influencing the mobility factor were more associated with internal factors including complementarity of contributions, relative size of the partners, and the complexity of the key skills and competencies identified.

In terms of the extent to which the levels of imitability influenced the intent of a partner firm, no responses cited imitation as a viable alternative to address a situation where low levels of mobility had been identified. However, where evidence of mobility existed of some key skills or competencies in the product-focused category, some level of imitation was recognized in conjunction with mobility (33 per cent responses). This was mainly to assist in the development of particular skills or competencies between partners:

> We do imitate each others reservations systems, we developed modifications to ours after learning about the partner's ... we get ideas from them and develop them.

A further 6.5 per cent of respondents who had already been identified as either pursuing largely mobile objectives, or had the intent to buy the partner out, also appeared to use imitation to compound the process. Thus, rather than being an alternative to mobility, it was argued from the analysis that imitability should be seen as a more externally-oriented extension of the mobility factor. These aspects should therefore be considered as acting together as, or as part of, the same continuum of influence, condoning or reinforcing the cooperative/competitive emphasis.

In response to the research question posed in this respect, it was therefore considered that the ease of imitability does significantly influence the competitive/cooperative intent of an entrant firm, but should be considered as an extension of the mobility factor rather than an entirely separate variable.

The Level of Uniqueness

Previous literature has suggested that, to varying extents, all resources and capabilities are unique due to the different levels of efficiency, utility or superiority with which they are used by a particular organization. It is the level of uniqueness that can, therefore, influence the cooperative/competitive intent of a partner firm.

A number of factors were identified from the data which influenced the extent to which a particular key skill or competence might be considered to be unique. The most significant included the reputation of the partner, the relative size of the partner firm, the existing network the partner firm belonged to, and the cultural understanding or locational advantage of a particular geographic region. These characteristics could reduce alternative options for the entrant firm. From the data collected, 32 per cent of responses identified that some level of uniqueness did exist in terms of a partner firm's market presence, thus strongly relating this driver to locational access or existing network entry. This significantly limited the choice of partner:

> We don't come empty handed. We come along and say if you let us in you will become a member of a worldwide network... we have 300 operations around the world.

A further 11.8 per cent of respondents suggested that skills development was partially specific and therefore to some extent reliant upon the selected partner. This most frequently related to a particular partner's skill of operating within, or understanding of, the local market. An additional 10 per cent of responses noted an element of uniqueness in respect of technology development. In these cases the partner firm was viewed as critical in providing a key part of the technological skills relevant to the relationship.

Just over 10 per cent of all partnerships surveyed were planned to result in a buy-out by one of the partners in the future. All of these were notable in respect that the partner being bought out retained a significant level of uniqueness in their key skills or competencies relevant to the partnership. A further 34 per cent of the relationships recognized that both partners contributed unique skills or competencies to the relationship. They were thus pursuing objectives which could not be achieved through another partner. These relationships were planned to remain stable with no anticipation of take-over or disbandment by either firm involved:

> Both are equal partners, each has one element which is needed by the other for them to work, this provides a good symmetry, neither is dominant.

In contrast, an additional 17 per cent of the partnerships in the survey had recently been disbanded. It was notable that all of these were rated as having a low level of uniqueness in terms of the key skills or competencies brought to the partnership.

With reference to the research question posed, it was therefore considered that the level of uniqueness of a key skill or competence can significantly influence the level of competitive or cooperative intent of an entrant partner. However, where both partners are characterized by equally high levels of unique resources or competencies, this can encourage a higher level of stability within the venture and, in that context, both competitive and cooperative approaches may be generated within a relationship by this driver.

The Level of Value

The value of a key resource or capability of a partner firm had been identified from the literature as influencing the level of competitive/cooperative intent adopted by the entrant partner. Analysis of the population data indicated that a significant number of objectives associated with the market-focused category of drivers were viewed by respondents as highly valuable. Market presence was noted in 96 per cent of responses, with gaining of market size, the ability to leapfrog political barriers, and achieving competitive defence all cited in 45–48 per cent of responses:

> It has cost us very few international customers but we have been able to get a world-wide distributor through (our partner), so this is value added success around the world.

Noticeably, 17 per cent of the respondents in this category identified value as being fundamental to their individual organization, rather than to the mutual partnership. Over half of these were later dropped by their partner and the relationship terminated. The remaining respondents, who claimed mutual advantage, were scheduled for take-over by their partner.

Between 58 and 69 per cent of respondents identified a high level of value associated with the product-focused category of drivers. However, the emphasis upon individual rather than mutual value was even higher here, with 73 per cent citing technology development, and 100 per cent of respondents noting that individual acquisition of skills development, should it occur, would be most valuable when transferred to their own organization, rather than as part of the mutual relationship:

> It is not only cultural awareness, but in technical skills, in economic, taxation, law etc, all have to be improved to benefit the organization, this is our aim. Alliances allow skills gain, it is an element.

A number of factors were cited which were seen to limit the extent to which value could be transferred to an individual partner. Of the responses, 28.3 per cent and 18.3 per cent respectively cited the scope and size of the respective partner as being a key limitation in terms of value-creation to the individual firm. This was largely in relation to the broadening of the product/service range, and to gaining market size, presence and knowledge in a previously unrepresented geographical or product area. Also, 16.7 per cent of responses noted the cost involved and the consequent cost/benefit of the investment in terms of its perceived future contribution to the organization:

> The value our partner brings is significant. We cannot transfer or imitate this as costs are too high.

Synergies already generated by the mutual relationship, regulatory barriers and the pace at which transfer could be undertaken were also noted as key limiting factors. Thus it may be suggested that it is the value as perceived by the entrant firm which will influence the extent to which a competitive approach will be adopted by that partner. However, this value will be judged in relation to the benefits/limitations of transfer which are identified.

With reference to the research question posed, analysis of the data therefore suggested that the extent of the *perceived relative* value of a partner firm's key resources and capabilities can contribute towards a cooperative/competitive intent to be pursued by an entrant partner.

The Level of Transparency

The level of openness, or transparency of a partner firm, the literature suggests, will have a direct influence upon the realizability of a cooperative/competitive approach by an entrant partner. Initial investigation of this aspect focused on identifying the factors in a relationship that influenced transparency. These were found to operate at two different levels. At one level were those factors which were determined by the initial assumptions and agreements of the partnership, and a second level could be associated more with ongoing operational issues. Both levels are discussed in detail below.

From the initial-assumptions level of factors, the most frequently noted in the dataset was the perceived permanence of the partnership (15 per cent of respondents). This was thought to encourage a more flexible and open approach to the partnership and encouraged more commitment although it could take time to achieve. Equity investment – noted by 10 per cent of the respondents – was also viewed as a tangible sign of permanence in this respect:

> It is felt that equity involvement produces longer lasting links…This creates a symbolic value and strengthens the relationships…The learning aspect is existent all the time but the overall aim is to achieve complementarity and aim to develop together.

Trust and clear recognition of expected mutual benefit was also noted by 12.5 per cent and 5 per cent of respondents respectively as encouraging a greater level of openness and cooperation within the relationship:

> We also have a China venture which is not making much at present, it has no focus on gaining trust and loyalty. It is very key that you trust your partners.

At the operational – or ongoing – level, 20 per cent of respondents noted that the level of communication had an influence upon the level of transparency which could be achieved. Where this was poor it created barriers, or at the very least extended the length of time needed to gain expected returns from the partnership. Emphasis upon staff exchange and joint training were also noted by 15 per cent of the respondents:

> You need to make sure that the key people in the office are experienced to other people in the partnership, not isolated. See that people understand they are part of a big family.

The need for regularity and frequency of meetings, alongside the need to establish and develop a good operational structure for the partnership where clear mutual goals were identified and supported (15 per cent and 7.5 per cent of respondents respectively) were also seen as having a direct bearing on transparency levels.

The data also evidenced that different levels of transparency could be attributed to different industries. Levels of transparency were considered to be relatively lower in the telecommunications industry, than with the insurance or airlines industries, with 13.8 per cent of respondents from the telecommunications sector registering disappointing levels of transfer achieved against expectations. As this sector is currently characterized by a greater level of competitive dynamics and environmental uncertainty, this is likely to be a reflection of a more defensive stance by firms in this industry.

Thus in terms of the research question it was deduced from the data that the level of transparency of a partner firm can enable/disable the competitive or competitive intent of an entrant partner. However, the extent to which this is seen to occur will depend upon the original expectation level set by the entrant partner, and will be influenced by the dynamic context of the industry environment.

The Level of Complexity

The level of complexity, or integration between the partners is also a key factor which was identified for consideration. From the data, complexity was found to consist of a number of elements including: integrated technical assistance, equity investment, shared systems, network membership, shared operations, joint training, joint board arrangements and shared marketing. Of these, shared technological skills and assistance were found to be the most common interlinking aspect, noted by 20.2 per cent of respondents:

> They [the partners] have also increased what they do together in terms of information exchange, technical overheads and general handling so there are economies in synergies achieved in this respect.

Equity investment and shared systems were also high on the list, with 18.3 per cent of respondents noting these as significant. A further 15.4 percent noted the use of network membership and joint technical assistance. For small firms in particular, the network advantage was seen as a significant factor; for some of these it even provided a protected market within which they could operate and develop their expertise:

> In future there are likely to be three global alliances. These will be in a strong position to gain economies of scale, so that will happen, but there will be a lot of infrastructure needs too so profit will be based more on value added success. We have the market hand there as we can supply infrastructure services for global services and find a niche within a partnership.

It was found from the data that different aspects of interlinking approaches could be related to different areas of realized intent. Factors associated with network membership, joint marketing, training and joint board membership appeared to encourage purely cooperative realization of intentions. In contrast, where equity investment, technical assistance, shared systems and operations existed there was evidence of mixed levels of cooperative and competitive strategies being achieved. Firms with a clear integrative focus solely upon technical integration had the highest levels of competitive realization of intent at 36.4 per cent of responses. The number of interlinkages was also relevant. 72.7 per cent of respondents with four to six aspects interlinked reflected both cooperative and competitive characteristics which tended to result in both a stable and a learning approach to the relationship.

With reference to the research question posed, it can therefore be deduced that the level of complexity does support the pursuit of a cooperative/competitive intent but will depend upon the extent and type of interlinkages established.

The Level of Cultural Compatibility

Literature on business partnerships identified that national and/or corporate differences can have an impact on the ability of either partner to realize a chosen cooperative or competitive approach. Where low levels of compatibility exist this can encourage a lack of commitment to a long-term relationship and, therefore, facilitate a competitive perspective. Conversely where high levels of compatibility are evident, a longer-term cooperative approach can be more easily established. Analysis of the sample data showed that 58.6 per cent of respondents noted corporate culture as significant in forming and maintaining a good relationship, whilst 44.8 per cent identified the need for high levels of national cultural compatibility in this context.

Problems stemming from poor national and corporate culture were acknowledged in 20.7 per cent of responses, which caused a strain on the relationship:

> You experience a different business culture. If someone with a German business culture is confronted in a meeting the German tends to be careful, but UK and US people tend to be typically more open … (the partner) is not a typical [our organization] culture, though it is very conservative, they may have to change.

Despite fairly widespread recognition of the problems associated with cultural incompatibility, the interview data showed that a number of factors acted to limit the possible choice of partner, thus sometimes leading to little alternative for a firm than to enter a partnership with some level of recognized incompatibility existent. The most significant of these was the need to gain agreement from, and availability of, a chosen partner. Thus there was a need for both partners to recognize potential benefits from the relationship. The relative size of the partner was a further recognized limiter of partner choice. Where a culturally compatible partner was relatively small, it was often rejected due to its inability to offer the size advantages being sought. Conversely, a much larger partner could impose too much control or dominate a smaller organization:

> Governments and large organizations like to deal with other large organizations, it is difficult for small companies to make alliances ... cultural differences can get in the way.

The level at which the agreement for partnerships was made, alongside geographical/market requirements and language restrictions, are also influencing factors on partner choice, thus affecting the selection process further:

> [The partner] is strong in Germany, we can use this. Also politics precluded an alternative of working with a non-German company. You need them to lobby for you in that country.

Despite these limitations, evidence from the survey confirmed that where partners had achieved good cultural matches, this had a strong positive impact on intent realization. Of respondents pursuing positive, long-term cooperative and competitive learning approaches, 83.3 per cent noted a high level of corporate and national compatibility.

Of those firms that reported low levels of corporate and national compatibility, 85.7 per cent were pursuing short-term competitive intents focusing on skill or competence acquisition. For some, cultural incompatibility had developed over time as both partners had grown apart. As a result fewer benefits were being gained by the partners and increasingly competitive approaches could be seen to be developing with some of these:

> There is also a difference in culture now. We used to have a common interest ... everyone was working for the same thing. Now we all have a different philosophy.

In terms of the research question posed earlier, it was therefore suggested from the evidence summarized above that although sometimes difficult in reality to achieve, cultural compatibility does influence the extent to which a cooperative/competitive intent can be pursued within a partnership.

The Level of Experience

It has been argued that a higher level of experience of partnering will lead to increasing levels of confidence and understanding of how to manage and use the relationship to the best advantage. It is therefore worth considering the influence of experience upon the realization of an entrant partner's intent.

The data was analysed to compare different levels of experience within the population. Of the respondents, 61.5 per cent said they had high or significant levels of experience in partnering (classified as 15 years or over). At the lower end, only 19.2 per cent felt they were inexperienced in this respect (classified as less than 7 years). In relation to the approaches to the partnership pursued, 33.3 per cent of the firms with high or significant levels of experience were pursuing a complex, stable cooperative and competitive learning approach to the relationship. These relationships were gaining from long-term synergies of the partnership and also benefiting from skill/technology exchange. Only 19.2 per cent of the inexperienced firms were in the same position. In comparison, 40 per cent of those with little experience found the relationship was prematurely disbanded compared with only 16.6 per cent of the experienced firms.

There was, however, evidence that the level of experience should also be considered in connection with the level of learning in an organization. In this respect, size was a relevant factor. Larger organizations appeared to find it more difficult to learn from previous partnership experiences, and to disseminate this throughout the organization. Additionally, poor communication and an unsupportive organizational culture could throw up additional barriers to learning:

> Where people who work for you have experience of bad alliances this is a good learning experience we can use. We do have a meeting which is supposed to look at problems with past ventures as part of its meaning, however I think information on mistakes or where things go wrong with alliances is very badly shared. Although we are trying to learn, we are just not very good at it yet.

In response to the research question posed it can therefore be considered from the evaluation above that the level of experience of partnering relationships can enable/disable the ability of an entrant firm to exercise a cooperative or competitive intent. However, the extent to which it does so will also be influenced by the learning ability within the organization.

FINAL DISCUSSION AND CONCLUSIONS

The dynamic and complex nature of the strategic alliance can engender both cooperative and competitive responses from the partners involved. These responses can prove to be a decisive factor in establishing the basis of the partnership and, in its potential direction, orientation and success. In response to this, this research was undertaken in an attempt to gain more understanding of what influences the intent with which partners enter and operate within an alliance arrangement in service-sector industries. The ultimate aim was to improve understanding of these issues and therefore to encourage more successful management of this form of organizational arrangement in this sector in the future.

Taking a resource-based view for the investigation, the research confirmed that levels of mobility, imitability, uniqueness and value all contribute towards the overall cooperative/competitive intent with which an entrant partner will view, and attempt to operate within, an alliance relationship. However, mobility and imitability, although both recognized as relevant forces acting upon the intent of a partner, were found to be directly linked, the imitability aspect simply reflecting a more externalized form of mobility. It was also concluded that the extent to which these factors influenced a level of cooperative and/or competitive intent was also related to the level of complexity and rate of development of the technological environment and the particular dynamics and characteristics of the industry.

Where a key skill or competence of a partner was considered to be relatively unique, was transferable in some form, and was not mirrored by the other partner's contribution to the alliance, this could engender a competitive approach by the other partner. However, where this manifested itself in a straightforward appropriation strategy, any potential longer-term synergistic benefits were lost to both partners. In contrast, where transfer proved to be problematic or where both partners brought relatively unique contributions to the relationship, a more mutual longer-term, synergistic approach was adopted by both partners. In the more productive of these relationships the competitive aspect of intent was then used as a more positive learning vehicle.

In terms of value, intent was strongly influenced by the extent to which mutual or individual value was considered to provide the greatest benefit, skills and technology-transfer tending to be viewed as providing more individual than mutual benefits once the relationship was established. The overall intent adopted was, however, also influenced by the relative size, scope or market/industry influence of the partner. Where this was extensive or the partner had strong network links, the pursued intent tended to be on a more cooperative basis, with the competitive factor used in a more positive, learning approach.

The factors noted above provided the basis for the development of a cooperative/competitive matrix (see Figure 2.3). With reference to the matrix, where cooperative and competitive influences on intent by a partner were low (box 1), the relationship had little to sustain itself from that partner's perspective and could be expected to be disbanded by the partner in the near future. This relationship was described as static as it had little dynamic sustainability or potential.

Where the cooperative approach by a partner had a high influence but few competitive influencers were present, they would be expected to pursue a synergistic relationship which could focus upon value-creation between the partners involved (box 2). At the opposite extreme where the competitive influencers took priority with little cooperative emphasis present, a short-term value-appropriation strategy to the partnership could be expected to be pursued (box 4).

In situations where both cooperative and competitive drivers exerted significant and relevant levels of influence upon the intent of a partner, this appeared to generate a longer-term synergistic relationship which also succeeded in converting the acquisitive competitive approach into a dynamic learning approach towards the relationship (box 3). This box on the matrix was labelled 'dynamic' as it reflected both the learning element in the relationship whilst also representing partners who would try to move the relationship over time towards a mutually-agreed merger or friendly acquistion as both firms developed increasing linkages and synergies between the partners involved.

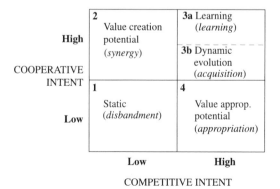

Figure 2.3   The cooperative/competitive matrix

However, it was found that the ability to realize any of these particular strategies needed to be related to the second set of drivers identified from the study. These included the extent to which the partner firm allowed access to its skills and resources (transparency), the complexity, level and type of interlinkages between the two partners, national and corporate cultural compatibility (within the limitations of choice available), and the prior experience of partnering. In these respects the level of openness of the partner firm was identified as being relative to the initial expectations of the entrant partner. It could also be reduced where the industry was experiencing highly dynamic and uncertain characteristics. Equally, the level of experience had to have been translated into a learning element within the organization to be relevant in this context.

The matrix demonstrates that in plotting an entrant partner's driven objectives and subsequent position on the matrix, and relating this to the perceived driven objectives of the other partners in the alliance, any differences in intentions of the partners involved which could prove to be incompatible in the relationship can be clearly identified. Additionally, it highlights relative positions where the full potential of a relationship may not be realized and therefore could provide grounds for readdressing an alliance strategy. It also allows a view of the relationship as the dynamic entity it is by providing facility for a projection of its development. It can, therefore, also assist in providing recognition and mapping future potential changes between alliance partners' aims and objectives, given the known influences on intent discussed above.

In order to address the potential pitfalls of alliance relationships it is therefore recommended that potential alliance partners consider the basis of a potential relationship in terms of the above factors. These factors also require constant review given the importance of the changing dynamics of both the business environment and industry characteristics identified. Change in any of the above factors could indicate a change in the cooperative/competitive interest of a partner firm. It is also worth considering a review of the relationship in positions where potential value or benefits are being missed. In this respect, efforts by both partners to achieve a stable, 'dynamic' position where both cooperative and competitive approaches are providing added value can be seen to offer the most significant potential.

AREAS FOR FUTURE RESEARCH

This chapter has reported an exploratory project into the drivers of intent in service-sector strategic-alliance relationships. In terms of future research, quantitative studies building on the findings of this study would add further validation to the work currently completed. It would also be valuable to compare and contrast the existing results with research on alliance relationships in service-sector organizations within the rapidly developing industrialized economies of the Far East such as China where the influence of relationships is much more forceful and socially related. Extension to encompass other service-sector industries additional to the three investigated here would also help to broaden the research and provide additional insights in this field. Finally, consideration of a comparison between manufacturing and service-sector organizations in terms of the model suggested in this research would help to provide further insights into successful management of the alliance phenomenon.

Notes

1. These costs might include both financial and non-financial costs such as the loss of specific knowledge or those associated with uncertainty, or supplier/buyer power.
2. 'Partner firm' being the 'other' partner in the alliance and 'entrant firm' representing the firm from which the perspective is being viewed.
3. It should be noted that value should be measured both in terms of the initial added value benefit, and in the level of sustainability of that benefit that can be maintained (Grant, 1991).
4. The author would like to acknowledge the contribution of Professor Yves Doz in developing the sub-group classifications for the focus adopted here.
5. It should be noted that these categories were not mutually exclusive and many companies evidenced more than one objective in the data collected.

References

Akehurst, G. (1989) 'Service Industries', in P. Jones (ed.), *Management in Service Industries* (London: Pitman).

Badaracco, J. L. (1991) *The Knowledge Link* (Mass.: Harvard Business School Press).

Baker, T. (1994) *Doing Social Research* (London: McGraw Hill).

Barney, J. B. (1991) 'Firm Resources and Sustained Competitive Advantage', *Journal of Management*, vol. 17: 99–120.

Berg, S. V. Duncan, J. and Friedman, P. (1982) *Joint Venture Strategies and Corporate Innovation* (Cambridge, Mass.: Oelgeschlager, Gunn and Hain).

Bleeke, J. and Ernst, D. (1991) 'The Way to Win in Cross-Border Alliances', *Harvard Review*, November–December: 127–35.

Devlin, G. and Bleackley, M. (1988) 'Strategic Alliances – Guidelines for Success', *Long Range Planning*, vol. 21(5): 18–23.

Doz, Y. and Hamel, G. (1998) *Alliance Advantage* (Boston, Mass.: Harvard Business School Press).

Goodman, R. L. (1990) 'Insurance: Bold Leaps in a Game of Inches', *McKinsey Quarterly*, no. 4: 112–31.

Grant, R. M. (1991) 'The Resource-Based Theory of Competitive Advantage: Implications for Strategy Formulation', *California Management Review*, vol. 33(3): 114–35.

Gray, B. and Yan, A. (1992) 'A Negotiations Model of Joint Venture Formation, Structure and Performance', *Advances in International Comparative Management*, vol. 7: 41–75.

Hamel, G. (1990) 'Competitive Collaboration: Learning, Power and Dependence in International Strategic Alliances', unpublished thesis, University of Michigan.

Hamel, G. (1991) 'Competition for Competence and Inter-partner Learning within International Strategic Alliances', *Strategic Management Journal*, vol. 12: 83–103.

Harrigan, K. R. (1988) 'Joint Ventures and Competitive Strategy', *Strategic Management Journal*, vol. 9: 141–58.

Hay, M. and Williamson, P. (1991) *The Strategy Handbook* (London: Basil Blackwell).

Hennart, J. F. (1988) 'A Transaction Costs Theory of Equity Joint Ventures', *Strategic Management Journal*, vol. 9: 361–74.

Jarillo, J. C. (1988) 'On Strategic Networks', *Strategic Management Journal*, vol. 9: 31–41.

Jones, P. (1989) *Management in Service Industries* (London: Pitman).

Kogut, B. (1988) 'Joint Ventures: Theoretical and Empirical Perspectives', *Strategic Management Journal*, vol. 9: 319–32.

Lei, D. (1993) 'Offensive and Defensive Uses of Alliances', *Long Range Planning*, vol. 26(4): 32–41.

Lei, D. and Slocum, J. W. (1992) 'Global Strategy Competence-Building and Strategic Alliances', *California Management Review*, Fall, vol. 35: 81–97.

Lorange, P. and Roos, J. (1992) *Strategic Alliances Formation, Implementation and Evolution* (Oxford: Blackwell).

Lorange, P., Roos, J. and Bronn, P. S. (1992) 'Building Successful Strategic Alliances', *Long Range Planning*, vol. 25(6): 10–18.

Lynch, R. P. (1990) 'Building Alliances to Penetrate European Markets', *Journal of Business Strategy*, March–April: 4–8.

Lyons, M. P. (1991) 'Joint-ventures as Strategic Choice – a Literature Review', *Long Range Planning*, vol. 24(4): 130–44.

Mahoney, J. T. and Pandian, J. R. (1992) 'The Resource-Based View Within the Conversation of Strategic Management', *Strategic Management Journal*, vol. 13: 363–80.

McGee, J. E., Dowling, M. J. and Megginson, W. L. (1995) 'Cooperative Strategy and New Venture Performance: The Role of Business Strategy and Management Experience', *Strategic Management Journal*, vol. 16: 565–80.

Mohr, J. and Nevin, J. R. (1990) 'Communication Strategies in Marketing Channels: A Theoretical Perspective', *Journal of Marketing*, vol. 54: pp 36–52.

Mohr, J. and Spekman, R. (1994) 'Characteristics of Partnership Success: Partnership Attributes, Communication Behaviour, and Conflict Resolution Techniques', *Strategic Management Journal*, vol. 15: 135–52.

Mowery, D. C., Oxley, J. E. and Silverman, B. S. (1996) 'Strategic Alliances and Interfirm Knowledge Transfer', *Strategic Management Journal*, vol. 17: 77–92.

Parkhe, A. (1993) ' "Messy" Research, Methodological Predispositions, and Theory Development in International Joint Ventures', *Academy of Management Review*, vol. 18(2): 227–68.

Pekar, P. and Allio, R. (1994) 'Making Alliances Work – Guidelines for Success', *Long Range Planning*, vol. 27(4): 54–65.

Penrose, E. T. (1985) *The Theory of the Growth of the Firm: Twenty Five Years Later*, (Uppsala: Acta Universitatis Upsaliensis).

Peteraf, M. A. (1993) 'The Cornerstone of Competitive Advantage: A Resource-Based View', *Strategic Management Journal*, vol. 14: 179–91.

Porter, M. E. and Fuller, M. B. (1986) 'Coalitions and Global Strategy', in M. E. Porter (ed.), *Competition in Global Industries* (Boston: HBS Press).

Segal-Horn, S. (1989) 'The Globalisation of Service Firms', in P. Jones (ed.), *Management in Service Industries* (London: Pitman).

Vickers, J. (1985) 'Pre-emptive Patenting, Joint Ventures, and the Persistence of Oligopoly', *International Journal of Industrial Organization*, vol. 3: 261–74.

Williamson, O. E. (1975) *Markets and Hierarchies: Analysis and Antitrust Implications* (New York: Basic Books).

Part II
Issues of Concern for International Collaboration: Internal Matters

3 Autonomy and Effectiveness of Equity International Joint Ventures (EIJVs)

William Newburry, Yoram Zeira and Orly Yeheskel

INTRODUCTION

This chapter utilizes data collected from a sample of 412 EIJVs located in China, the USA, Britain, Hungary and Israel to examine the effects of multiple dimensions of autonomy on EIJV effectiveness. Study results suggest that numerous measures of autonomy are correlated with IJV effectiveness including: permitting EIJVs to formulate strategic business plans independently, permitting IJVs to implement strategic business plans independently, permitting EIJVs to develop local human resources management (HRM) policies, structuring the EIJV so that it has a dominant parent, and ensuring that an IJV is less resource-dependent. Additionally, there is a positive correlation between EIJV age and effectiveness and a negative relationship between parent company goal similarity and EIJV effectiveness. The chapter concludes with a discussion of our results as well as future research.

The issue of how much autonomy, if any, to grant an equity international joint venture (EIJV) is currently a major issue faced by both researchers and practitioners. A literature review reveals conflicting findings regarding the correlation between autonomy and effectiveness. Experienced CEOs of multinational corporations (MNCs) have also reached conflicting conclusions. Some CEOs concluded that 'parents should make it as easy as possible on alliance managers by ignoring details and allowing them to operate as a separate entity' (Gates, 1993: 23). Others 'maintain that parents should be involved in daily management', without delegating an excess amount of authority (Gates, 1993: 23). Application of these opposing viewpoints has implications regarding the way EIJVs are managed as well as on their patterns of interactions with stakeholders in their host countries. This chapter expands upon previous work by the study authors to examine whether autonomy constructs previously examined in limited country settings apply on a worldwide basis. Previous work has indicated that a theory on EIJV autonomy may be developed which transcends parent country culture (see Newburry and Zeira, 1999).

For the purpose of this examination, an equity international joint venture (EIJV) is defined as a separate legal organizational entity representing the partial holdings of two or more parent firms, in which the headquarters of at least one is located outside the country of operation of the joint venture. This entity is subject to the joint control of its parent firms, each of which is economically and legally independent of the other (Shenkar and Zeira, 1987: 547). While more specific autonomy dimensions will be discussed later in this chapter, autonomy generally refers to the level of freedom that an EIJV has to operate without parent company interference. Starting from an underlying assumption that EIJVs receive their basic mission from their parent companies (as specified and constantly updated in their documents of incorporation), this chapter operates under the premise that autonomy is a multidimensional construct and that these dimensions are each related to EIJV effectiveness.

Within this chapter, we empirically examine a number of potential autonomy variables and their relationship with EIJV effectiveness based upon a sample of 412 EIJVs located in China, the USA, Britain, Hungary and Israel. The following section develops a series of six hypotheses based upon various dimensions of autonomy. This section is followed by a discussion of the study's methodology. Next, we present the findings of this research study. Finally, we conclude with a discussion of our results as well as future research.

HYPOTHESES DEVELOPMENT

The following section outlines a series of six hypotheses that relate to various dimensions of autonomy within multinational corporations.

Business Strategy Development

Chandler (1962: 13) defined strategy as '... the determination of the basic long-term goals and objectives of an enterprise, and the adoption of courses of action and the allocation of resources necessary for carrying out these goals'. Similarly, Learned *et al.* (1969: 15) defined strategy as 'the pattern of objectives, purposes, or goals and major policies and plans for achieving these goals, stated in such a way as to define what business the company is in or is to be in and the kind of company it is or is to be'. Ackerman (1994) found that inadequate strategies were the number-one cause of joint venture failure. Since strategy is such a central concept to any organization, it is not surprising that it is commonly discussed with respect to EIJVs. For example, Hamill and Hunt (1993) identified two main reasons for EIJV failure as attempts by one partner to limit the delegation of authority and disagreements over operating strategies, policies and methods. They noted that while centralized authority may be necessary to integrate an EIJV into an MNC's overall strategy, 'failure to delegate decision-making power, however, will be resented at [the] local level and will create pressures for decentralization' (1993: 257). Additionally, Bleeke and Ernst (1993: 25) concluded that 'a partnership is best able to resolve or avoid conflicts when it has its own management team and a strong board with operational decision-making authority'. They also found that allowing an EIJV flexibility in formulating its strategies and procedures enables it to quickly analyse opportunities and threats within its host-country environment. These sentiments are echoed by other authors who have found that autonomy in strategy formulation improves EIJV effectiveness (for example Harrigan, 1985; Lyles and Reger, 1993; Zeira and Parker, 1995; Newburry and Zeira, 1999). Based on the above, we suggest the following hypothesis:

Hypothesis 1 EIJVs which have the freedom to develop and implement business policies independently will be more effective than IJVs which have less freedom to do so.

Business Policy Implementation

Jemison (1981: 605) noted that strategy implementation was closely aligned with 'the understanding and development of systems to operationalise the desired strategies'. Zajac (1990) expressed the viewpoint that while strategy implementation has generally been studied independent of its context, this may be an artificial segregation, since appropriate implementation tactics are often determined by context. Within the EIJV context, Bleeke and Ernst (1991: 132) found that 'operating decisions are best made by managers whose sole focus is the JV'. Similarly, Xuan and Graf (1996: 73) noted that 'parent companies should stay behind and should not intervene in the decision making of the JV executive'. The authority to implement strategy autonomously was also found to positively affect EIJV effectiveness by numerous other researchers (for example Killing, 1983; Harrigan, 1985; Hamill and Hunt, 1993; Lyles and Reger, 1993; Zeira and Parker, 1995; Newburry and Zeira, 1999). This argument logically follows from all of the reasons stated within hypothesis 1. Additionally, the necessity seems to be amplified as strategy implementation inherently involves interaction with the community where the strategy will be implemented. Thus, hypothesis 2 is proposed as follows:

> *Hypothesis 2*   EIJVs which have the freedom to implement their strategic business plans independently will be more effective than IJVs which lack the freedom to do so.

Local-based HRM Practices

As noted by Schneider and Barsoux (1997: 128), 'any international company hoping to implement a global strategy must choose the human resource policies and practices that will best support that strategy... Unfortunately, the same policies will not produce the same effects in different cultural contexts'. Inkpen and Li (1999) noted that 'we continue to be surprised at how many firms involved in international joint ventures are inadequately prepared to deal with national culture issues'. Antoniou and Whitman (1998) found that success of SinoWestern EIJVs was based upon the ability to understand the values of the ventures' human resources. Typical work behaviours vary across cultures, as do appropriate managerial styles. Managers of global companies must be sensitive to managerial problems associated with misperceptions and misinterpretations across cultures (see for example Adler, 1991). Adopting a polycentric HRM system allows managers to be more sensitive to the cultural beliefs and attitudes of local populations and, accordingly, reduces the risk of these problems and any reduced effectiveness that may be associated with them. Similarly, numerous authors have found that it is important for EIJV parent companies to maintain a commitment to polycentric HRM policies (for example Pucik, 1988; Lane and Beamish, 1990; Zeira and Shenkar, 1990; Zeira and Parker, 1995; Newburry and Zeira, 1999). Accordingly, our third hypothesis is proposed as follows:

> *Hypothesis 3*   EIJVs which have the freedom to independently develop and implement local-based HRM practices will be more effective than those which lack the freedom to do so.

Top Executive Participation in Parent Company Policy-making Meetings

Participation generally refers to the degree to which employees in an organization are involved in decision-making processes. In the case of EIJVs, it could be said to pertain to the degree to which EIJVs are involved in making decisions regarding the EIJV. As noted by Cordery (1998: 402), 'participation may be said to increase as the degree of subordinate influence over decisions increases from no influence … to joint decision making'. Participation may be seen as an indicator that a joint venture has established a separate identity from its parents. Akerman (1994) noted that joint ventures with more separate identities were generally more satisfied with their overall effectiveness. Within the loosely-coupled system of an EIJV and its parents, participation in parent company meetings serves as an indicator of parent company confidence in the ability of an EIJV top managerial team to make meaningful contributions in the decision-making process for the EIJV. Two ways in which these contributions can occur are through the transfer of knowledge regarding the local joint venture marketplace (Si and Bruton, 1999) and by providing knowledge obtained from the EIJV's other partners (Shenkar and Li, 1999; Larsson *et al.*, 1998). Accordingly, it is suggested that when this occurs, EIJVs will be more effective. Accordingly, hypothesis 4 is proposed as follows:

Hypothesis 4   IJVs whose top executives are allowed to participate more in parent company policy-making meetings will be more effective than IJVs whose top executives participate less in parent company meetings.

Resource Dependence

Gates (1993: 20) stated that 'the most effective means of maintaining control is simply to keep the alliance dependent on the parent's contribution'. Lyles and Baird (1994) found that assistance from the foreign parent had a positive relationship with EIJV effectiveness. Indeed, many EIJVs are formed with the main objective of combining resources from the EIJV parents (for example Contractor and Lorange, 1988; Llaneza and Garcia-Canal, 1998). If these resources are not provided, the joint venture is likely to fail. However, being too dependent upon resources and assistance may also lower an EIJV's autonomy. Harrigan (1985: 335) noted that 'unless the child was allowed to stand on its own … it could not hope to operate autonomously'. An EIJV that depends upon its parents for most resources has no ability to act independently. Without autonomy, an EIJV tends to find it difficult to adapt to an uncertain environment, which in turn may inhibit EIJV effectiveness. While the issue of dependence is one of considerable debate, numerous authors have described the necessity to decrease

IJVs dependence in order to increase their effectiveness (see for example Koot, 1988; Bleeke and Ernst, 1991). Thus, hypothesis 5 is proposed as follows:

> *Hypothesis 5*   EIJVs which are less dependent upon their parents for resources will be more effective than those which are more dependent.

Dominant Parent

The question of whether an IJV should be managed by a single dominant parent versus being jointly managed by a combination of parents is one of great debate. Killing's (1983) seminal work found that EIJVs with dominant parents were more successful EIJVs. Similarly, Salant and Shaffer (1998) found that unequal investments by joint venture profits produced higher overall profit for the venture than when investments are equal. Newburry and Zeira (1999) also found that dominant parents were more effective. Looking specifically at foreign parent dominance, Appell *et al.* (1999) advised that foreign firms going into China should maintain dominant control of their joint ventures. In contrast, Lyles and Baird (1994) found a negative relationship between foreign parent dominance and EIJV performance. Classifying a parent as dominant implies that the parent is deeply involved in the daily operations of its EIJV(s). However, in practice, this is usually achieved by appointing its managers to the most important key positions in the EIJV and providing them with the autonomy to run the venture.

As noted by Killing (1983) and Hoon-Halbauer (1994), the parent assuming the dominant position should be the one that possesses the capabilities necessary to effectively run the EIJV. It might be noted that while the EIJV dominant parent is not necessarily the foreign parent, these parents often do dominate since they generally possess some type of necessary input that is unavailable in the local market. It is suggested here that with the comfort of their own personnel in charge, dominant EIJV parents will give their EIJV managers the ability to pursue actions autonomously. Combined with a clear sense of direction (due to the managers' close ties to the parent company), it is thus proposed that these EIJVs will be more effective. Accordingly, we propose hypothesis 6 as follows:

> *Hypothesis 6*   EIJVs that are managed by the appointees of their dominant parents will be more effective than those without such a management style.

METHODS

The study reported here is a part of a larger ongoing international comparative study which has been conducted by one of this paper's authors since 1985 to understand ways of increasing EIJV effectiveness. The following sections describe the questionnaires used within our study, the operationalizations of our dependent variables, our test procedures, and our respondents.

Questionnaires

As the main basis for gathering data for this study, prevalidated questionnaires were sent to EIJV CEOs. We mailed the questionnaires to the CEOs since we consider them to be key informants due to their role as liaisons between parent companies and their EIJVs. Due to their unique role, they have an intimate knowledge of how parents interact among themselves as well as with their EIJVs, since they are responsible for achieving the goals specified within their documents of incorporation (Rafii, 1978). This approach to data gathering is widely accepted in this field (for example Hannan and Freeman, 1984; Carter, 1990). The questionnaire items enabled EIJV managers to rate the extent to which various EIJV characteristics and procedures were typified within their organization and the extent to which the EIJVs achieved various goals.

Independent, Dependent and Control Variables

The independent variables within our study were operationalized as follows. Each was measured by a single item on a five-point Likert scale.

BUSSTRAT (H1) measures the degree to which an EIJV develops and implements business strategy independently of its parent organizations. **IMPLPLAN** (H2) measures the degree to which an IJV implements its business policy independently of its parent companies. **LOCALHRM** (H3) measures the degree to which an EIJV develops and implements human resource practices independently based on host-culture characteristics. **PARMTGS** (H4) measures the extent to which top EIJV managers participate in most parents' policy meetings concerning the EIJV. **RESDEP** (H5) measures the extent to which the EIJV depends on one or more parents for most resources. **DOMPAR** (H6) measures the degree to which an EIJV has a dominant parent with appointees responsible for running the venture independently regardless of the parent's equity ownership.

Our control variables were operationalized as follows. **LOGAGE** represents the log of the age of the EIJV in years. **LOGSIZE** is generated as the log of the number of employees in the EIJV. **SAMEGOALS** relates to whether the parent companies established the EIJV to achieve similar goals, with responses ranging from almost completely similar goals to goals are almost completely dissimilar. **INCORP** measures the degree to which the EIJV has very detailed documents of incorporation.

The main dependent variable in our analysis is EIJV effectiveness. Following in the path of previous authors who have shown self-rated measures of effectiveness to be well-suited to studying EIJVs (Geringer and Hebert, 1989; Anderson, 1990), our questionnaire respondents were asked to rate the extent to which their EIJVs accomplished the following effectiveness measures:

A   achieve their goals as specified and up-dated in their documents of incorporation;
B   meet the expectations of their stakeholders;
C   have a growing market share;
D   are financially profitable;
E   meet targeted growth objectives;
F   meet targeted profit objectives.

Effectiveness measures B through F were chosen because our content analysis of EIJV documents of incorporation indicate that they are the most frequently mentioned goals (see also Dobkin *et al.*, 1994). These measures of EIJV effectiveness are widely accepted in the literature (Killing, 1983; Schaan, 1983; Beamish, 1984), and their results have been found to correlate significantly with financial measurements of the same variables (Dess and Robinson, 1984; Geringer and Hébert, 1989, 1991). Additionally, as noted in Zeira and Parker (1995), usage of a variety of measures helps account for the fact that companies from different countries often pursue different objectives. For the EIJVs in our sample, the internal reliability of the six items was found to be quite high (Cronbach alpha = 0.83), suggesting a common underlying factor.

Considering this internal consistency among the six measures and the magnitude of the correlation of A with the other five (B–F) measures (0.83), the subsequently reported statistical analyses were initially run utilizing only the first dependent variable, goal achievement as specified and updated in the documents of incorporation. This variable is subsequently reported as **GOALS** and is measured on a five-point scale, with responses ranging from five (achieved all goals) to one (achieved no goals). Since different EIJVs are established to achieve different goals, this appears to be a more accurate effectiveness measure than utilizing specific effectiveness measures. All the other subgoals are shared by most, but not all, EIJVs. As an additional test of our data, a general effectiveness index was created by averaging across the remaining five items of our survey and reported below as **INDEX5**.

Test Procedures

We tested our hypotheses by running Pearson correlations between our hypothesized autonomy measures and EIJV effectiveness. In addition to testing the existence of individual relationships between each of the hypothesized variables and the two measures of effectiveness (GOALS and INDEX5), a set of hierarchical linear-regression models was run to determine the best possible combination of factors for predicting EIJV success.

FINDINGS

Summary Statistics

Table 3.1 presents summary means and standard deviations for the dependent variables, GOALS and INDEX5, the six hypothesized independent

Table 3.1   Summary statistics for independent, dependent and control variables

	N	Mean	Std. devn	Min	Max
Dependent variables					
GOALS	404	3.723	0.917	1	5
INDEX 5	341	3.882	0.780	1.4	5
Autonomy variables					
BUSSTRAT (H1)	408	3.152	1.304	1	5
IMPLPLAN (H2)	408	3.721	1.143	1	5
LOCALHRM (H3)	412	3.925	0.952	1	5
PARMTGS (H4)	340	2.812	1.378	1	5
RESDEP (H5)	338	3.435	1.283	1	5
DOMPAR (H6)	412	3.364	1.422	1	5
Control variables					
IJVAGE	410	7.127	6.492	1	55
IJVSIZE	410	2.501	0.726	0.3	4.5
SAMEGOAL	409	2.190	0.982	1	5
INCORP	410	3.698	1.119	1	5

variables (in the order hypothesized) and the control variables. Responses for the independent and dependent variables were given on a five-point scale. For the variables relating to our six hypotheses, BUSSTRAT (H1), IMPLPLAN (H2), LOCALHRM (H3), PARMTGS (H4), RESDEP (H5) and DOMPAR (H6), a score of five indicates strong agreement with the previously stated variable descriptions. The same statement applies for the control variable INCORP. LOGAGE and LOGSIZE are self-explanatory. For SAMEGOAL, a score of five indicates that an EIJV's parent companies have goals that are almost completely similar, while a score of one indicates that goals are almost completely dissimilar.

Table 3.2 presents Pearson correlations for the dependent variables, GOALS and INDEX5, the six hypothesized independent variables and the control variables. There are strong significant positive correlations between the autonomy measures, BUSSTRAT (H1), IMPLPLAN (H2) and LOCALHRM (H3) and both our measures of effectiveness. These results give strong preliminary support for hypotheses 1, 2 and 3. DOMPAR (H6) is also significantly correlated with IMPLPLAN in the case of the INDEX5 effectiveness variable, but not in the case of GOALS. While the DOMPAR correlation with GOALS is not significant, it remains in the hypothesized direction. Thus, partial support is obtained for hypothesis 6 as a result of the Pearson correlations. Table 3.2 shows no significant correlation between either PARMTGS (H4) or RESDEP (H5) and either effectiveness measure. Thus, no support for these hypotheses can be interpreted as a result of the Pearson correlations.

With respect to the other variables in the matrix, the control variables EIJVAGE and SAMEGOAL are both significantly correlated with both dependent variables. EIJVSIZE is also correlated with INDEX5, but not with GOALS.

Regression Analyses

Table 3.3 summarizes the regression analyses for our GOALS and INDEX5 dependent variables. Presented in the table are models with only our control variables and models presenting both the control variables and the hypothesized variables. For the model with GOALS as a dependent variable the partial F-statistic that measures the contribution of the hypothesized variables given that the control variables are in the model, is 11.7 and its p-value is 0.0001. For the model with INDEX5 as a dependent variable, the partial F-statistic is 17.46 and its p-value is 0.0001. In both cases the contribution of the hypothesized variables is highly significant. These statistics indicate that collectively our autonomy variables provide a high

Table 3.2   Pearson correlations of dependent, independent and control variables

	INDEX 5	GOALS	FORM PLAN	IMPL PLAN	LOCAL HRM	PARMTGS	RESDEP	DOMPAR	EJJV AGE	EJJV SIZE	INCORP	SAME GOAL
INDEX 5	1.000											
GOALS	0.731***	1.000										
BUSSTRAT	0.331***	0.247***	1.000									
IMPLPLAN	0.374***	0.333***	0.432***	1.000								
LOCALHRM	0.230***	0.189***	0.185***	0.220***	1.000							
PARMTGS	-0.109	-0.028	-0.029	-0.005	-0.121	1.000						
RESDEP	-0.068	-0.080	-0.039	-0.007	-0.127	-0.063	1.000					
DOMPAR	0.109**	0.056	0.055	-0.072	-0.178	-0.071	0.518***	1.000				
EJJVAGE	0.126**	0.181***	-0.007	0.037	0.043	0.102*	-0.165	-0.168	1.000			
EJJVSIZE	0.124**	0.055	0.061	0.119	0.112	-0.150***	-0.077	-0.093	0.154	1.000		
INCORP	0.048	0.029	-0.027	0.173	0.057	-0.031	0.014	0.150***	0.085*	0.026	1.000	
SAMEGOAL	-0.114**	-0.122*	-0.005	-0.043	-0.177	-0.047	0.083	0.154***	-0.044	-0.133***	-0.121	1.000

*** $p < 0.01$; ** $p < 0.05$; * $p < 0.10$.

Table 3.3   Results of hierarchical regression analysis of autonomy variables on EIJV effectiveness as measured by GOALS and INDEX 5 (for each regression the table presents the standardized estimates (beta) and the adjusted R-Square)

	GOALS		INDEX 5	
	Only control variables	*Control and autonomy variables*	*Only control variables*	*Control and autonomy variables*
EIJVAGE (Control)	0.210***	0.255***	0.125**	0.173***
EIJVSIZE (Control)	0.056	0.002	0.107*	0.039
SAMEGOAL (Control)	−0.152***	−0.155***	−0.080	−0.071
INCORP (Control)	0.009	0.022	0.027	0.049
BUSSTRAT (H1)		0.120**		0.169***
IMPLPLAN (H2)		0.267***		0.265***
LOCALHRM (H3)		0.093*		0.155***
PARMTGS (H4)		−0.062		−0.092*
RESDEP (H5)		−0.133**		−0.163***
DOMPAR (H6)		0.262***		0.300***
Adj. *R*-square	0.063	0.228	0.027	0.264
N	307	307	312	312

$*p < 0.1$; $**p < 0.05$; $***p < 0.01$.

degree of explanatory power above that provided by the control variables. This is also indicated by the significant improvement in r-square from the control models to the hypotheses models. In the GOALS models, the r-square increases from 0.063 to 0.228 as a result of our hypothesized variables. In the INDEX5 models, the r-square increases from 0.027 to 0.264.

Looking at the individual hypotheses, five of the six hypotheses received at least marginal support for both dependent variables. The strong support for hypotheses 1, 2 and 3 in both the Pearson correlations and the Table 3.3 regressions is consistent with Newburry and Zeira (1999) and the other previous authors mentioned in the development of these hypotheses. The fact that these variables are also highly correlated with each other indicates that they might be part of a common underlying factor, as was previously found in Newburry and Zeira (1999). Thus, it appears that this study is able to extend previous study results to a broader world sample.

While DOMPAR (H6) is only marginally significant in the Pearson correlations, and RESDEP (H5) is not significant (although its correlation coefficient is in the hypothesized direction), both of these variables achieve strong significance in both the GOALS and INDEX5 regression analyses. In interpreting these results it should be noted, however, that resource-dependence and dominant parent are highly correlated (0.518). This may be causing the regression model to overestimate their significance. The strong correlation between the two indicates that they might also be part of one overarching autonomy dimension. The only hypothesis that was not supported at all was hypothesis 4, which dealt with EIJV top-executive participation in parent company policy meetings about the EIJV.

DISCUSSION AND DIRECTIONS FOR FUTURE RESEARCH

Overall, our analyses find support for the majority of the variables within our hypotheses, providing strong support for the overall assumption that EIJV autonomy is associated with EIJV effectiveness. This result occurred across a broad sample of EIJVs from multiple national contexts.

Looking more specifically at the results for the individual hypotheses, three activities were consistently significant in both the Pearson correlations and the regression analyses. These activities were: BUSSTRAT – the degree to which an EIJV develops and implements business strategy independently of its parent organizations; IMPLPLAN – the degree to which an IJV implements its business policy independently of its parent companies; and LOCALHRM – the degree to which an EIJV develops and implements human resource practices independently based on host-culture characteristics. These three activities are highly correlated, indicating that they might form a single autonomy dimension, which we will refer to here as **strategic autonomy**. This dimension may be described as an indication that the EIJV is free to act free from parental influence, a commonly used general definition of autonomy.

In addition to being highly correlated, the three activities listed above might also be said to represent three levels of autonomy: high, medium and low. High autonomy is hypothesized to indicate the freedom to formulate and implement the strategic business plan of the EIJV. Medium autonomy indicates the freedom to formulate and implement only in certain functional areas, such as human resource management (HRM), marketing or finance. Low autonomy indicates possessing no freedom to formulate, but only freedom to implement strategic business plans.

The only hypothesis that was not supported at all was hypothesis 4, which dealt with EIJV top-executive participation in parent company policy meetings about the EIJV. The negative coefficient for this hypothesis in both the Pearson correlations and the Table 3.3 regressions is interesting because it indicates that EIJV CEOs do not consider top-executive participation as important for their EIJVs to be effective. While it is not totally clear why this result may be occurring, one possible rationale is that EIJV CEOs may believe that their presence at parent company meetings involves a role of simply being aware of their parents' international problems, thus decreasing their ability to be highly competitive in order to make affiliates more productive, and so on. Related to this point, participating in discussions of parent organizations can enable the EIJV to have a broader picture, and this is actually a way of integrating all kinds of subsidiaries. Participation in parent company meetings means taking into account the goals, needs and problems of all the affiliates of the MNC. Accordingly, the group dynamics in these meetings support integration and discourage CEOs from following policies of differentiation. This may also diminish the CEOs' abilities to achieve unique competitive advantages within their EIJVs. Again, this may be a method of increasing overall multinational effectiveness, without necessarily improving specific EIJV performance. An additional rationale may be that the CEOs perceive the need to attend these meetings as an indicator that they have to negotiate with their parent companies for authority over items that they believe should be under their control without the necessity to meet with parent companies. Again, according to this rationale, participation at these meetings may be perceived as less than optimal.

Our final two hypotheses were both strongly supported in the regression analyses. This occurred despite the fact that RESDEP (H5) was not supported in the Pearson correlations, and DOMPAR (H6) was supported in only the Pearson correlation with INDEX5. These two variables are more highly correlated than any other combination of our six autonomy variables (0.518) and, taken together, may provide evidence of a second dimension of EIJV autonomy, which we will refer to here as **structural autonomy**. This dimension concerns attributes that indicate the degree to which an IJV is structurally dependent upon its parent companies. In the case of resource dependence, the connection to this variable is relatively clear. In the case of whether the EIJV has a dominant parent, the rationale may relate to the fact that when an EIJV has a dominant parent, it effectively depends on only one parent, instead of two. As noted in the justification for this hypothesis, classifying a parent as dominant implies that the parent is deeply involved in the daily operations of its EIJV(s). However, since this is usually achieved by appointing its transferees to the most important key positions in the EIJV and providing them with the autonomy to run the venture, EIJVs with a dominant parent might actually be less dependent.

As can be seen in Figure 3.1, combining the two autonomy dimensions into a two-by-two matrix allows us to classify EIJVs into four categories.

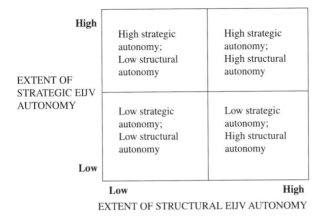

Figure 3.1   Two dimensions of EIJV autonomy

It would be useful for future research to specifically examine these four categories and their relationship to EIJV effectiveness. In addition to the above recommendation, this chapter also produces several other implications for future researchers. First, more research is needed into the temporal aspects of the autonomy variables and EIJV effectiveness; that is, whether the significance of one preceded the significance of the other. Second, our current research indicates that autonomy is a construct that is multidimensional and future research is needed to further define the dimensions of this construct. Third, additional research is needed to address the specific cases where EIJVs should be evaluated at one level of analysis versus another.

References

Ackerman, L. D. (1994) 'Managing the Image of the Joint Venture', *Directors and Boards*, vol. 18(2): 47–9.

Adler, N. J. (1991) *International Dimensions of Organizational Behavior*, 2nd edn (Belmont, Col.: Wadsworth Publishing).

Anderson, E. (1990) 'Two Firms, One Frontier: On Assessing Joint Venture Performance', *Sloan Management Review*, vol. 31(2): 19–29.

Antoniou, P. and Whitman, K. (1998) 'Understanding Chinese Interpersonal Norms and Effective Management of Sino–Western Joint Ventures', *Multinational Business Review*, vol. 6(1): 53–62.

Appell, A., Jenner, R. and Hebert, L. (1999) 'Taking a Conservative Approach when Entering the China Market', *Journal of Global Marketing*, vol. 12(4): 65–78.

Beamish, P. W. (1984) 'Joint Venture Performance in Developing Countries', unpublished doctoral dissertation, the University of Western Ontario.

Bleeke, J. and Ernst, D. (1991) 'The Way to Win in Cross-border Alliances', *Harvard Business Review*, vol. 69(6): 127–35.

Bleeke, J. and Ernst, D. (1993) *Collaborate to Compete* (New York: John Wiley).

Carter, N. M. (1990) 'Small Firm Adaptation: Responses of Physicians' Organizations to Regulatory and Competitive Uncertainty', *Academy of Management Journal*, vol. 33(2): 307–33.

Chandler, Jr., A. D. (1962) *Strategy and Structure: Chapters in the History of the Industrial Enterprise* (Cambridge, Mass.: MIT Press).

Contractor, F. J. and Lorange, P. (1988) 'Why Should Firms Cooperate? The Strategy and Economics Basis for Cooperative Ventures', in F. J. Contractor and P. Lorange (eds), *Cooperative Strategies in International Business* (Lexington, Mass.: Lexington Books): 31–53.

Cordery, J. (1998) 'Participation', in N. Nicholson, R. Schuler and A. H. Van de Ven (eds), *Blackwell Encyclopedic Dictionary of Organizational Behavior*, revd edn (Malden, Mass.: Blackwell): 402.

Dess, G. G. and Robinson, R. B. (1984) 'Measuring Organizational Performance in the Absence of Objective Measures: The Case of Private-held Firm and Conglomerate Business Unit', *Strategic Management Journal*, vol. 5(3): 265–73.

Dobkin, J. A., Burt, J. A., Krupsky, K. J. and Spooner, M. J. (1994) *Joint Ventures with International Partners: Structure and Negotiation with Forms* (Washington, D.C.: Butterworth).

Gates, S. (1993) *Strategic Alliances: Guidelines for Successful Management*, Report no. 1028 (New York: The Conference Board).

Geringer, J. M. and Hébert, L. (1989) 'Control and Performance of International Joint Ventures', *Journal of International Business Studies*, vol. 20(2): 235–54.

Geringer, J. M. and Hébert, L. (1991) 'Measuring Performance of International Joint Ventures', *Journal of International Business Studies*, vol. 22(2): 249–65.

Hamill, J. and Hunt, G. (1993) 'Joint Ventures in Hungary: Key Success Factors', *European Management Journal*, vol. 11(2): 238–47.

Hannan, M. T. and Freeman, J. H. (1984) 'Structural Inertia and Organizational Change', *American Sociological Review*, vol. 29: 149–64.

Harrigan, K. R. (1985) *Strategies for Joint Ventures* (Lexington, Mass.: Lexington Books).

Hoon-Halbauer, S. K. (1994) *Management of Sino-foreign Joint Ventures* (Lund University Press).

Inkpen, A. and Li, K.-Q. (1999) 'Joint Venture Formation: Planning and Knowledge-Gathering for Success', *Organizational Dynamics*, vol. 27(4): 33–47.

Jemison, D. B. (1981) 'The Importance of an Integrative Approach to Strategic Management Research', *Academy of Management Review*, vol. 6(4): 601–8.

Killing, J. P. (1983) *Strategies for Joint Venture Success* (New York: Praeger).

Koot, W. T. M. (1988) 'Underlying Dilemmas in the Management of International Joint Ventures', in F. J. Contractor and P. Lorange (eds), *Cooperative Strategies in International Business* (Lexington, Mass.: Lexington Books).

Lane, H. W. and Beamish, P. W. (1990) 'Cross-Cultural Cooperative Behavior in Joint Ventures in LDCs', *Management International Review*, vol. 30: 87–102.

Larsson, R., Bengtsson, L., Henriksson, K. and Sparks, J. (1998) 'The Interorganizational Learning Dilemma: Collective Knowledge Development in Strategic Alliances', *Organization Science*, vol. 9(3): 285–305.

Learned, E. P., Christensen, C. R., Andrews, K. R. and Guth, W. (1969) *Business Policy: Text and Cases*, revd edn (Homewood, Ill.: Irwin).

Llaneza, A. V. and Garcia-Canal, E. (1998) 'Distinctive Features of Domestic and International Joint Ventures', *Management International Review*, vol. 38(1): 49–66.

Lyles, M. A. and Baird, I. S. (1994) 'Performance of International Joint Ventures in Two Eastern European Countries: The Case of Hungary and Poland', *Management International Review*, vol. 34(4): 313–29.

Lyles, M. A. and Reger, R. K. (1993) 'Managing for Autonomy in Joint Ventures: A Longitudinal Study of Upward Influence', *Journal of Management Studies*, vol. 30(3): 383–404.

Newburry, W. and Zeira, Y. (1999) 'Autonomy and Effectiveness of Equity International Joint Ventures (EIJVs): An Analysis Based upon EIJVs in Hungary and Britain', *Journal of Management Studies*, vol. 36(2): 263–85.

Pucik, V. (1988) 'Strategic Alliance with the Japanese: Implications for Human Resource Management', in F. J. Contractor and P. Lorange (eds), *Cooperative Strategies in International Business* (Lexington, Mass.: Lexington Books): 487–98.

Rafii, F. (1978) 'Joint Ventures and Transfer of Technology to Iran: The Impact of Foreign Control', unpublished doctoral dissertation, Harvard University.

Salant, S. W. and Shaffer, G. (1998) 'Optimal Asymmetric Strategies in Research Joint Ventures', *International Journal of Industrial Organization*, vol. 16(2): 195–208.

Schaan, J. L. (1983) 'Parent Control and Joint Venture Success: The Case of Mexico', unpublished doctoral dissertation, University of Western Ontario.

Schneider, S. C. and Barsoux, J.-L. (1997) *Managing Across Cultures* (Herts: Prentice Hall Europe).

Shenkar, O. and Li, J. (1999) 'Knowledge Search in International Cooperative Ventures', *Organization Science*, vol. 10(2): 134–43.

Shenkar, O. and Zeira, Y. (1987) 'Human Resources Management in International Joint Ventures: Directions for Research', *Academy of Management Review*, vol. 12(3): 546–57.

Si, S. and Bruton, G. (1999) 'Knowledge Transfer in International Joint Ventures in Transitional Economies: The China Experience', *Academy of Management Executive*, vol. 13(1): 83–90.

Xuan, G.-L. and Graf, G. (1996) 'Key Issues in the Creation of International Joint Ventures with China', in A. G. Woodside and R. E. Pitts (eds), *Creating and Managing International Joint Ventures* (Westport, Conn.: Quorum).

Zajac, E. J. (1990) 'CEO Selection, Succession, Compensation and Firm Performance: A Theoretical Integration and Empirical Analysis', *Strategic Management Journal*, vol. 11: 217–30.

Zeira, Y. and Parker, B. (1995) 'International Joint Ventures in the United States: An Examination of Factors Related to their Effectiveness', *The International Executive*, vol. 37(4): 373–93.

Zeira, Y. and Shenkar, O. (1990) 'Interactive and Specific Parent Characteristics: Implications for Management and Human Resources in International Joint Ventures', *Management International Review*, special issue no. 30: 7–22.

4 Learning in International Joint Ventures

David Pollard

INTRODUCTION

A wide variety of companies have favoured the international joint venture (IJV) as a strategic route into new foreign markets and/or new technologies and products, the trend being evident in the increasing number of new ventures over the past few decades. This trend has brought with it a burgeoning literature, mainly devoted to strategic choice factors and other 'upstream' activities such as partner choice and the formation of the venture (see also Chapter 2). Latterly, performance aspects, control and other managerial issues have been the subject of increased scholarly activity, as have joint venture networks. An aspect of collaboration that has only recently attracted the attention of academics and practitioners alike is that of how learning and the development of knowledge occurs in IJVs.

One unfortunate outcome of a relatively young but rapidly expanding literature is the plethora of approaches employed in studying IJVs, bringing with it wide disagreement on the use of terminology. These factors affect theory-building and render empirical study more problematic, a state of affairs roundly criticized by Parkhe (1993). In some studies, the terms 'strategic alliance' and 'joint venture' are used synonymously; in others the terms are defined along the lines of formal and informal relationships or equity and non-equity ventures. In this chapter, 'international joint ventures' means those organizations which are set up by two or more independent partner organizations, each partner engaging in the decision-making activities (Geringer, 1988, 1991) but the extent of that engagement depending on the nature of the venture (Ditta, 1988; Kogut and Singh, 1988). Also, one or more partner organizations have headquarters outside the venture's country of operation or if the venture has significant levels of operation in more than one country (Geringer and Hébert, 1989).

Engaging in joint ventures affects the way the partner companies do business (Levinson and Asahi, 1995). A fundamental question for IJVs is how to acquire and develop knowledge gained through collaboration in the development of competencies related to the competitive advantage which engagement in collaboration brings. For organizations to acquire and develop knowledge, some input from a partner firm (perhaps involving technology transfer) is generally necessary. A transfer of knowledge between partners occurs during the life of the venture, not just in the initial stages of formation, but the nature of knowledge is likely to differ as the venture matures. Such collaborative knowledge can be utilized in the current venture and also subsequently, especially in the context of a collaboration network. Learning and the transfer of knowledge within an IJV has proved problematic because of a range of difficulties, which are explored later in the chapter.

As learning and knowledge development occur at various stages in the life of a joint venture, a life-cycle approach is taken in this chapter. The life-cycle approach is extended later to include networks of ventures and particular combinations of partner firms, such as when two companies from different countries collaborate to enter a market foreign to both of them. The international nature of IJVs necessarily involves cross-cultural issues and their effect on learning and knowledge transfer, an area significantly underrepresented in the IJV literature. The chapter also addresses additional factors such as technology transfer, the importance of trust and the evolution of IJVs.

Towards the end of the chapter, case studies are employed to illustrate some of the principles developed. The case evidence is derived from the author's involvement with organizations operating IJVs in the Czech Republic, Thailand and China as well as from selected published sources. The case studies cover a range of countries and operating conditions, and bring an important practical element into the discussion of learning in joint ventures, in terms of the recognition of the importance of learning by management and particular implementation issues.

LEARNING AND KNOWLEDGE DEVELOPMENT

Although the concept of organizational learning was introduced over 40 years ago, it is only recently that the subject has attracted significant interest from academics and practitioners alike. Both organizational learning and learning in organizations are the subject of some controversy in terms of definition and scope (see for example Senge, 1990; Schein, 1993; Nonaka and Takeuchi, 1995, 1998).

Crossan and Inkpen (1994) suggest a three-level model in understanding learning in organizations, viz. individual, group and organizational, an approach utilized in a later section. The model helps to explain that the corpus of an organization's knowledge is greater than the sum of the knowledge of individuals within the organization. It is in linking and leveraging individual and collective learning that the company progresses over time and is able to resist changes in personnel and leadership and retain its cultural identity. There is therefore a strong link between company culture and the acquisition and development of knowledge.

Examining the roots of organizational knowledge is problematic because the content, processes and the networks that exist are often difficult to define. Whereas managers would readily agree that organizational learning is important, it would be difficult for them to describe exactly how learning occurs and is accumulated as knowledge at various levels, or indeed, the processes that exist to support knowledge development. The design of knowledge systems often ignores the more subtle aspects of individual-knowledge acquisition and also is unable to incorporate tacit knowledge; explicit knowledge being much easier to replicate in knowledge-management systems. The 'western' approach, which tends to concentrate on explicit knowledge, has been criticized by Nonaka and Takeuchi (1998), driven, or so they claim, by traditions which date back to the Scientific Management movement. In contrast, they argue that Japanese firms are much better at determining the importance of tacit knowledge and evolving procedures for its acquisition and development.

The difference between tacit and operational knowledge is a fundamental issue in considering knowledge transfer. Operational knowledge can be transferred through written routines and instructions, but tacit knowledge is often highly content-specific; existing in an individual's memory as accumulated beliefs and experience, and often only invoked when circumstances dictate. This experience can only be effectively transferred to others through some measure of personal interaction. It should be noted, however, that explicit and tacit knowledge is not a dichotomy, rather the opposite ends of a continuum. Nonaka and Takeuchi (1998) suggest that a key challenge for organizations is how to convert tacit knowledge into explicit knowledge that can be incorporated more easily into organizational knowledge and also simplify technology and knowledge transfer.

It is argued that managers should be facilitators for knowledge creation, for knowledge development requires management of both learning integration and the development of integrating mechanisms, dealing with both emergent knowledge and the growth of stored knowledge. This extends to managing knowledge and continual education, ultimately linking to innovation and creativity; that is, innovation and creativity flow out of knowledge. The guidance and interest of the company's top management is vital in both enabling and promoting knowledge development.

INTERNATIONALIZATION AND LEARNING

Learning aspects of internationalization have generally been neglected in the literature (Tsang, 1999), although learning has been considered a dimension of internationalization for some time. Johanson and Vahlne's (1977) study is perhaps one of the most famous that specifically alludes to learning, in this case learning on the part of managers that drive internationalization decisions. Although the model has been criticized, the issue of international knowledge acquisition and development is still relevant to organizational development overseas. Internationalization is a learning process in itself as firms extend the nature of international operations and have to deal with increasing complexity.

International operations present a number of learning opportunities and challenges for the companies, for example dealing with cultural differences in the context of working practices and procedures, management decision-making and the transfer of technology. Learning in the international arena may be more complex and 'the need to operate internationally represents the greatest current change challenge' for organizations (Torrington and Holden, 1992: 20). However, given the greater internationalization of markets, international learning is no longer a choice but a necessity.

Internationalization often involves transferring technology from one part of the firm to another, or to another company in a collaboration strategy. The transfer of technology involves significant commitment on the part of firms in both the cost of transfer which usually includes the use of expatriate staff to provide training and a commitment to manage the changes necessary to incorporate new technology in existing corporate working patterns. The learning context of IJVs necessarily involves the transfer of learning across borders and issues developed in this section will be further discussed in that context.

INTERNATIONAL JOINT VENTURES –
THE LEARNING CONTEXT

Learning occurs in all IJVs, yet studies of the subject did not flourish until after Hamel's (1991) paper on the determinants of competence-building in strategic alliances. More recently, Crossan and Inkpen (1995) have similarly argued that learning is important for joint ventures because it is vital to their success. The nature of such learning, how effectively knowledge is gained and used and what the partner organizations have to do to ensure that knowledge is utilized and developed effectively, are important questions for organizations. However, it seems that some organizations fail to pay sufficient attention to learning processes or neglect to exploit the learning opportunities presented (Inkpen, 1998).

A number of problems arise when examining learning in IJVs because the range of settings and purposes of ventures is relatively extensive. Generally, IJVs are not just temporary but they have differing time horizons, some exploiting short-term market opportunities while others develop and become major long-term competitors in their own right. Parkhe (1993) argues that a differentiation can be made from partner firms who enter into ventures with the sole objective of acquiring technology and those who have a wider range of motivations. In the former case, once the technology transfer objective has been met, the purpose of the alliance is satisfied and there is no point in pursuing it. The second group is of alliances which tend to be longer-term in nature and which involve a more complex level of learning and learning development. This may result in both a significant level of organizational learning and strengthening of the collaboration. In this way, the partner organizations may develop additional innovations and use the IJV as a springboard for other activities. Institutional learning and knowledge-management development by the venture as a whole is perhaps the next stage in this quest.

By definition, an IJV implies partnership between independent and separate firms. It follows, therefore, that partner independence, culture (organizational and national), management-style differences and strategic imperatives will affect collaborative processes including the transfer of information and learning. Learning to work effectively with a partner company's culture and management style as well as operational differences poses a number of learning opportunities for both management and staff. Companies who are used to controlling activities themselves may find difficulty in setting up mechanisms to transfer knowledge, or to foster the sharing of knowledge acquired from participating in the venture within other parts of the organization.

Interorganizational working and pathways for information flow, linking and bridging between organizations to affect learning, the flow of learning and therefore organizational learning (Levinson and Asahi, 1995) are required, as is an assessment of the skills or learning gaps. As the collaboration matures, it may move away from concentrating on knowledge acquisition to knowledge development, entailing the modification of information pathways and perhaps shifting attention to increased two-way flows of knowledge.

In the early stages of the venture, the transfer of learning and information might have ethnocentric tendencies. In many instances, the provider of the technology supplies training in an expatriate or home-base setting. Later, collaborative learning may take place, with the technology provider learning more about the venture and its market. However, it has to be said that some companies seem to approach such ventures with an arrogance of superior learning and rarely consider learning from the recipient. If this learning 'return loop' is ignored by organizations, then firms may not achieve the benefits achievable through the venture and, in some cases, may threaten the venture's existence. The significant number of IJV failures, coupled with other problems in successfully setting up the venture, leads to a high degree of instability, the level of which may vary with the individual firm's experience of joint ventures. Firms who develop knowledge of dealing with such instability may stand a better chance of participating in further successful ventures.

Not all IJVs have clear purposes or roles within partner-company strategy. Conflicts within parent companies may arise because resources are devoted to ventures at the expense of other activities, resulting in negative attitudes on the part of managers, leading to obstructions in the progress of the venture. Such undercurrents affecting the interaction of individuals within companies can therefore adversely affect learning and knowledge development. In fact, learning might be actively discouraged in the hope that the collaboration would underperform and so be brought to an end.

LEARNING AND KNOWLEDGE DEVELOPMENT IN INTERNATIONAL JOINT VENTURES

One of the key motivations for a company entering collaborative ventures is to gain knowledge (Inkpen, 1998; Kogut, 1988), and as soon as practicable (Hamel, 1991). An important question is how mutually to increase capabilities within collaborations, which goes beyond the processes of knowledge acquisition to knowledge development. Crossan and Inkpen (1994) argue that learning is a competitive imperative and that learning should be recognized as important in building new competencies.

As mentioned earlier, learning occurs at various stages during the lifecycle of the IJV; that is, strategic analysis, partner selection, venture negotiations, technology transfer activities and the acquisition of venturing skills and management acumen all involve knowledge acquisition. On a more developmental level, issues of joint control, transfer of innovative ideas and a mutual approach to strategy also involve learning. It is important to recognize that the 'downstream' activities will be affected by the 'upstream' activities, for example poor partner selection would affect both the evolution of the venture and knowledge development within it.

Parkhe (1993) suggests that learning in collaborative environments is also related to diversity in partner characteristics, for example differences between the partners may be a greater spur to learning than similarities. This may seem paradoxical since significant differences between partner firms in IJVs are often associated with problems in working effectively together. Such differences could include cross-cultural elements.

In IJV learning and knowledge development, two processes are important; knowledge acquisition and integration into the firm's knowledge base (Huber, 1991) and the development of new knowledge through the actions of the collaborating entities (Nonaka and Takeuchi, 1998; Powell *et al.*, 1996). Gyndwali (1999) argues that the literature is heavily weighted towards knowledge acquisition from partner organizations and comparatively little attention has been given to the institutionalization of knowledge nor to its transfer to other collaborations in a network. Crossan and Inkpen's (1994) model of learning at individual, group and organization levels is useful in examining learning processes and knowledge development in IJVs in more detail.

Individual Level

As learning begins at the individual level, understanding learning that originates from the interaction of individuals in collaborative ventures as opposed to formal methods is important. Such interactions can be very complex in nature and scope and depend on the roles of actors and the place of their individual activities in the life-cycle of the venture. Acquisition and the subsequent creation of knowledge in IJVs begins at the very beginning of the process, the creation of knowledge incorporating both single-loop and double-loop learning.

The methods of the transfer of knowledge and its context are important. Informal learning occurs through the development of working relationships and personal contacts, and can be an important means of transferring tacit as opposed to explicit knowledge. Interactions between individuals become larger in scale and faster in terms of speed as more and more actors in the organization become involved; this process has been described as a spiral of organizational knowledge creation (Nonaka, 1994). It is the formal mechanisms that tend to predominate in the literature (and attract management attention), very few studies distinguish between explicit and tacit knowledge or discuss its relevance to knowledge creation and transfer.

The acquisition of learning at the individual level is often difficult in IJVs despite the best intentions of management, neither is it always as successful as intended. Learning is also not always intentional, for instance people learning to cope with particular operational difficulties that were not anticipated. There is a danger that this corpus of knowledge will continue to reside at the individual level and, if not shared or formalized, will be in danger of being lost because it is often taken for granted by individuals.

The more tacit is the nature of knowledge, the more difficulty there will be in transferring the knowledge even in a supportive environment, as, for example, people may not be able to articulate their learning effectively. Individuals may not realize that they may be called upon to transfer their knowledge at a later date and some people may have to be trained for this role. Difficulties in transferring tacit knowledge could be overcome by providing specific opportunities for interaction between individuals within the collaboration.

Group Level

This brings the discussion on to people learning through interactions in 'groups' of two or more individuals. These could be formal learning groups, but more often than not are informal groups of individuals sharing knowledge of mutual importance in various parts of the venture. As learning resides at the individual level until prompted to share, such sharing has to be facilitated. The need to overcome barriers to learning at group level is important, such as a lack of openness (Crossan and Inkpen, 1994). Trust between people and their relative status (the latter an important barrier in some countries) is also a consideration in fostering the effective sharing of information.

Organizational Level

In IJVs, challenges at organizational level include the filtering, integration and institutionalization of knowledge within the collaboration, and eliminating knowledge that has become obsolescent. There are also considerations of management involvement which brings into question how management assess the importance of learning as part of collaborative activity. The time involved in collecting, assessing and incorporating knowledge is also important, especially if a strategic imperative is time-dependent.

At the organizational level, collective learning becomes independent of individuals; for example the collective experience resists the impact of people leaving and leadership changes. Acquisition of new knowledge is complex as learning objectives and requirements may differ within the venture. Moving from single-loop learning to double-loop learning which challenges 'taken for granted' assumptions and can result in a deeper level of knowledge may be important in generating new knowledge.

As one organization shares knowledge with others in an IJV, opportunities can be taken to amplify, modify and clarify knowledge in the supplying firm's contexts. For knowledge to migrate across a venture, however, knowledge connections must exist between the parents and the venture. Organizational boundaries have to be 'permeable' to allow the transfer of knowledge (Crossan and Inkpen, 1994), and knowledge transfer can become an important capability (Hamel, 1991; Kogut, 1988). Connections between partner collaborating firms require management support to foster the flow of knowledge. Bridging between venture organizations does not imply linear transfer of knowledge; interaction and iteration are also important.

The development of organizational knowledge could also be built not on differences, but on shared understanding. As a collaboration matures and the venture organizations build trust and learn more about each other, such shared knowledge could be a platform for developing new knowledge because the firms are likely to have developed basic understanding about each other's skills, and so on. It is perhaps tempting to think that it is only the organization that receives new technology or the benefit of western management methods in developing economies that achieves a significant pay-off from participating in IJVs. But as Stenton (1996) argues, all partners have the opportunity to learn; perhaps this learning is different but even firms transferring propriety technology have an opportunity to learn about organizational methods of other countries and about new markets.

Knowledge connections can be created through formal and informal relationships between individuals and groups (Inkpen, 1996). Whilst these connections provide a basis for transferring individual knowledge to organizations and ultimately to organizational knowledge, the connections too are part of organizational knowledge. Connections do not have to become formal to be incorporated; indeed the formalization of previously informal channels might negatively affect their use.

The facilitation of learning and the acquisition of new skills are cultural issues which collaborating firms should consider as part of the collaborative commitment. Lyles (1988) argues that collaboration between organizations can result in a growth or learning and also assist learning processes. Perhaps priority and status of learning in the IJV could be signalled through reward processes, job or role appraisal, and the development of knowledge 'champions', thereby consolidating the important message that the company fosters learning.

Properties that make learning difficult to manage also make it difficult to replicate and therefore create or action competitive advantage. Difficult learning situations may therefore be of strategic benefit to the company, provided they can overcome the difficulties better than competitors.

At the individual, group and organizational levels, evaluation of learning is necessary to decide whether to retain and integrate it or reject the new knowledge as irrelevant. There is a danger that new knowledge will be rejected, for example, when it meets established routines or rigorous control mechanisms that might conflict with the new knowledge. Crossan and Inkpen (1994) warn against poor evaluation of learning in another sense, choosing knowledge available at minimal cost which might be counterproductive, as against spending more on knowledge that would be useful for future use. They further suggest that performance, rather than learning outcome measurement, may be another obstacle in indicating poor performance in the short term to show that learning has not or could not occur. An emphasis on a need for early profitability can also cloud the issue because firms do not look beyond the start-up period. Crossan and Inkpen (1994) suggest that learning and improved performance is not immediately related, learning requires time to be gained and assessed before its impact is felt.

Unfortunately in many IJVs, should performance decline, learning is impeded. Should poor performance in the IJV inhibit or starve learning of resources or motivation (Crossan and Inkpen, 1994), a long-term perspective is required. Short-termism is not commensurate with a developing learning environment although some alliances are short-term in nature and have different goals. Certainly those collaborations which intend to develop should take into consideration that learning is for the future as well as for the present. Poor partner performance on the other hand might lead to collaborating organizations ignoring a learning potential, as the partner is perceived as not worth learning from.

The importance of knowledge management in IJVs could be vital. Many now argue that knowledge is the modern competitive currency, firms dealing with the increasing speed of competition (Hedlund, 1994) and wishing to sustain competitive advantage need to effectively mobilize knowledge assets. In collaborative environments, knowledge management involves the transfer of knowledge between the individual firms (Bresman *et al.*, 1999) and crucially with the venture partners working together to increase their total knowledge. Such knowledge management activities are complex enough within the same national environment but the transfer of knowledge management to foreign locations poses further difficulties (Bresman *et al.*, 1999). The opportunities are significant as discussed earlier, as international collaboration provides additional opportunities for learning that can be transferred to other markets and that can enhance collaborative networks.

LEARNING IN INTERNATIONAL JOINT VENTURES – CROSS-CULTURAL ISSUES

By their very nature, cross-cultural issues are inherent in learning and the transfer of knowledge within an IJV. The context can be further complicated; for example, Pan and Tse (1996) studied two foreign companies collaborating to enter a third market (China) in cooperation with a local company. This type of collaboration raises a number of fascinating learning issues, both in learning to collaborate and learning about the new market and the venture partner in that market. Pan and Tse discuss issues of cultural distance and collaboration motivations amongst others.

The transfer of knowledge across borders has a long history (Pollard and Tayeb, 1997) contrasting with more recent interest in cross-cultural aspects of learning in IJVs. In what little research that has been undertaken, there remains a diversity of approaches to the study of cross-cultural issues in IJVs, contributing to a lack of recognition of the importance of country differences in collaborative working and learning.

IJVs bring together firms of different national origins, cultures and political bases (Parkhe, 1991) causing considerable diversity in firm-specific characteristics that might be linked to each firm's national heritage. In the previous section it was noted that inter-firm diversity might inhibit the ability to work jointly and effectively unless the firms can overcome their differences, cross-cultural differences included. It means that, perhaps, ventures from culturally-dissimilar countries have a higher potential for learning, although such learning will require more effort and commitment from management.

One difficulty facing researchers and arguably practitioners in any cross-cultural situation is the problem of identity (Tsang, 1998). People interpret situations and actions in a cultural framework and it is all too easy to add one's own cultural perspectives to an international setting. This can manifest itself in a culturally-bound interpretation of management issues, and errors in understanding or action might not be realized until a problem occurs. An example might be in not properly regarding the seniority of a partner firm's senior manager, leading to a loss of status or face. Disregarding the effect of '*guanxi*' in Chinese ventures, for example, could also lead to ineffectiveness when considering learning networks and learning in groups.

The importance of learning transfer at various stages of a venture's life-cycle has been shown to be important for knowledge and collaborative development. Interaction between individuals and the transfer of knowl-edge is carried out in an environment of cultural differences, whether they are in face-to-face contact or not. 'The provision of knowledge, the expec-tations of its recipients and the implementation of new techniques all have significant cultural dimensions' (Pollard and Tayeb, 1997: 68). Transferring knowledge involves crossing national boundaries in such a way that it is effectively received and this has implications for the management of path-ways of learning between collaborating organizations.

Pollard and Tayeb (1997) note significant cultural effects on the transfer of learning across borders. In the context of this discussion, both learning acquisition and learning development would be affected. In the acquisition of learning, local procedures for learning and learning styles themselves would differ. In terms of learning development, aspects of cultural similar-ity, collective or individualistic approaches and the relative positions of peo-ple in the collaborative venture might be relevant. The main point is that cultural differences should be appreciated and that learning and knowledge development processes are designed accordingly. The four knowledge man-agement processes identified in Inkpen and Dinur's 1998 study – technology sharing, interorganizational interaction, personnel transfers and strategic integration – all have cross-cultural dimensions, which could affect both explicit and tacit learning. In considering the personnel transfer process, for example, the way knowledge is gained, the content of the knowledge and even the questions asked could be affected by national differences.

As noted earlier, Nonaka and Takeuchi (1998) argue that Japanese orga-nizations recognize that tacit knowledge is important and whereas suggest that many western managers are more accustomed to dealing with explicit knowledge. Tacit knowledge is very difficult to communicate, the more embedded it is in processes, the more difficult it is to transfer. In IJVs, the transfer of tacit knowledge may be relatively time-consuming and involve the supplier in significant cost, in terms of expatriate relocation and on-site training for example.

EXPATRIATE DEPLOYMENT AND LEARNING

Expatriate deployment or the location of staff overseas for a period of time has been researched relatively extensively, although learning aspects have not been as fully explored. In this section, the role of the expatriate as 'expert' in learning transfer is a good example of the impact of cross-cultural differences impacting on the transfer of knowledge across borders. The expatriate's contribution to organizational learning on return from knowledge-transfer assignment has also not been well-explored.

Expatriate staff can gain valuable knowledge from working in venture operations abroad as 'experts' or indeed as management of the venture. Such knowledge could be shared with others, for example in preparing the next expatriates for their role. They could also be a valuable source of knowledge concerning the working practices and management priorities of the partner organization. Examples are the partner's attitudes to working within the joint venture, decision-making processes, and use of venture information and priorities for action.

Expatriate 'experts' are often used to assist in knowledge transfer situations, spending periods of time training local staff in new skills and routines. Some companies (see cases for an example) provide training at their establishment for venture employees, the main disadvantages being cost and the absence of key personnel abroad for a period of time. However, this type of training, whilst disruptive, can be very effective for knowledge transfer and might also lead to the development of personal relationships and links, something for which expatriate deployment is not so well-suited.

Several technology transfer-based studies allude to the importance of the 'expert' as a mechanism for learning and knowledge transfer. However, expatriate assignments are not always successful and factors such as culture shock, organizational cultural differences, family and social difficulties and poor preparation for the deployment are well-known problem areas. Yet, technology transfer implies that technological capability on the part of the employee is the critical factor when choosing an individual for the task. It seems, therefore, that technical ability is not the only factor, other attributes are required of the person concerned. The person concerned should be able to deal with the cultural differences that will be met and, importantly also, be able to impart knowledge effectively to others. Much the same goes for other personnel such as managers who are tasked with particular activities within the venture but outside their home country.

This role of 'expert' raises a number of cross-cultural concerns. The expert may be perceived as an outsider and as someone to be obeyed, rather than as a teacher and a source of knowledge, which will affect their approach to knowledge. The ability to transfer technology within a collaboration could be adversely affected if care is not taken in this area. In IJVs, the expatriate will be perhaps working with partner personnel, calling for additional skills in dealing with consensus rather than control.

Having considered the role of expatriates as 'experts' in technology transfer, we move on to consider learning and knowledge aspects contained in the technology transfer process itself.

TECHNOLOGY TRANSFER AND LEARNING

Many IJVs are specifically created to acquire or to transfer technology to new situations and markets, especially in developing economies. The discussion in this section concerns how technology is transferred, protection of technology and the often neglected issue of the technology provider taking advantage of learning opportunities; that is, learning in technology transfer can be a two-way process, although the literature is rather biased towards provision.

Technology transfer is more complex than just providing 'hard' technology such as equipment, transfer includes 'soft' technology in the form of procedures, instructions and professional knowledge. Many organizations provide detailed training in the use of their technology within the venture and/or within the supplying parent organization but perhaps neglect tacit knowledge. On-site training at the technology supplier's base has the advantage of including tests for understanding and interpersonal contact that helps transfer inherently tacit knowledge but requires time. Another common way of transferring technology is through the use of expatriate 'experts' (discussed above) who are supplied by the technology provider, often for medium-term deployment.

There are several factors that will affect the transfer of knowledge, many of which have been dealt with earlier such as the nature of the venture, its location, the strategic positions of the collaborating companies, and so forth. Just like partner differences discussed earlier, the technology gap, far from being obstructive, could be a spur to learning. Much depends on the motivation of the collaborating firms and the staff involved. Organizations are understandably protective of their knowledge assets, especially if the IJV partner is a current or potential competitor. Some commentators have sought to warn of the dangers of what they see as a giving away of competitive competencies. One means of protection is to 'ring-fence' technology to be transferred within the venture agreement and limit access to particular areas of technology involved in the venture and to separate other company operations not relevant to it. The level of trust will affect the transfer of knowledge and restrictions could endanger this flow of information as well as leading to problems at a higher level between the participating companies. It is to this question of trust that we now move.

THE IMPORTANCE OF TRUST IN LEARNING WITHIN IJVs

Early research into IJVs discussed trust as an important factor in dealing with collaborating firms within a venture and also the role of trust in the success of the venture (Morgan and Hunt, 1994). It was also argued that trust could be built up through interaction over a period of time but that it had to be an area of management focus, it was too important to allow unconsidered development.

The link between learning and trust was alluded to earlier in the context of sharing information in groups; trust helps the transfer of knowledge and information over company boundaries and out to collaborating firms. In the same way, a life-cycle approach would perhaps show trust developing alongside learning, that is trust facilitates learning but trust is also a matter for learning in itself – the trust of employees in their working environment, trust in partners in sharing technology, and trust when dealing with other managerial colleagues.

The initial stages of setting up the IJV can be relatively slow because of the need to build up trust on the part of venture managers. The building of trust does not stop at managerial levels but may also be important whenever staff work together within IJVs, bringing meaning and a firm basis for the development of effective learning relationships (Ring and Van de Venn, 1994; Ottati, 1994). Buckley and Casson (1988) argue that learning in collaboration involves a high level of trust between partners which also helps organizational effectiveness and promotes continuing relationships between the firms. Peng and Heath (1996) argue that trust is especially important in transformational ventures because of the uncertain nature of the business environments. As the venture evolves, then, trust can be built up through a range of personal contacts and a reinforcing of those contacts over time, involving an exchange of knowledge, mainly tacit in nature. Evolutionary aspects of learning in IJVs are addressed in the following section.

LEARNING AND THE EVOLUTION OF THE INTERNATIONAL JOINT VENTURE

It was suggested earlier that learning and knowledge development change as the venture matures. This section examines the developing role of learning as the venture moves from a position of concentrating on learning acquisition to providing learning opportunities for the partner organizations and the development of knowledge in the venture as well as in other sections of the collaboration. Firms often enter into ventures with learning as an explicit objective, which means that such an objective, although espoused in the rationale of the venture, receives surprisingly little management attention. Even if it does attract attention, it may be of a transitory nature with post-implementation learning relatively ignored.

In a developing collaboration, opportunities exist for partners to assess each other's skills and knowledge over a period of time and not just in the context of getting the venture up and running. Subsequent developments could see partner organizations exploiting their strengths (Crossan and Inkpen, 1994) to mutual strategic benefit. This could be the result of venture partners learning together and growing together, as opposed to learning acquisition which is more a feature of the early stages of the venture – although knowledge acquisition would still be important for many firms. Such collaborative growth might be seen as one of the hallmarks of successful venturing.

For collaborative growth to occur, firms have to manage the process, and particularly learning and knowledge development. Prioritizing and fostering learning and making thinks happen is vital for such development as the proper evaluation and institutionalization of knowledge. Zucker (1977) suggests that as inter-firm cooperation continues, informal contacts and mutual understanding are likely to be institutionalized into routines, and Ring and Van de Venn (1994) suggest that the longer the duration of the venture the more likely that the commitment of the partners will be formalized. Doz (1996) suggests that there is a dearth of research concerning the evolution of strategic alliances and that it is necessary to consider the role of learning in alliance evolution. An aspect of IJV evolution that is becoming more common is the growth of networks, the learning aspects of which are discussed next.

LEARNING AND NETWORKS

Much of the foregoing discussion in this chapter has related to single ventures with two or more partners. The development of IJVs, however, has given rise to the creation of networks of ventures engaged in by individual firms and a web of different alliances. This development adds further complexity to managing collaborative ventures at various levels, for example the development of specialist venture managers, control and performance factors and potential conflict within the network as well as managing from the centre of a collaborative 'web'. Such networks grew through the utilization of the IJV form to meet flexible competitive demands (Joshi and Inkpen, 1996) and may supersede contemporary notions of global firms (Crossan and Inkpen, 1994).

As a strategic tool, network growth can be differentiated from generic growth and acquisition (Peng and Tan, 1998). For example, Toshiba possesses more than two dozen alliances with competitor firms (Joshi and Inkpen, 1996). In networks, life-cycles will vary; at any given time some ventures will be new, others mature, with a mixture of both long and short-term horizons, perhaps indicating a portfolio approach to managing the network. Collaborative networks provide opportunities for transferring knowledge and experience gained from involvement in previous ventures (and further developing those ventures), showing that competencies gained in working with partners can be transferred to new situations such as experience gained in partner selection and negotiations, for example. Gyndwali (1999) discusses knowledge acquisition and the integration of the new knowledge into the existing knowledge base; the development of new knowledge through the activities of the collaborating entities is relevant to organizational learning. This view is supported by Powell *et al.* (1996), who suggest that learning in networks could be a function of both access to knowledge and capability to develop new knowledge.

The growth and transfer of knowledge can have the effect of making further venturing more efficient and less costly for the firm concerned. This implies that there is a transfer of accumulated knowledge on managing and operating IJVs as a process as well as the specific product of production-related knowledge. However, networks bring challenges not only for knowledge transfer but also additional knowledge acquisition and management in an environment of added complexity.

Inkpen and Dinur's (1996) study of networks identified the need for firms to develop IJV competencies and, importantly, transferring learning back from the venture to the parent, for example concerning what works and what doesn't. This feedback of information is vital if the partner firm wishes to develop other partnerships in addition to possible knowledge development elsewhere in the business. Such a setting provides a complex web of knowledge-building and a fascinating area for further research.

Networks can fail if expanded too soon. Tsang (1999) relates the case of a Singapore-based company which opened up four joint ventures in quick succession in a new market (China), and within a short time half of them were closed down. He claims that they moved too quickly, not taking time to learn from initial experience in the market. Thus the development of a series of ventures runs the risk of not only overextending the company, but leads to adverse experience which might have a knock-on effect on later venturing processes. Taking time to learn from experience, however, has to be balanced against first-mover considerations and other strategic issues.

CASES

This section contains a short commentary on IJVs to develop some of the principles discussed in earlier sections. Three are from the author's research and the other is drawn from the IJV literature.

Case 1

This was a Norwegian joint venture with a Chinese company near Shanghai, set up with an existing state-owned company to produce power generation equipment. The Norwegian partner provided technology as well as one of the joint venture CEOs and the human resource manager (the Chinese partner providing the other joint-CEO). Technology transfer was effected through a series of expatriate deployments. As the venture developed, expatriate presence for technology transfer was reduced and it was planned to phase out the permanent presence in favour of occasional visits, as operations demanded.

Having commenced operations and transferred the necessary technical skills, the venture management looked to develop additional skills in the workplace, realizing that technology transfer was only one factor contributing to the venture's success. The human resources management (HRM) manager was keen to promote effective working practices within the venture including communications, and to raise awareness concerning the importance of the venture.

In approaching these issues, the HRM manager asked supervisors what skills they considered important for the venture and what problems they considered detracted from the venture's effectiveness. Based on their responses, a series of training sessions was devised to explore the significant aspects identified and to help provide a framework for further discussions within the plant. The sessions set out aspects of the nature of joint ventures and collaborative working, working together within the venture, communications, skills development and the importance of learning. The sessions were well-attended and attracted a good deal of interaction between presenters and those attending.

The case provides two main insights. One is the need to continue and consolidate the learning process after the initial technology transfer; indeed some staff members suggested that a good deal of learning had still to be done. Secondly, it shows the importance of a management commitment to provide not only resources for learning development but also in playing their part in indicating its importance for the future of the venture.

There is still a long way to go. The institutionalization of knowledge concerned with a range of operations is going to be a very complex undertaking and it was clear that technical routines, whilst important in an industry where each product is made to order and there is a great deal of inherent variability, are only part of the knowledge-base of the venture.

Case 2

In the Czech Republic, Mendex (a fictitious name) were manufacturers of small components for a range of applications who entered into a joint venture with a German concern. The Czech company was motivated by anticipation of technology transfer in order to compete more effectively in an increasingly competitive market.

The technology transfer was essentially two-fold. One aspect was production and product technology, the transfer being aided by the inherent skill and maintaining levels already existing in the Czech company. German 'experts' provided on-site training and opportunities were provided for some training to be effected in Germany.

The second aspect of technology transfer was much more problematic for the Czech concern. Their existing computer systems were incompatible with the German system and the hardware was incapable of handling the transaction volume and other characteristics demanded by the German production system. The German company provided new hardware and software needed to operate the venture in much the same way as they operated in Germany. Unfortunately, the visiting 'experts' seemed to operate with a 'take-it-or-leave-it' attitude, and this led to conflict with Czech staff and affected the time taken to make the changes. A high level of staff turnover was experienced in the departments affected and much training effort was wasted. There was no attempt to prepare incoming 'experts' for the task in hand, technical expertise and availability being the main criteria for selection.

This case illustrates that problems can exist in transferring knowledge if the nature of the transfer is not considered beforehand. New knowledge, to be transferred successfully, requires a supportive environment where people are motivated to learn, albeit with a firm direction for the learning being provided.

Case 3

A company in the east of Scotland recently entered into a joint venture with one of its customers in Thailand to manufacture machinery previously supplied from Scotland, so as to take advantage of the Thai company's knowledge of the Southeast Asian market and to reduce costs. The agreement was 'ring-fenced' in the context of the technology to be transferred; the agreement was for access to basic, non-sensitive technology, which protected assets and also had the effect of reducing the complexity of technology transfer and assisting start-up.

The Thai company had been dealing with the Scottish partner for a number of years and there had been a good history of interpersonal contact between the staff, a factor which managers felt was a considerable advantage in setting up the venture. As part of the initial phase, managers from the Thai partner visited Scotland for discussions with managerial and technical staff. This was followed by a visit for Thai staff recruited for the manufacturing processes, these people spending some months in Scotland being trained by domestic staff in the technical aspects of production. Management felt that this training had the advantage of transferring not just operational knowledge but also the more tacit elements, and also that they could check understanding during discussions with the Thai contingent.

At the same time, Scottish staff were visiting Thailand and it was anticipated that such visits would continue as the venture progressed. The venture was implemented recently with few reported problems and management has been happy with the initial transfer of learning. Plans are now being developed to extend market penetration to other countries in Southeast Asia.

Case 4

Gutmann (1995) reports learning aspects of the Volkswagen–Skoda collaboration where significant use was made of expatriate staff. Skoda had a lack of economic knowledge and management skills but possessed an educated and skilled workforce. Prior to the commencement of the venture, Skoda management had been more autocratic in style.

Initially, the use of expatriate staff created scepticism and antagonism but there was a degree of motivation and readiness to learn on the part of Skoda employees. The main issues identified were how to build efficiency and exploit the partners' strengths as well as how to transfer know-how. It could have been achieved through the importation of foreign managers, but in Skoda it was done by a combination of project work, coaching and what they termed 'tandem management'.

In projects, key tasks were undertaken by bicultural project teams within a defined time period of 3–6 months. Expatriate staff members from Volkswagen were installed to support projects and to offer coaching if necessary. Projects included performance appraisal, creating a new management culture and a restructuring of HRM. Tandem management involved an expatriate manager and a local manager working together for a limited period of time of approximately three years. The task was to develop the professional and management skills of the local manager, with the aim being for him to manage the department independently. The expatriate manager effectively became a knowledge mediator and coach. It was seen as important in the tandem management for both persons to have the same objective and move in the same direction. Learning aspects of tandem management included the importance of cultural understanding and problems arising from wrong selection and the inadequate preparation of both parties.

Local managers showed high motivation, a willingness to learn and to profit from the expatriate managers. Some arrogance problems were experienced which could be a serious barrier to learning and communications. Crossing the cultural divide between the two groups was necessary, as Germans communicating only with Germans would have been undesirable. Language training was provided and staff members were encouraged to develop working relationships.

Tandem management that allows for a supportive know-how transfer is more effective than seminars (see for example Gutmann, 1995). It provides for interaction on joint areas of daily work, the joint solving of problems and the joint experience of success. The exercise also involved the importance of understanding traditions, attitudes and behaviour. Early involvement of people and joint working included confrontation with responsibility. The exercise also helped to accelerate integration and allowed for assignments for local managers in other plants. From the Volkswagen side there was considerable investment involved and a long-term horizon was taken.

IMPLICATIONS FOR MANAGERS IN IJVs

Although discussion in this chapter so far has discussed both theoretical and practical issues allied to learning and knowledge development in IJVs, the purpose of this section is to identify the significant implications of the discussion for managers in IJVs concerned with their creation and evolution.

Learning begins at the very start of the joint venture and occurs during the various stages of its evolution. Since most learning is acquired by individuals, both the acquisition and also, importantly, the sharing of this knowledge becomes an important management consideration. Despite the theoretical wrangling associated with the concept of the learning organization, the incorporation of knowledge within the organization is desirable for the evolution of the venture, transfer to other venture opportunities or within the network, as well as to other areas of the firm's operations. This entails a proactive and supportive approach to learning and knowledge development commensurate with the strategic importance of the venture and the organization's own strategies.

The development and nurturing of links within the collaboration is necessary to maintain and further develop channels of communication and information flow. Many channels are informal and work best that way, but still require management attention as well as more formal channels. Of course, these links occur in a variety of settings, not necessarily managerial in nature, and staff members should be encouraged to foster interorganizational links too. The transfer of tacit knowledge as opposed to explicit knowledge should attract management attention because of the relative difficulty of transfer and the need to develop tacit knowledge into explicit knowledge as the venture evolves.

As IJVs necessarily involve companies from other countries, cross-cultural considerations are necessary. For those companies who operate abroad this may not seem a major issue, but managing in an international collaboration is different from managing in a subsidiary. The transfer of learning and knowledge has significant cross-cultural dimensions, which can hinder the effectiveness of transfer if not given due credence. Collaboration involves a measure of trust in working with other independent firms and it has been shown that trust is important in another context, that of sharing knowledge. Trust tends to develop over the life-cycle of the venture and adds to cross-venture communication and learning in itself. Trust is built by paying attention to people in other organizations within the venture, which of course takes time.

Technology transfer brings with it considerations of how the transfer is to be effected and also how the supplier of technology can learn from the transfer, not just the recipient. If expatriate staff are used, they should be selected on criteria additional to technical expertise. They will gain in knowledge whilst on deployment and will be a good source of information on returning to the company. Some companies fail to take advantage of such staff members in importing knowledge from the venture and using it elsewhere. At the same time there is a danger of an ethnocentric approach which would act against the supplying organization learning anything at all. Assigning capable local managers to other tasks within the collaboration might be another advantage that could be taken into account, as happened in the Skoda case. Such redeployment of managers allows for the circulation of learning within the collaboration.

As IJVs evolve, there is perhaps a temptation to lessen the attention paid to individual ventures. However, it is later in the life-cycle that knowledge development takes place and new opportunities for the venture appear. The emphasis has then moved from knowledge acquisition to knowledge development, calling for a different type of management involvement.

Learning by one partner can shift the balance of power in an IJV (Inkpen and Beamish, 1997); thereby changing the relative engagement in the venture is one of the inherent problems in technology transfer collaborations. This change is better anticipated at an early stage and considered as a natural aspect of the evolution of such ventures. The giving-over of roles to local staff is a natural development, given that in the initial stages of technology transfer the use of expatriate staff will be necessary, although this may not be a long-term need and not with the same numbers of people deployed.

Finally, networks were examined as opportunities for the transfer of venture knowledge to other settings. This calls for different skills on the part of managers. Managing a network of organizations or managing in such a network is demanding in terms of flexibility and a systemic and strategic perspective which considers the implications of relevant decisions throughout the network is often necessary.

Much research evidence and practical experience points to the importance of senior management recognizing the importance of learning in collaborative contexts and ensuring that adequate resources are provided for both knowledge acquisition and development. The role of senior managers as facilitators is important and learning should become part of the culture of the collaboration. This also involves the recognition of the importance of learning from other venture partner's activities as well as from the venture itself. If learning is an important element of corporate objectives, then some means of measurement of progress in acquiring such learning would be important.

CONCLUDING REMARKS

This chapter has examined learning in international joint ventures from a number of viewpoints. The perspective has been one of evolution and instability, both of which characterize many modern ventures, and in a cross-cultural context which is only beginning to be explored. Learning in international joint ventures is a dynamic field that merits significant further research in the future. Learning and knowledge development have an important role in achieving the objectives of companies and, in the context of this discussion, a role in the success of collaborative ventures also, in line with Doz's comments, the evolution of collaborations has not met with much research input to date. Longitudinal studies that investigate change in IJVs over a period of time are highly desirable in order to bridge an important gap in the literature.

Inkpen (1998) suggests that the failure of firms to take advantage of venture learning opportunities can be explained by (1) a failure to put knowledge connections in place, (2) the knowledge itself proved problematic and (3) that the parent company did not facilitate the transfer and development of knowledge. As many organizations enter into joint ventures in order to gain new knowledge (and perhaps new technology), it seems that intent is not backed up by commitment and facilitation of learning. The case studies discussed earlier showed commitment and management support.

The importance of learning has been discussed in the context of IJVs. However, management do not always understand how knowledge is acquired and incorporated in organizational systems and processes. Explicit knowledge is easier to deal with in that it can be incorporated into a range of documents and settings, tacit knowledge presents more difficulties in transfer.

The creation of an IJV implies learning opportunities which vary according to the nature and purpose of the venture. It seems that the ability to learn and learn quickly provides significant strategic and competitive advantage. However, as Inkpen (1998) warns, learning should not be assessed purely through 'bottom-line' criteria as it is likely that, in the short term at least, resources will have to be deployed for longer-term gain.

Partner organizations gain more that just knowledge pertaining to the venture; learning can be transferred to other parts of the business, including other ventures. For this to occur, however, it is important to build learning pathways within the firm and to support such learning, and increase its strategic value. As ventures evolve and trust is built up between the collaborating organizations, more sophisticated and wider content-learning is possible (for example in the Chinese case discussed above). Trust is therefore an important consideration, not just for overall venture management but to facilitate knowledge development. Building trust across borders is more complex but is an important source of learning in itself.

The case studies, while showing a relatively high level of commitment on the part of managers, also show that imparting new knowledge requires commitment and an appreciation of partner firms' cultures and norms. The transfer of learning can be adversely affected by poor selection of staff or an overly-ethnocentric approach.

The literature on learning in IJVs is set to develop further and perhaps more interest will be generated in cross-cultural aspects of learning and the evolution of these ventures. If strategic intent is to be matched by results, then perhaps learning in IJVs will command management attention and scholarly activity alike.

References

Buckley, P. and Casson, M. (1988) 'A Theory of Co-operation in International Business', in F. Contractor and P. Lorange (eds), *Co-operative Strategies in International Business* (Lexington, Mass.: Lexington Books).

Bresman, H., Burkinshaw, J. and Nobel, R. (1999) 'Knowledge Transfer in International Acquisitions', *Journal of International Business Studies*, vol. 30(3): 439–62.

Chen, R. and Boggs, D. J. (1998) 'Long-term Co-operation Prospects in International Joint Ventures: Perspectives of Chinese Firms', *Journal of Applied Management Studies*, vol. 7(1): 111–27.

Crossan, M. M. and Inkpen, A. C. (1995) 'Promise and Reality of Learning Through Alliances', *The International Executive*, vol. 36(3): 263–73.

Ditta, D. K. (1988) 'International Joint Ventures: A Framework for Analysis', *Journal of General Management*, vol. 14(2): 78–91.

Dodgson, M. (1993) 'Learning, Trust and Technological Collaboration', *Human Relations*, vol. 46(1): 77–96.

Doz, Y. (1996) 'The Evolution of Co-operation in Strategic Alliances: Initial Conditions or Learning Processes?' *Strategic Management Journal*, vol. 17 (Summer): 55–84.

Farhang, M. (1996) 'Managing Technology Transfer to China', *International Marketing Review*, vol. 14(2): 92–105.

Fedor, K. and Werther, W. (1995) 'Making Sense of the Cultural Factors in International Alliances', *Organization Dynamics*, vol. 23(4): 33–49.

Geringer, J. M. (1988) *Joint Venture Partner Selection: Strategies for Developed Countries* (Westport, Conn.: Quorum Books).

Geringer, J. M. (1991) 'Strategic Determinants of Partner Selection in International Joint Ventures', *Journal of International Business Studies*, vol. 22(1): 41–62.

Geringer, J. M. and Hébert, L. (1989) 'Control and Performance of International Joint Ventures', *Journal of International Business Studies*, vol. 20(2): 235–54.

Gutmann, B. (1995) 'Tandem Training – the Volkswagen–Skoda Approach to Know-how Transfer', *Journal of European Industrial Training*, vol. 19(4): 21–4.

Gyndwali, D. R. (1999) 'Interorganizational Learning Dynamics: Roles of Networks on Knowledge Creation', paper presented at the Third International Conference on Organizational Learning, Lancaster University, June.

Hamel, G. (1991) 'Competition for Competence and Inter-Partner Learning International Strategic Alliances', *Strategic Management Journal*, vol. 12: 83–103.

Hedlund, G. (1994) 'A Model of Knowledge Management and the N-form Corporation', *Strategic Management Journal*, vol. 15 (Summer): 73–91.

Hofstede, G. (1992) 'Motivation, Leadership and Organization: Do American Theories Apply Abroad?', *Organizational Dynamics*, vol. 22(Summer): 98–122.

Hong, J. (1999) 'Cross-Cultural Influence on Organizational Learning: The Case of Japanese Companies in China', paper presented at the Third International Conference on Organizational Learning, Lancaster University, June.

Huber, G. P. 'Organizational Learning: The Contributing Processes and the Literature', *Organizational Science*, vol. 2: 89–115.

Inkpen, A. C. (1996) 'Creating Knowledge Through Collaboration', *California Management Review*, vol. 39(1): 123–40.

Inkpen, A. C. (1998) 'Learning, Knowledge Acquisition and Strategic Alliances', *European Management Journal*, vol. 16(2): 223–9.

Inkpen, A. and Beamish, P. (1997) 'Knowledge, Bargaining Power and the Instability of International Joint Ventures', *Academy of Management Review*, vol. 22(1): 177–202.

Inkpen, A. and Dinur, A. (1998) 'Knowledge Management Processes and International Joint Ventures', *Organization Science*, vol. 9(4): 454–68.

Johanson, J. and Vahlne, J. E. (1977) 'The Internationalization Process of the Firm. A Model of Knowledge Development and Increasing Foreign Market Commitments', *Journal of International Business Studies*, vol. 8: 23–33.

Joshi, M. P. and Inkpen, A. C. (1996) 'Co-operation in a Competitive World, A Framework of Global Strategic Alliances', *Competitive Intelligence Review*, vol. 7(2): 46–55.

Kogut, B. (1988) 'Joint Ventures: Theoretical and Empirical Perspectives', *Strategic Management Journal*, vol. 9: 319–32.

Kogut, B. and Singh, K. (1988) 'The Effect of National Culture on the Choice of Entry Mode', *Journal of International Business Studies*, vol. 19: 411–30.

Levinson, N. S. and Asahi, M. (1995) 'Cross National Alliances and Interorganizational Learning', *Organizational Dynamics*, vol. 24(2): 50–63.

Lyles, M. (1988) 'Learning Amongst Joint Venture-Sophisticated Firms', in F. J. Contractor, and P. Lorange (eds), *Co-operative Strategies in International Business* (Lexington, Mass.: Lexington Books).

Morgan, R. M. and Hunt, S. D. (1994) 'The Commitment–Trust Theory of Relational Marketing', *Journal of Marketing*, vol. 58(3): 20–38.

Nonaka, I. and Takeuchi, H. (1995) *The Knowledge Creating Company* (Oxford: Oxford University Press).

Nonaka, I. and Takeuchi, H. (1998) 'The Knowledge-Creating Company', in C. Mabey, G. Salaman and J. Storey (eds), *Strategic Human Resource Management* (London: Sage).

Ottati, G. D. (1994) 'Trust, Interlinking Transactions and Credit in the Industrial District', *Cambridge Journal of Economics*, vol. 18(6): 529–46.

Pan, Y. and Tse, D. K. (1996) 'Co-operative Strategies Between Foreign Firms in an Overseas Country', *Journal of International Business Studies*, vol. 27(5): 929–47.

Parkhe, A. (1991) 'Interfirm Diversity, Organizational Learning and Longevity in Global Strategic Alliances', *Journal of International Business Studies*, vol. 22(4): 579–601.

Parkhe, A. (1993) 'Messy Research, Methodological Predispositions and Theory Development in International Joint Ventures', *Academy of Management Review*, vol. 18(2): 227–69.

Peng, M. W. and Tan, J. J. (1998) 'Toward Alliance Post-Socialism: Business Strategies in a Transitional Economy', *Journal of Applied Management Studies*, vol. 7(1): 145–9.

Peng, M. W. and Heath, P. S. (1996) 'The Growth of the Firm in Planned Economies in Transition: Institutions, Organizations and Strategic Choice', *Academy of Management Review*, vol. 21(2): 492–528.

Pollard, D. and Tayeb, M. H. (1997) 'National Culture and Teaching Management Practices', in U. Gröner, H. M. de Jongste, U. Kracke and H. Senne (eds), *Wirtschafts-wissenschaft: Anwendungsorientierte Forschung an der Schwelle des 21. Jahrhunderts (Economic and Business Studies – applied research on the threshold of the 21st century)* (Heidelberg: R.v. Decker's Verlag): 57–69.

Powell, W. W., Koput, K. W. and Smith-Doerr, L. (1996) 'Interorganizational Collaboration and the Locus of Innovation: Networks of Learning in Biotechnology', *Administrative Science Quarterly*, vol. 42: 35–67.

Ring, P. S. and Van de Ven A. H. (1994) 'Developmental process of Co-operative Interorganizational Relationships', *Academy of Management Review*, vol. 19(1): 90–118.

Schein, E. H. (1993) 'On Dialogue, Culture and Organizational Learning', *Organizational Dynamics*, vol. 22(2): 40–51.

Senge, P. M. (1990) *The Fifth Discipline: The Age and Practice of the Learning Organization* (London: Century Business).

Stenton, G. (1996) 'Management Education Models in Europe: Diversity and Integration', in M. Lee, H. Letiche, R. Crawshaw and M. Thomas (eds), *Management Education in the New Europe* (London: International Thompson Press).

Torrington, D. and Holden, N. (1992) 'Human Resource Management and the International Challenge of Change', *Personnel Review*, vol. 21(2): 19–30.

Tsang, E. W. K. (1997) 'Choice of International Technology Transfer Mode: A Resource-based View', *Management International Review*, vol. 37(2): 151–69.

Tsang, E. W. K. (1998) 'Inside Story: Mind Your Identity when Conducting Cross-Cultural Research', *Organization Studies*, vol. 19(3): 511–16.

Tsang, E. W. K. (1999) 'Internationalization as a Learning Process: Singapore MNCs in China', *Academy of Management Executive*, vol. 13(1): 91–107.

Zucker, L. G. (1977) 'The Role of Institutionalization in Culture Persistence', *American Sociological Review*, vol. 42 (October): 726–43.

Part III
Issues of Concern for
International Collaboration:
The Cultural Challenge

5 Merging Organizational Cultures: Lessons for International Joint Ventures

Thora Thorsdottir

INTRODUCTION

This chapter discusses corporate culture and the acculturative process during business acquisitions, drawing on the findings of an empirical study which investigated four acquisitions. The chapter gives an overview of the main paradigms and definitions of corporate culture and acculturation. Anthropological theories are compared with one another and applied to the business context. The research findings are then analysed from a cultural perspective and anthropological models applied to the process and outcome of each case. The study takes a levels approach to culture and develops models which can be applied to acquisitions.

Although the cases were domestic acquisitions, the findings have an even greater significance for international joint ventures where cultures vary immensely. It is argued that discrepancies between desired mode of integration between the partners have to be considered with greater sensitivity to ensure a successful outcome.

DIFFERING VIEWS AND PARADIGMS

Organizational culture is a term borrowed from anthropology, but researchers have not yet been able to develop a universally acceptable approach to the study of culture or even consistency in definition of culture (Sathe, 1983, 1986). Woods (1989) states there are few theoretical agreements, and this is evident in a review of the literature. There are many debates within the organizational culture literature which have also been apparent in cultural anthropology. This is due to the complexity and ambiguity of the concept.

Allaire and Firsirotu (1984) mention the popularity of looking at organizations as 'little societies'; social systems with socialization processes, social norms and structures. 'It is within this very broad metaphor that the concept of culture in organizations takes its significance' (1984: 193). They divide the schools of thought into two main categories; those who assume the culture is meshed into the social system and those who conceive the cultural system to be ideationally different to the social system.

Often, due to external pressures organizations will respond by changing their policies, structures, or formal system of goals, but these change efforts are often unsuccessful, because the cultural system (that is, structure, values, myths) will not be congruent with the new changes in the formal system. This will often cause severe dysfunctions and difficulties in coping with changed circumstances.

Smirchich (1983a) differentiates between those researchers who view culture as a 'critical variable' (culture being either an independent or dependent, external or internal variable) and those who look at culture as a 'root metaphor for conceptualising organizations.' Schneider (1990) differentiates between the phenomenal and the ideational perspectives. The former, he states, focuses on observable behaviours and artefacts such as rites, rituals and stories, and the latter focuses on shared meanings, symbols and values; these are often taken-for-granted or are preconscious beliefs or assumptions held by organization members. Sathe (1983, 1986) differentiates between the ideational and the cultural adaptionist schools in anthropology. Again, the ideational is that which is shared in the minds of 'community' members and the adaptionist (like the phenomenal school mentioned earlier) focuses on the directly observable behaviours of members, that is patterns of behaviour, speech and the 'use of material objects'.

Functionalism has been the main 'paradigm' used in the social sciences, especially organization studies (Morgan and Smirchich, 1980; Morgan, Frost and Pondy, 1983). The limitation with mechanistical and organismic metaphors is that they do not catch this complexity and only assume that man/groups respond as 'machines' and 'organisms'. Functionalist perspectives or paradigms may seem functionally more lucrative from perhaps a methodological and operationalizable point of view, but the more idealistic or interpretive 'paradigms' are richer, and to those holding those views the only way in which human activity can be properly studied.

LEVELS OF CULTURE

The concept of culture having many levels or multiple dimensions has been proposed by several theorists (Schein, 1984, 1986a,b; Martin and Siehl, 1983; Dyer, 1982; Lundberg as cited in Woods, 1989; Sathe, 1986; Deal and Kennedy, 1982; Bourcier, 1987; Kilmann, 1984, Pettigrew, 1990).

Sathe (1986) states that looking at culture in terms of levels assumes that culture is something an organization *is* rather than *has*.

Rousseau (1990) states that culture 'has many elements, layered along a continuum of subjectivity and accessibility' (1990: 157). The deeper and more unconscious the element of culture the more difficult it is to uncover or surface. These layers or levels range from artefacts through to fundamental assumptions, which are the deepest most inaccessible levels. In between these levels are the patterns of behaviour, behavioural norms and values. Artefacts are the material objects which represent or reflect the physical manifestations of culture (that is, logos). The 'patterns of behaviour' are the functions of organizations that are observable to outsiders and whose purpose is to solve basic organizational problems. The 'behavioural norms' are the members' beliefs regarding acceptable and unacceptable behaviour. This may be observable to outsiders but would need information directly from members. The 'values' are the priorities of certain outcomes. This requires information directly from members. The 'unconscious assumptions' are not obvious, even to members. This level is the most difficult to study, for it is not manifest under normal circumstances.

According to Schein (1986a,b) espoused values lead to certain behaviours which in turn may or may not solve the group's problems (of internal integration and external adaption). If the behaviour does solve the problems consistently, the espoused values then become an assumption and will be taken for granted (dropping out of awareness). Assumptions, according to Schein, are learned responses that originated as espoused values. Not all espoused values necessarily lead to basic assumptions.

ACCULTURATION – THEORIES IN ANTHROPOLOGY

According to Padilla (1980), the literature on acculturation in anthropology has accumulated since the turn of the century, but there continues to be a lag in theory-building around the concept. Psychological consequences of acculturation have been common in the literature on acculturation (that is, stress). Like other culture researchers, those that study acculturation have either taken a qualitative or quantitative approach. Anthropologists emphasize the changes in cultural patterns, whereas social psychologists emphasize the more individual experiences and adaptation strategies. Berry (1980b) states that writing on acculturation has appeared as early as 1880, but states that there are four major formulations of the concept. Some similar themes have emerged through all these definitions. Acculturation can be discussed from the point of view of nature, course, level, measurement and adaptation. Each will now be considered in turn. This is based on Berry (1980a) whose work has since been adapted within the acquisition literature (Altendorf, 1986; Nahavandi and Malekzadeh, 1988; Cartwright and Cooper, 1990).

The group must consider several issues during acculturation: 'Is my cultural identity of value to be retained?' and 'Are positive relations with the larger (dominant) society to be sought?' Both these questions require a yes/no reply and, by contrasting the different alternatives, one comes up with four distinct varieties of acculturation which are shown in Table 5.1. Assimilation and integration are two different examples of adjustment. Rejection is a type of reaction and deculturation is a form of withdrawal.

In the case of assimilation, the new culture is adopted without the retention of any of the original culture. In the case of integration, the old cultural identity is kept and the individual/group still moves towards the new culture (accepts both). The final two options are negative; the new culture is rejected in both. In the first the original culture is kept but in the latter neither the original nor the new culture are adopted; this is accompanied by confusion and anxiety, both individual and collective.

When the group's right to choose the form of acculturation is taken into account, the possibilities above become even greater. Each of the four modes of acculturation have two different possibilities depending on whether the acculturation mode was forced or voluntary. Table 5.2 illustrates the different possibilities when choice is taken into consideration. Multiculturalism and pluralism are two forms of integration; the former refers to the voluntary and valued aspect of having both the old and accepting the new culture, whereas the latter refers to the forced element of the same phenomenon. 'Melting pot' and 'pressure cooker' are two forms of assimilation; the former refers to the voluntary aspect of adapting to the new culture and rejecting one's own, whereas the latter refers to the forced element, when groups are coerced into taking on the new culture

Table 5.1 Dichotomous answers to questions of acculturation

Varieties of acculturation	*Retention of cultural identity?*	*Positive relationship to dominant society?*
Assimilation	No	Yes
Integration	Yes	Yes
Rejection	Yes	No
Deculturation	No	No

Source: Berry (1980a): 14. Reprinted with permission.

Table 5.2   Varieties of acculturation as determined by group response

Varieties of acculturation	Retention of cultural identity?	Positive relationship to dominant society?	Group right to choose options?
Multiculturalism	Yes	Yes	Yes
Pluralism	Yes	Yes	No
Melting pot	No	Yes	Yes
Pressure cooker	No	Yes	No
Withdrawal	Yes	No	Yes
Segregation	Yes	No	No
Marginality	No	No	Yes
Ethnocide	No	No	No

Source: Berry (1980a): 16. Reprinted with permission.

and rejecting its own. Withdrawal and segregation refer to rejection of the new and retention of the original culture; the former refers to voluntary rejection, whereas the latter refers to forced distinctiveness and separation by the dominant culture. Like the above, deculturation can also be either forced or voluntary. The former is what Berry (1980a) calls 'ethnocide' and the latter is 'marginality', where marginal groups continue to exist and resist change.

THE SOCIAL SCIENCE RESEARCH COUNCIL'S VIEW OF ACCULTURATION

Acculturation in anthropology has mostly been researched on the acculturation of natives; Aborigines in Australia (Sommerlad and Berry, 1970); Amerindians in Northern Canada (Berry, 1976 as cited in Berry, 1983); the Quebecois in Canada (Berry, 1983); colonization (Newson, 1976) and Barter Island Eskimos in Alaska (Chance, 1965).

The Social Science Research Council* (SSRC, 1954) in an exploratory overview of the topic of acculturation, divide the concept of acculturation into four 'principal facets':

(1)   the characterization of the properties of the two or more autonomous Cultural Systems which come into contact;
(2)   the study of the nature of the Contact Situation;

* Now Economic and Social Research Council.

(3) the analysis of the Conjunctive Relations established between the cultural systems upon contact; and

(4) the study of the Cultural Processes which flow from the conjunction of the systems (1954: 975).

The research findings discussed in this chapter are based on a study of four acquisitions, viewed as the four principal facets suggested by the SSRC suggested above; autonomous systems coming into contact; the nature of the contact situation; the relations established during contact; and finally the acculturation process.

Berry (1983) differentiates between *mobile* groups on the one hand, and *sedentary* groups on the other. Table 5.3 shows the different types of acculturating groups due to variations in freedom of contact and mobility. Berry (1983) suggests that each of the above groups will acculturate in different ways (individual differences may also be found). The sedentary groups are less likely to assimilate to the host culture and are more likely to integrate with or reject it. The original culture is more likely to be maintained to some extent. In the context of an acquisition, the mobile groups can be thought of as those targets that are physically integrated with the acquirer, whereas the sedentary groups are those that remain autonomous, physically separate, subsidiaries, and so forth. This would include acquired companies that remain physically separate and do not change location following acquisition. Refugees are perhaps not a good metaphor in the case of acquisitions unless one compares it with acquired companies that are in financial trouble or are seeking a 'white knight' acquisition. This could include rescue situations where the target was up for sale. The term refugee has the connotation of fleeing *from*; that is, the original culture is the driving force of the mobility, not the host culture itself.

Table 5.3 Four types of acculturating groups due to variations in freedom of contact and mobility

Freedom of contact	Mobility	
	Mobile	*Sedentary*
Voluntary	Immigrants	Ethnic groups
Forced	Refugees	Native peoples

Source: Berry (1983): 70. Reprinted with permission.

In the context of an acquisition, it is questionable whether the freedom of contact can ever be completely voluntary; degree of physical integration of the target is presumably dependent on the strategy of the acquirer, although the extent to which the acquired employees are willing to integrate or assimilate will ultimately affect the success of acculturation, the level of acculturative stress experienced, and the degree of resistance to the change process. Berry and Annis (1974) and Berry (1983) state that greater acculturative stress will be characteristic of migratory, low population density and low stratification societies, while lesser acculturative stress will be characteristic of more sedentary and stratified societies. In organizational terms, this could be translated as: target employees that are physically integrated with the acquirer will experience more acculturative stress than those that remain physically separate. Migratory could also be understood as those groups that are constantly moving around. In the context of an acquisition, this would mean companies or subsidiaries that are constantly changing owners or being acquired and sold, only to be sold and acquired again.

ACCULTURATION AND ACQUISITIONS

From the above discussion one can see how much of the anthropological literature on acculturation of both groups and individuals can be applied to the context of mergers and acquisitions. Researchers in the field of mergers and acquisitions have adapted the Berry (1980a) model of acculturation in one form or another (Buono and Bowditch, 1989; Cartwright and Cooper, 1992; Nahavandi and Malekzadeh, 1988; Louis, 1990; Bastien, 1987 citing Harris and Moran, 1979; Sales and Mirvis, 1984).

Nahavandi and Malekzadeh (1988) propose that 'the degree of congruence between the acquirer and the acquired organizations' preferred modes of acculturation will affect the level of acculturative stress. The latter will in turn either facilitate or hinder the implementation of the merger' (1988: 79). They suggest that the *congruence* between the desired mode of integration between the two companies is more vital to the success of the acquisition than the mode of acculturation *per se*. Nahavandi and Malekzadeh (1988) adopted Berry's (1980a,b, 1983) model of acculturation to the context of acquisitions. It is a modified version in that the *attractiveness* of the acquirer is used instead of 'positive relationship to dominant society sought'. They use the term *Separation* instead of *Rejection*. Table 5.4 shows this adaptation of Berry's above model.

Table 5.4   Acquired firm's modes of acculturation

Perceptions of the attractiveness of the acquirer	How much do members of the acquired firm value preservation of their own culture?	
	Very much	*Not at all*
Very attractive	Integration	Assimilation
Not at all attractive	Separation	Deculturation

Source: Nahavandi and Malekzadeh (1988): 83. Reprinted with permission of ACAD and MGMT. Nahavandi and Malekzadeh (1988) had not tested this model empirically, but made some suggestions and propositions.

A STUDY OF ACQUISITIONS FROM A CULTURAL PERSPECTIVE

The findings discussed in this chapter are based on a study conducted by the author as part of a doctoral thesis. Four case studies were conducted of integrated acquisitions. The corporate cultures of acquiring and target companies were analysed using both qualitative and quantitative methods, and the nature of the contact situation was explored as well as the outcomes. The aim was to analyse the importance and relevance of organizational culture in the context of corporate combinations (Table 5.5).

Interviews were conducted to assess the forms of *group* acculturation; the process and states. The four principal facets of acculturation as suggested by the Social Science Research Council (1954) were explored in the context of acquisitions. Berry's (1983) model ('Adaptive Options Available to Non-Dominant Groups during Acculturation') is explored in the context of acquisitions. Nahavandi and Malekzadeh's (1988) model based on the perceptions of the attractiveness of the acquirer and the extent to which preservation of the original culture is valued, is tested in the context of group acculturation. The final adaptive states are observed.

The case studies were comparable in that the acquisitions took place in the same year, were located in the same region and the purpose was physical integration. The size of the companies varied as well as the industries they were in. In order to maintain confidentiality, the names of the companies are not revealed; the findings will be discussed mainly in aggregate terms to ensure anonymity. This was agreed with the companies involved in the study. A brief background and cultural analysis of each acquisition will be discussed, followed by more detailed discussion on the overall

Table 5.5   Levels of culture observed in the present study

Level, from the manifest to the deepest	Characteristics
Artefacts	The material objects that reflect the physical, observable manifestations of culture (i.e. physical symbols, logos)
Behavioural norms	Beliefs regarding acceptable and unacceptable behaviour. Native-views are needed to understand these
Values	The priorities of certain outcomes (i.e. whether or not to take risks). Native-views are needed to understand these
Unconscious basic assumptions	Taken-for-granted and the deepest level of culture which is not manifest under 'normal' circumstances

Source: Adapted from Rousseau (1990).

findings and relevance to the models discussed previously. The contents of the cultures as seen by the acquired employees are discussed in this section. Acquisition success was evaluated subjectively by both acquirer and target employees.

Cultural Analysis of Acquisition 1 – Consumer Wholesale

The contents of the cultures as seen by the remaining acquired employees are illustrated in the following discussion. Acquirer1's emphasis was on brands and brand-building, whereas the target had emphasized their old heritage and prestige of the company name rather than the brands themselves. But Target1's aspirations had been to become more brand-oriented; already we can see that Acquirer1 had something that could benefit the target.

The greatest difference observed between the two companies (apart from the size – the acquirer being a large multinational) is with regard to emphasis on *brands*. That is, Acquirer1 emphasized brands to a much greater extent than Target1. Marketing aimed to emphasize the image that a particular brand should evoke; each brand would have a different image, and these brands are what are important not the Acquirer1 name. Target1, on the other hand, emphasized the Target1 name as the brand. The emphasis was put on the Target1 name and the prestige and glamour that surrounded it. It was a very old-fashioned company that emphasised its history; it was strict with regard to procedures, policies and decision-making (for example all decisions had to be authorized at formal, regular meetings) (see Table 5.6). In Acquirer1, on the other hand, the aim was to be innovative, creative, entrepreneurial; 'If you think something will benefit the company then do it and ask later' (finance director).

Acquirer1 emphasized that small was beautiful. In this way, although it was a multinational company it was broken down into so-called 'strategic business units' that functioned separately and independently of each other. This enabled the company to remain closer to the customer, enhance the family feeling within the company and to enable Acquirer1 to have the strength of a multinational but the flexibility and innovativeness of a small group. This also minimized bureaucracy. This structure is also likely to

Table 5.6   Native's views of acquirer and target

Level of culture	Original (target) culture	Acquirer's culture as seen by target employees
Artefacts	Prestigious office showing company tradition	Glass cases showing all the bottles and labels (brands). Display photos of brands and origin 'museums' established
Behavioural norms	'Overstock'. Internally focused. Ritual with regards to decision-making – lots of procedures – regular meetings to decide things – must ask permission to do things and authorize decisions	Do, and then ask later. Externally focused. Be creative and innovative if you think it will benefit the company
Values	Prestige and value diplomats and embassies – up-market customers	It is only worth investing in brands that give sufficient return. The target worked on lower margins and were less successful. 'Small is beautiful'. 'Closer to the customer'
Basic assumptions	The target name is the product – old-established name selling to prestigious customers – slightly old-fashioned	We never sell the concept of the company – the image of the brand is what we sell – innovation and marketing is the key

have minimized the culture shock for the acquired Target1 employees. Target1, which was much smaller, was integrated into various units of Acquirer1 which were independent and functioned separately. The added bureaucracy and change associated with entering a much larger, multinational company will have been minimized due to the particular structure of Acquirer1.

In this particular acquisition, the acquirer wanted the target to adopt Acquirer1's ways of doing things; they believed Target1's old-fashioned way would not have worked. Acquirer1 considered that their own way of doing things (being creative and innovative and staying in small units) is what made them successful. Target1 had to learn to be entrepreneurial as well.

Acquirer1 had used project teams to integrate the various functions. Induction courses were used to teach the new methods. They were very professional in their post-acquisition management and offered a lot of outplacement help to those being made redundant (95 per cent of those being made redundant had jobs to go to). Target1 themselves were happy with the acquisition. Target1 management realized that they had to become brand-oriented in their marketing to survive. They knew that Acquirer1 were very strong in brands which was a benefit for Target1. The cultural differences in this acquisition (as seen by the target) were obvious, but the target was *willing* to change.

Cultural Analysis of Acquisition 2 – Production

This acquisition was made in order to replace lost turnover rather than being part of an overall strategy. The target were completely different, both in terms of customers and aims. Acquirer2 emphasized growth more than profit whereas Target2 had emphasized profit. There were also a great deal of cultural and other fundamental differences between the two groups involved in this acquisition. According to the employees interviewed, the acquirer did not understand them and their market (Table 5.7).

This acquisition was the least successful as judged by the target. This is in accordance with Kitching (1973) who found that acquisitions of this type (where the technology is the same but the customers are different) are the least successful of all the strategic types.

From Table 5.7 one can see that there were immense differences between these two companies with regard to issues such as production, marketing and sales. The clients of the acquirer were prestigious and needed specialized products which were not mass-produced. They were expensive products and a lot of care put into each production. Acquirer2 was more

Table 5.7   Native's views of acquirer and target

Level of culture	Original (target) culture	Acquirer's culture as seen by target employees
Artefacts	List of clients. Company very structured	Acquirer's name implies prestige. Prestige around author list. Very unstructured set-up
Behavioural norms	Mass produce cheap goods quickly for less-specialized market. Costs assessed before agreement to produce. Tight budget control	Few, expensive products for very specialized market. Did not cost out projects ahead of time
Values	Profit stressed mostly. Price must be cheap – customers not well-off. Group cohesiveness valued	Quality and prestige more important than profitability – add to price – these are rich clients
Basic assumptions	Business tightly run – rigorous systems in a tight market. Important to get goods out in time. Marketing very important. Cost very important	Take risks – think big; big investments. Top end of the market – we are having an easy time; no tight systems. Product must be perfect; 'Strive for perfection'. Quality first and money second

concerned about prestige and quality than about profitability. The company was not tightly run, a lot of risk was taken and no costing out was done beforehand. The price of the goods were often increased simply because it was felt that the client could afford it.

Target2 on the other hand, was the exact opposite. The clients were less well-off and not as demanding; goods were mass-produced cheaply with the aim of keeping prices low; costs were assessed beforehand and there was tight budget control. There was also a lot of time pressure to get products out quickly. There appear to be many different ways in which the two cultures could clash if one was forced to assimilate with the other. It is unlikely that these fundamental differences could ever be merged smoothly, and this is something that Acquirer2 seemed to overlook initially. After the clashes had occurred, Acquirer2 management finally realized that Target2 could not adopt their methods even if they wanted to. The differences were so fundamental to the survival of each type of product that they could not have functioned in any other way. Acquirer2 learned more from Target2 and the acculturative process was eventually the acquirer moving more towards assimilation with the target.

The Target2 employees did not feel that the acquirer had been sympathetic towards them and they felt that the acquirer did not understand their culture and needs and those of their customers. Apart from the discrepancies in culture and Acquirer2's unsuccessful attempt to force assimilation, there had not been an obvious benefit to the Target2 employees with regards to the present acquisition.

Cultural Analysis of Acquisition 3 – Manufacturing

Acquirer3 was in the acquisition business and had an overall acquisition strategy; the acquisition of Target3 fitted in with this strategy. The motive was to tidy up the marketplace and regulate pricing. Although the product life-cycle was considered mature, the finance director was very much aware of that; in spite of it the acquisition was made in order to get an even larger share of a declining market.

There were also clear reasons behind the sale from the target's point of view. The employees felt that the owners, who were to retire, did not want outsiders running their company. They did not seem to care about the employees; only the owning family. The target appeared to have been run for the benefit of the family and employees were not happy with the way they had been treated there. Acquirer3 seemed to be completely different in a positive way. It was a large company, but did give the impression that they were more professional.

Although there were differences in structure, there was a 'Role' culture in that each employee had a specific role to perform on his machine. The job itself therefore did not change much for the employees. Acquirer3 also did a good job of communicating intentions to employees. From Table 5.8, one can see that although Target3 had been considered very autocratic and Acquirer3 democratic, the two companies were based on 'role' cultures in that they were factories where each worker performed his/her role on a specific machine. The day-to-day jobs did not change much. Some employees even took their own machines with them to the new plant.

The structure of the two companies was completely different; one being a family-run company and the other a large multinational. In Target3, the family only cared about their own family members; no outsider was allowed to become part of management. Target3 were also not very professional. In Acquirer3, things were a lot more professional. Although there was a very structured set-up where the foremen wore white, the management was approachable and there was a cooperative atmosphere.

Table 5.8   Native's views of acquirer and target

Level of culture	Original (target) culture	Acquirer's culture as seen by target employees
Artefacts	Cramped, dirty conditions, over-stocking	Clean conditions. Foremen wear white. A lot of space
Behavioural norms	Management does not say hello – rarely ever seen on shop floor. People volatile – problems never solved fast enough – foremen conflicting. Empire-building non-cooperative management	Management friendly. Foremen not seen to work. Cooperative atmosphere
Values	Family-run company; management only cares about their family. 'Whole company seems to be run for the benefit of the family'	Very structured; employee levels visible; but management seen to care about us. Approachable management
Basic assumptions	Autocratic, dictatorial. Paternalistic-authoritarian. Role culture; do your role and do not question. Not progressive – only family members got ahead	Democratic – role culture; do your role but can question. Supervision is good. Be organized

The working conditions, employee/management relations and the general climate improved immensely. The benefit of this acquisition for the remaining acquired employees was realized *after* cultural contact occurred (there were initially many reservations due to relocation). The rules were brought about by 'formal indoctrination of the new procedures and reasons for them' (the finance director of acquirer). Manufacturing was very disorganized in Target3. The approach to culture change was slow and gradual, and proved successful. This had been done before the employees had been relocated (teaching employees to be organized and the importance of clean and spacious working conditions).

Cultural Analysis of Acquisition 4 – Service Industry

This acquisition was part of the acquirer's expansion plan. Target4 had what they needed in terms of accounts, but they were less professional; however, Target4 wanted to become more professional and selective with regard to their choice of accounts. They were willing sellers. Although they were a very small, tightly knit group, they realized there was a need for change in their very competitive market. Target4 had to become more professional and competitive to survive.

The acquired management openly discussed the acquisition with their employees before it took place. As was stated, in such a small group it is difficult to keep secrets and neither were publicly quoted. The acquisition process, however, was more difficult than anticipated. The acquirer was arrogant and their procedures were very strict. It was also difficult for the employees to handle the transition into a much larger organization. However, the target in this case benefited from the acquisition in that it had access to prestigious accounts and improved its reputation, but there were some difficulties in being accepted by Acquirer4's employees.

Table 5.9 illustrates the cultural differences between these two companies. Target4 had been a very small, fairly unprofessional company where

Table 5.9   Native's views of acquirer and target

Level of culture	Original (target) culture	Acquirer's culture as seen by target employees
Artefacts	Target4 accounts which Acquirer4 wanted. Employees have company cars; bigger fish in smaller pond	The symbol of the company and all that it entails
Behavioural norms	Small group; make your own coffee. Communications open and verbal. Cooperative. Not strict on spending	More structured procedures; industry regulations. Stricter, more professional and competitive. Communications written. Strict on spending; tight control
Values	Old family feeling; we are all in this together	We are professional; value the prestige and image; arrogant towards less prestigious companies
Basic assumptions	Relaxed about who customers are; clients through friends and family – don't have to write things down; just remembered. We are laid back here	Discipline is necessary. Must be strict with regard to choice of clients. Only certain clients are acceptable. All spending must be accountable (industry is an undisciplined world – but we are disciplined). 'We are the best'

they were not strict on spending or in their decision on who should be their clients, whereas Acquirer4 was the opposite. They had very strict policies in accepting new accounts. Although Acquirer4 was a bigger company and the Target4 employees and management missed the good old days when things were tightly knit within a small group and one was a bigger fish in a smaller pond, they did realize that things had to change. They were in financial trouble and they had to become more professional.

The differences in culture between these two companies were due to differences in size and to the stricter regime of the acquirer. These were differences that Target4 were aware of, anticipated and were willing to adopt. The resistance came from the acquirer itself. The difference in culture *per se* did not affect the acculturative process or stop Target4 from wanting to assimilate; the problem came from the host culture.

Comparison of Group Acculturation across Cases

Nahavandi and Malekzadeh (1988) discuss the various modes of acculturation in acquisitions; these are based on Berry's (1983) original models of acculturation in anthropology. The basic forms are integration, assimilation, separation and deculturation, each being further divided into two groups depending on whether the approach was forced or voluntary. As discussed in the literature review on acculturation, there are eight different varieties of acculturation. Based on Berry's (1980a,b) model, the acquisitions in the present study can be grouped according to whether the target wanted to retain its own cultural identity; whether there was a positive relationship to the dominant society; and whether the target had a right to choose the relationship. This can be seen in Table 5.10, where the far-right column shows the type of acculturation.

As Table 5.10 shows, the group acculturative state on contact is not always the same as it is in its final adaptive state after conflict. Sometimes there is no conflict. The type of acculturation can and does change throughout the process. The differing *acculturative* states vary in *type* as well as degree. In some instances, the initial choice of acculturation may turn out to be the least practical mode as the physical integration occurs. The mode of acculturation changes with the degree of contact. The mode of acculturation also changed when those being acculturated strongly opposed the new culture and rebelled against having to assimilate (Target2). The acquirer eventually realized that it was better for the acquired group to maintain its original way of working.

Today, the targets have a positive relationship (as a group) with the acquirer. The groups have adjusted after acquisition and hence one could

Table 5.10   Group acculturative states initially, on contact and today

Name of target	Retention of cultural identity	Positive relationship with acquirer	Group right to choose option	Type of acculturation
Target1	No	Yes	No	Assimilation; Pressure cooker
Target2	*Initially*: Yes	*Initially*: Yes	*Initially*: No	*Initially*: Integration; Pluralism
	On contact: No	*On contact*: No	*On contact*: No	*On contact*: Deculturation; Ethnocide
	Today: Yes	*Today*: Yes	*Today*: Yes	*Today*: Integration; Multiculturalism
Target3	No	Yes	No	Assimilation; Pressure cooker
Target4	*Initially*: Yes	*Initially*: Yes	*Initially*: No	*Initially*: Integration; Pluralism
	On contact: No	*On contact*: No, due to acquiring employees	*On contact*: No	*On contact*: Deculturation; Ethnocide
	Today: No	*Today*: Yes	*Today*: No	*Today*: Assimilation; Pressure cooker

conclude that the final acculturative state seen in Table 5.10 is the 'ultimate' adaptive state reached. The less resistance existing today and the more symbiotic the relationships between the groups, the more likely that the group has reached its adaptive state.

On contact, there are several ways in which a group can react – modes of adaptation. These are adjustment, reaction and withdrawal. The so-called adaptive state, which comes after the contact and conflict states could also be one of either adjustment or withdrawal. Reaction is more likely to occur on contact and during conflict and will lead to an end-state of either withdrawal or adjustment to the host culture. The reaction and withdrawal situations on contact can vary. In the Target2 case, the reaction and hence conflict was due to clashing cultures. In Target4, the reaction and conflict came from the *acquiring* employees. There was minimal conflict in the Target3 and Target1 cases where the acquired group adjusted on contact.

Both the Target2 and the Target4 groups could have reached an adaptive state of withdrawal had the conflicts not been resolved. In the Target4 case, Acquirer4 eventually accepted them and those causing the conflict gradually retired. This allowed Target4 to reach an adaptive state of adjustment. If this had not occurred, a form of ethnocide could have occurred.

In the Target2 case, things could have gone drastically wrong. Since the group was not willing to assimilate with the host culture, and they were initially not given a choice, the forced assimilation could have led to ethnocide as well (the most drastic form of deculturation). Unlike the case of Target4 where the adaptive state was adjustment (to management's original intentions of assimilation), the Target2 group reached a different form of adjustment. The original motives were *assimilation with the acquirer*; to which Target2 group withdrew (*withdrawal*). As a reaction to the conflict which arose on contact, the management decided that if any form of adjustment was to be reached, the acquisition had to be changed from an integrated one to a more autonomous form. The adaptive forms of adjustment in autonomous acquisitions are the two forms of integration (multiculturalism and pluralism).

Cultural Compatibility and Level at which Discrepancy Occurs

The four cases were analysed culturally from the native's points of view. The original culture and the host culture (as seen by the natives as they came into contact with the acquirer) were studied. The question one must ask is – at what *level* do the incompatibilities occur and what is their nature? It was suggested that incompatibilities can occur at any of the four levels of culture: artefacts, behavioural norms, values and basic assumptions. It was also suggested that the *deeper* the level at which this discrepancy occurs, the greater the conflict and the more difficult it is to assimilate the target with acquirer. Another question one must ask is: 'What is the *nature* of the incompatibilities?' That is, are the cultures similar, different or opposing? The findings of the study are illustrated in Table 5.11.

Table 5.11 shows that Acquirer2 is the one acquisition where the cultures were opposing at every level. Although the Acquirer3 case was also opposing at every level, it is only opposing at the level of basic assumptions if the *host* cultures are considered. The nature of the employees' day-to-day job did not change. Referring back to the definition of culture, the assumptions that have worked repeatedly in the past in order to get the job done are in many ways still the same in the case of the Target3 employees. The actual culture clash at the level of basic assumptions would have been minimal. The behavioural norms and values would also have been similar

Table 5.11   Nature of cultural discrepancy and the levels at which
they occur across the cases

Level of culture	Acquirer1/ Target1	Acquirer2/ Target2	Acquirer3/ Target3	Acquirer4/ Target4
Artefacts	Different	Opposing	Opposing	Different
Behavioural norms	Opposing	Opposing	Opposing/ *similar* at level of sub-culture	Opposing
Values	Different	Opposing	Opposing/ *similar* at level of sub-culture	Different
Basic assumptions	Different	Opposing	Opposing with regards to overall cultures; *similar* at level of sub-cultures	Opposing

between Acquirer3 and Target3 if one considers the sub-cultures rather than the host. The nature of the job did not change for the individuals concerned.

The Acquirer1 and Target1 cultures were different, but only opposing at the level of behavioural norms. Target1 had been more old-fashioned and with strict procedures, whereas Acquirer1 was more externally focused – do, and then ask later. This did not cause many problems as the Target1 employees realized they had to change in order to become more competitive. At the level of basic assumptions, things were different but not opposing.

The Acquirer4 and Target4 cultures were opposing at the level of basic assumptions. The methods of performing the task in order to survive were opposing and so were the behavioural norms. The values were also very different, although not opposing as such. But, as in the Acquirer1 case above, the target realized the need for change (it was a seller-initiated acquisition where the target wanted to become more professional).

The Acquirer2 and Target2 cultures were opposing at every level ranging from artefacts to basic assumptions. Although opposing at the level of the host culture, the Acquirer3 and Target3 cultures were similar when the sub-cultures were considered. The nature of the role itself did not change. The two acquisitions where the cultures were *opposing* at the level of *basic assumptions* had greater problems with the acculturative process. The difference between these two cases on the other hand is that Acquirer4's target realized the need for change and the conflict came from the host. Once this problem was alleviated, things ran smoothly. In the Acquirer2 case the conflict came from the target, causing the acquirer to consider altering the mode of acculturation, assimilation not being possible.

At the level of sub-cultures, one could conclude that the culture 'fit' or compatibility was greatest between Acquirer3 and Target3. The acquisition process itself was relatively smooth compared to the acquisitions where the basic assumptions had been opposing. The Acquirer1 acquisition was also relatively smooth; the target company gave the highest rating of success. In the Acquirer2 case, the rating for the target success was lowest and the process was the least smooth of all the acquisitions in the study. As explained, the Acquirer4 basic assumptions were desirable to the target and the conflict subsided.

Cultural incompatibility did appear to be associated with the targets' ratings of success for the acquisition and with the smoothness of the process. The least smooth acquisition as rated by the author and the lowest ranking of target success was the case where the acquirer's and target's cultures were *opposing* at every level of culture. The smoothest acquisitions with least cultural conflict were those where the basic assumptions were *not* opposing. The acquisitions with *opposing* basic assumptions had greater problems and more conflict during integration. Cultural 'compatibility' was evident to the greatest extent in the Acquirer3/Target3 acquisition. Although compatibility as such was rarely observed between the cultures, incompatibility did cause problems, especially at the level of basic assumptions and where the cultures were opposing.

Discrepancies between Desired Modes of Acculturation

Nahavandi and Malekzadeh (1988) hypothesized that the *discrepancy* between the desired mode of acculturation between the target and acquirer has greater implications for conflict and resistance than the actual type of acculturation *per se*. The greater the discrepancy in desired mode of acculturation between the two groups, the greater the conflict. The differences between desired mode of acculturation between acquirer and target across cases can be seen in Table 5.12.

From the table one can see that there was a discrepancy between the desired mode of acculturation between acquirer and target in two of the cases; Acquirer2/Target2 and Acquirer4/Target4. In the latter case, the discrepancy was only between employees of the two companies; the acquiring *management* did want the target to assimilate. The employees who were the source of the conflict left eventually thus resolving the conflict;

Table 5.12   Discrepancy in desired mode of group acculturation
between acquirers and targets

Name of acquirer and target	Acquirer's desired mode of target acculturation	Target's desired mode of acculturation	Actual mode of target acculturation
Acquirer1/Target1	Assimilation	Assimilation	Assimilation
Acquirer2/Target2	Assimilation	Separation	Integration
Acquirer3/Target3	Assimilation	Assimilation	Assimilation
Acquirer4/Target4	Assimilation – separation from *host employees*	Assimilation	Assimilation

assimilation was eventually reached. In the Acquirer2/Target2 case, the discrepancy was a greater problem and did have implications for the smoothness of the acquisition process. Conflict and resistance was greatest in this acquisition.

Group Acculturative Process

In the case of Target3, the cultural conflict was minimal; there was adjustment both on contact and as an adaptive state. In the case of Target1, the acquisition was also considered a benefit and there was minimal cultural resistance; as above, the initial and the final states were adjustment. For Target4 there was a benefit of the acquisition as well as a realized need for change. Although Target4 wanted an adaptive state of adjustment, this could have ended with withdrawal due to hostility from the acquirer. In the Target2 situation there was no obvious benefit of the acquisition for the Target2 group, and on contact there was a great deal of cultural conflict. This conflict and management's aim of physical integration could easily have led to ethnocide. The *management of acculturation* in this situation is very difficult and risky.

In the case of physically integrated acquisitions this could be very risky and lead to the most severe type of withdrawal (deculturation). To hope for assimilation in this situation requires a lot of effort from management and a lot of risk. If still attempted, and not managed properly, ethnocide could occur. Rather than risking deculturation in an attempt to assimilate a physically integrated target, management could refrain from physically integrating the target and settle for an autonomous acquisition. The chance of adaptive adjustment is greater in the case of autonomous acquisitions than in the case of physically integrated targets (less scope for conflict). The management effort is also less and the risk is lowered due to minimal contact between the two entities. Even if withdrawal occurs, it is not as serious a problem to deal with as deculturation in the physically integrated situation.

Target2 had the lowest rating for target success. Eventually the group was allowed to choose its form of acculturation and they chose to be partly autonomous; complete symbiosis was not reached. They withdrew from the acquirer's original intentions of assimilation and physical integration; at the time of the study, they had almost reached a state of adjustment (multiculturalism) but there was still some tension which had to be resolved. It could either be argued that an adaptive state of withdrawal had been reached, or that an adaptive state had not yet been reached – multiculturalism could only be reached if matters were resolved.

I am suggesting ways in which the adaptive states of adjustment and withdrawal can be broken down depending on the management's acculturative intention (integrated vs autonomous) and the group's right to choose. The final adaptive state *adjustment* in the case of physically integrated acquisitions is a form of assimilation (either melting pot or pressure cooker, depending on the group's right to choose). The final adaptive state *withdrawal* in the case of physically integrated acquisitions is a form of deculturation (either marginality or ethnocide, depending on the group's right to choose). Where the acculturating group adjusts initially on contact (for example when the acquisition is of obvious benefit to the target or there is a realized need for change or there is minimal cultural conflict), the final adaptive state is most likely to be adjustment. Stress and conflict will be minimal and the acquirer's effort needed in the *management of acculturation* will be minimal. The risk of withdrawal as a final adaptive state will be minimal where adjustment occurs on contact.

Table 5.13, devised by myself using Berry's (1980a,b) types of acculturation, shows that where the aim is physical integration of the target, there is more at stake if things do not work. Where assimilation is forced, a form of deculturation could occur if the target does not want the same form of acculturation. The table suggests the ways in which an alternative adaptive state can be reached by either allowing the target to choose their own form of acculturation or lessening the degree of physical integration.

Table 5.13 shows these various adaptive states of adjustment or withdrawal depending on physical integration, the group's longing for a relationship with the acquirer and the group's right to choose. Although the

Table 5.13 Variations in group adaptive states depending on physical integration, the group's longing for a relationship and the group's right to choose

Whether or not the target is physically integrated with acquirer	Does group want a relationship with acquirer	Group adaptive state	Group right to choose	Group no right to choose	Type of acculturative state
Physically integrated targets	Yes	Adjustment	Melting pot	Pressure cooker	Assimilation
	No	Withdrawal	Marginality	Ethnocide	Deculturation
Physically Autonomous Targets	Yes	Adjustment	Multi-culturalism	Pluralism	Integration*
	No	Withdrawal	Withdrawal	Segregation	Separation

* Integration here refers to *cultural* integration, not the *physical* integration of a target with acquirer.

acquirer can decide whether a target is physically integrated or autonomous, and whether the group itself has a right to choose the form of acculturation, *adjustment* and *withdrawal* within those options will ultimately depend on:

(a)   the group's initial contact (adjustment, withdrawal, reaction)
(b)   how management reacts to reactions, withdrawal and conflict

Normally a target does not have a right to choose its form of accultura-tion. If the aim is physical integration and the group does not want the sort of relationship the acquirer wants it to have (as in the case of Target2), assimilation is unlikely to occur (at least not without much difficulty). The risk with continuing pursuit of physical integration and/or assimilation may lead to ethnocide as the group withdraws rather than adjusts. If the group continues not to want a relationship with the acquirer, the acquirer could either allow the group to choose (where marginality would become the adaptive state), or the group could remain physically separate where multiculturalism or pluralism would be a more desirable outcome for all concerned. Nahavandi and Malekzadeh (1988) suggested that the *incongruence* between the acquirer's and the target's desired mode of acculturation was more likely to cause conflict than the actual type of acculturation *per se*. This was illustrated very well in the Target2 case. Some forms of acculturation cannot occur when the differences are fundamental.

CONCLUSIONS

Several propositions can be put forth based on the issues raised in this chapter. In particular, there is a very strong case for considering the importance of corporate culture during acquisitions, as these findings illustrate its importance.

Although the sample consisted of domestic acquisitions, the issues raised apply to an even greater extent to cross-border acquisitions where the national cultures can vary immensely. In these situations the corporate and national/regional cultures will all influence the acculturative process. Differing views towards the acquirer/target may be greater and more difficult to assess, and physical distance may also make communications and efforts towards change more difficult. Although physical integration may not always be the aim, assessment and continual sensitivity is of utmost importance. The propositions can be summarized as follows:

- Discrepancies can occur at any level of culture (ranging from artefacts to basic assumptions).
- The level at which this discrepancy exists has greater implications than the discrepancy *per se*.
- The deeper the level at which cultural discrepancy occurs, the more difficult will be the process of change and assimilation. Discrepancy at the level of basic assumptions will lead to the greatest conflict.
- Apart from looking at the *level* at which the clash or discrepancy occurs, it is also necessary to ascertain the *nature* of the discrepancy; are the cultures opposing or just different?
- In order for the basic assumptions to change, there must first be a reason to change. There must be a felt need and the new methods have to be able to work repeatedly in the new context.
- There are circumstances where it is unlikely that two cultures could ever be merged at the level of basic assumptions. Where the basic assumptions that are being imposed can never work well enough to be taken for granted as part of the survival of the group, other measures should be taken. The degree of assimilation and/or degree of physical integration should in these situations be altered.
- Acquirers would benefit from knowing their own culture before acquiring, and as much as possible about the target as early as possible to be able to assess the 'fit' and/or be able to pinpoint possible cultural clashes beforehand.
- Cultural conflict occurs where the target does *not* favour the same mode of acculturation as the acquirer. The extent to which target members do or do not favour the acquirer's desired mode of acculturation

will determine the level of resistance and conflict experienced during the process.

- Cultural clashes account for serious problems especially when there is an attempt at forced assimilation. Acquirers should be sensitive to these issues and not force assimilation in situations where there are culture clashes at the level of basic assumptions. This is most important in the situations where the basic assumptions are *opposing* and where there is no perceived *benefit* for the target to change.

- If there is no initial benefit of acquisition for the target and/or there is no realized need for change, the likelihood of adjustment on contact is minimized. If on contact there is cultural conflict, this could also lead to reaction or withdrawal.

- Where the initial contact leads to immediate adjustment, the acquisition success for the target will be higher than in cases where there was reaction and/or withdrawal. Where the initial contact leads to reaction and/or withdrawal, the *final adaptive state* will determine the success of the acquisition as seen by the target. It is also more difficult to reach an adaptive state of adjustment. Adjustment will be more successful than withdrawal. Where adjustment is reached, the success will also depend on the difficulties and effort needed to reach this state.

- In physically integrated acquisitions where the acquirer wants to assimilate the target, a form of deculturation could occur where the target does not want to assimilate. It is necessary to be careful and ascertain whether the target wants a relationship with the acquirer before an attempt is made at assimilation. Where a relationship is not wanted, this view must be changed before an attempt at assimilation is made or an alternative mode of acculturation found.

- An adaptive state of adjustment is reached when the group and psychological/individual acculturative states are aligned. Where *assimilation* is to occur, a group adaptive state of adjustment is reached once the acquirer's basic assumptions are fully adopted and where individuals identify fully as members of the acquirer.

- The content of the cultures *per se*, the level, nature and degree of cultural discrepancy, the fluidity of the original frame, the extent to which physical integration is to occur and the type of acculturation that is to occur are all important factors in determining the smoothness of the acculturative process.

References

Allaire, Y. and Firsirotu, M. E. (1984) 'Theories of Organizational Culture', *Organization Studies*, vol. 5(3): 193–226.

Altendorf, D. M. (1986) 'When Cultures Clash: A Case Study of the Texaco Takeover of Getty Oil and the Impact of Acculturation on the Acquired Firm', unpublished PhD dissertation, University of Southern California.

Bastien, D. T. (1987) 'Common Patterns of Behaviour and Communication in Corporate Mergers and Acquisitions', *Human Resource Management*, vol. 26(1): 17–33.

Berry, J. W. and Annis, R. C. (1974) 'Acculturative Stress: The Role of Ecology, Culture and Differentiation', *Journal of Cross-Cultural Psychology*, vol. 5: 382–406.

Berry, J. W. (1980a) 'Acculturation as Varieties of Adaptation', in M. A. Padilla (ed.), *Acculturation; Theory, Models and Some New Findings* (Boulder, Col.: Westview Press).

Berry, J. W. (1980b) 'Social and Cultural Change', in H. C. Triandis and R. W. Brislin (eds), *Social Psychology; Handbook of Cross-Cultural Psychology*, vol. 5 (Boston: Allyn & Bacon): 211–79.

Berry, J. W. (1983) 'Acculturation: A Comparative Analysis of Alternative Forms', in R. Samuda (ed.), *Perspectives in Immigrant and Minority Education* (Philadelphia: University Press of America): 65–78.

Bourcier, C. (1987) 'Culture and Sub-Cultures: A Definition of Organizational Culture', unpublished working paper, University of Quebec, Montreal.

Buono, A. F. and Bowditch, J. L. (1989) *The Human Side of Mergers and Acquisitions: Managing Collisions Between People, Cultures, and Organizations* (San Francisco: Jossey-Bass).

Cartwright, S. and Cooper, C. L. (1992) *Mergers and Acquisitions: The Human Factor* (Oxford: Butterworth-Heinemann).

Chance, N. A. (1965) 'Acculturation, Self-Identification and Personality Adjustment', *American Anthropologist*, vol. 67: 372–93.

Cooper, C. L. and Cartwright, S. (1990) 'The Impact of Mergers and Acquisitions on People at Work: Existing Research and Issues', *British Journal of Management*, vol. 1: 65–76.

Deal, T. E. and Kennedy, A. A. (1982) *Corporate Cultures; The Rites and Rituals of Corporate Life* (London: Penguin).

Dyer, W. G. (1982) 'Patterns and Assumptions: The Keys to Understanding Organizational Cultures', Technical Report, TR-ONR-7, MIT, Sloan School of Management, Cambridge, Mass., June.

Harris, P. R. and Moran, R. T. (1979) *Managing Cultural Differences* (Houston: Gulf Publishing).

Kilmann, R. H. (1984) *Beyond the Quick Fix; Managing Five Tracks to Organizational Success* (San Francisco: Jossey-Bass).

Kitching, J. (1973) *Acquisitions in Europe: Causes of Corporate Successes and Failures*, Geneva: Business International S.A. Research Report 73-3.

Louis, M. R. (1990) 'Acculturation in the Workplace: Newcomers as Lay Ethnographers', in B. Schneider (ed.), *Organizational Climate and Culture* (San Francisco: Jossey-Bass): 85–129.

Martin, J. and Siehl, C. (1983) 'Organizational Culture and Counterculture: An Uneasy Symbiosis', *Organizational Dynamics*, Autumn: 52–64.

Morgan, G. and Smirchich, L. (1980) 'The Case for Qualitative Research', *Academy of Management Review*, vol. 5(4): 491–500.

Morgan, G., Frost, P. J. and Pondy, L. R. (1983) 'Organizational Symbolism', in L. R. Pondy, P. J. Frost, G. Morgan and T. C. Dandridge (eds), *Organizational Symbolism* (Greenwich, Conn.: JAI Press): 3–35.

Nahavandi, A. and Malekzadeh, A. R. (1988) 'Acculturation in Mergers and Acquisitions', *Academy of Management Review*, vol. 13(1): 79–90.

Newson, L. (1976) 'Cultural Evolution: A Basic Concept for Human and Historical Geography', *Journal of Historical Geography*, vol. 2(3): 239–55.

Padilla, M. A. (1980) 'The Role of Cultural Awareness and Ethnic Loyalty in Acculturation', in M. A. Padilla (ed.), *Acculturation; Theory, Models and Some New Findings* (Boulder, Col.: Westview Press): 47–85.

Pettigrew, A. M. (1990) 'Organizational Climate and Culture: Two Constructs in Search of a Role', in B. Schneider (ed.), *Organizational Climate and Culture* (San Francisco: Jossey-Bass): 413–33.

Rousseau, D. M. (1990) 'Assessing Organizational Culture: The Case for Multiple Methods', in B. Schneider (ed.), *Organizational Climate and Culture* (San Francisco: Jossey-Bass): 153–92.

Sales, A. L. and Mirvis, P. H. (1984) 'When Cultures Collide: Issues in Acquisition', in J. R. Kimberly and R. E. Quinn (eds), *Managing Organizational Transitions* (Homewood, Ill.: Richard D. Irwin): 107–33.

Sathe, V. (1983) 'Implications of Corporate Culture: A Manager's Guide to Action', *Organizational Dynamics* (Autumn): 5–23.

Sathe, V. (1986) 'How to Decipher and Change Corporate Culture', in H. R. Kilmann, M. J. Saxton and R. Serpa (eds), *Gaining Control of the Corporate Culture* (San Francisco: Jossey-Bass): 230–61.

Schein, E. H. (1984) 'Coming to a New Awareness of Organizational Culture', *Sloan Management Review* (Winter): 3–16.

Schein, E. H. (1986a) 'Are You Corporate Cultured?', *Personnel Journal* (November): 83–96.

Schein, E. H. (1986b) 'How Culture Forms, Develops and Changes', in H. R. Kilmann, M. J. Saxton and R. Serpa (eds), *Gaining Control of the Corporate Culture* (San Francisco: Jossey-Bass): 17–43.

Schneider, B. (1990) 'The Climate for Service: An Application of the Climate Construct', in B. Schneider (ed.), *Organizational Climate and Culture* (San Francisco: Jossey-Bass): 383–412.

Smirchich, L. (1983a) 'Concepts of Culture and Organizational Analysis', *Administrative Science Quarterly*, vol. 28: 339–59.

Smirchich, L. (1983b) 'Organizations as Shared Meanings', in L. R. Pondy, P. J. Frost, G. Morgan and T. C. Dandridge (eds), *Organizational Symbolism* (Greenwich, Conn.: JAI Press): 55–65.

Sommerlad, E. and Berry, J. W. (1970) 'The Role of Ethnic Identification in Distinguishing between Attitudes towards Assimilation and Integration of a Minority Racial Group', *Human Relations*, vol. 23(1): 23–29.

Social Science Research Council (SSRC) (1954) 'Acculturation: An Exploratory Formulation', *American Anthropologist*, vol. 56: 973–1002.

Woods, R. H. (1989) 'Restaurant Culture: Congruence and Culture in the Hospitality Industry', unpublished PhD dissertation, Graduate School of Cornell University.

6 National Culture and Cross-Border Partnerships

Monir H. Tayeb

INTRODUCTION

The extent to which national culture, especially that of foreign countries, influences a firm with overseas interests depends on the degree of its internationalization and on the aspects of its activities. For strategic alliances this relevance of culture is most pronounced at (1) the initial stages of partner selection, (2) negotiations between the would-be alliance partners, and then (3) later at the core values and strategic policies that they would develop jointly and the processes leading to their agreements on their characteristics, as crystallized notably in an IJVs' human resources management (HRM) (see for instance Meyer, 1993, for the implications of the national culture of partners on the processes of relationship and trust-building communication and management of meetings in a joint American–German project). These stages of cross-border cooperation require sensitivity to the cultural backgrounds of the parties involved. Cultural insensitivity here is a prescription of failure (Konieczny, 1994).

Chapter 1 discussed major sociocultural and political issues which provide the context within which the initial stages of cross-border partnerships take place. This chapter concerns the implications of national culture for negotiation and settle-down stages, notably HRM and other related management issues.

NATIONAL CULTURE AND NEGOTIATIONS

Negotiations in cross-cultural settings are a risky affair and mistakes can lead to disasters. As Usunier (1996) acknowledges, ignorance of the other party's culture is an obstacle to the implementation of a successful strategy in negotiations. If negotiating parties do not share common 'mental schemes', problems in negotiations become difficult to solve. The issue, quite rightly, has attracted much attention in the academic community as well as among practitioners.

In the past two decades or so there have been extensive cross-cultural studies covering various aspects of negotiations, such as differences in negotiating styles between participants from various countries (Graham *et al.*, 1994; Tse *et al.*, 1994), the effect of negotiation adaptation on business success (for example Francis, 1991) and the role of cultural awareness and sensitivity in successful negotiation and completion of business deals (Bonvillian and Nowlin, 1994; Gulbro and Herbig, 1996).

Communication with Others

Negotiations are, in essence, about communication with others and all that it entails, including commitment to achieving a mutually beneficial goal, exchange of information, understanding of and adjusting to partners' points of view while safeguarding one's principles, and generally working alongside one another on good terms for a period of time.

Within the context of business, more often than not a great deal is at stake, both financial and non-financial, in a negotiating situation, which as a result is usually highly charged with tension and frustration as well as hopes and aspirations. The situation can be exacerbated by culture-based miscommunications and misunderstandings. Miscommunication can arise when the message intended by the sender fails to resemble the message perceived by the receiver. Such an unintentional distortion could be caused by different life experiences of the parties involved, who might assign different meanings to the words or actions and interpret the message and its nuances differently (Howell, 1982; Ronen, 1986). As Tung (1993) points out, such different experiences are largely culture-based.

The manner in which information exchange and communication are structured in negotiations and other business encounters can reflect high and low contexting. In high-contexted nations there are far more hidden, unspoken and taken-for-granted meanings when people communicate with one another compared to people from low-contexted cultures (Hall and Hall, 1990). For example, in high-context cultures, such as the Japanese, people are generally rather slow getting to the point and do not expect to have to be very specific even when they do. They talk around the point. They think that intelligent human beings should be able to discover the point of a discourse from the context, which they are careful to provide. In contrast, low-context people are fast in getting to the point, tend to over-inform and are much more direct in delivering their message (Hall, 1989).

Unless one is familiar with these hidden meanings, cross-cultural business negotiations may become awkward affairs riddled with misunderstandings. Directness of a person from a low-context culture, for instance, could be perceived as rude by a person from a high-context culture who is accustomed to implicit, understated messages.

Attitudes to silence, as observed by Elashmawi (1989) in Japanese and American companies, is another cultural characteristic on which peoples differ from one another. In Japan, silence is a virtue. It is a time when the majority of Japanese sense the thoughts and feelings of the other, but to people from some other cultures silence is very uncomfortable and discourages them from communicating their feelings. Many Americans, for instance, view silence as an unnecessary interruption of the flow of communication and exchange of information, and tend to break it with arguments to press for agreements from each other. The end result of such a culture clash could be misunderstanding and conflict.

Within any given society, people might differ from one another as to how well they communicate with others in multicultural situations. In this connection, Ting-Toomey (1992) suggests that Howell's (1982) progressive five-stage model of communication competency can be applied to the process of cross-cultural communications:

Level 1   unconscious incompetence
Level 2   conscious incompetence
Level 3   conscious competence
Level 4   unconscious competence
Level 5   unconscious super-competence.

At one end of the continuum, unconscious incompetence may stem from a person's ignorance. Unconscious super-competence, located at the other end of the continuum, is characterized by great proficiency in handling cultural differences. A person of this level of competence is truly multicultural and multilingual and moves with spontaneity between one set of cultural norms and another (see also Tung, 1995, for a detailed analysis of these five stages and their application in diversity-management development).

Other People's Language

One of the major issues concerning negotiations with trade partners from other countries is language. Although it is not always necessary to know the partners' mother tongue, various research studies have shown that a correlation exists between successful company performance in winning new business in foreign markets, and the ability of the company to conduct its business in the language of the customer (see for instance Evans, 1994).

Generally, in multinational companies competence in foreign languages is most needed by those involved in export, marketing, sales, technical work, arranging a joint venture deal and any other activities aimed at establishing and facilitating trade between companies and institutions concerned. This is particularly crucial for IJVs because of the depth and breadth of the involvement of the parties concerned.

It is of course possible, and is precisely what many business people do, to hire an interpreter. But the knowledge of a partner's language or the use of an interpreter is not enough to create shared understanding between people from different cultural backgrounds. Language represents and expresses the culture, the value system behind it. Not knowing this underlying culture can cause problems. As Jankowicz (1994) points out, some people tend to underestimate the difficulties involved in the creation of shared understanding and scarcely recognize the issue of cultural differences. Jankowicz makes a further pertinent point in the context of the problems involved in teaching western management theories and practices to Polish managers. Using terminology taken from French literary criticism, Jankowicz makes a distinction between *langue* (language as translated) and *parole* (language as experienced in a given culture). If this distinction is not recognized by partners involved in multicultural dealings, misunderstanding is bound to happen.

In addition, it is worth noting that as Macquin and Rouzies (1998) argue negotiators do not always negotiate with someone from their own culture in the same way they do with someone from another culture. In other words, knowing how Chinese people negotiate with each other, for instance, will not give negotiating teams from other cultures much help in predicting how the Chinese will negotiate with *them*.

The present author is not aware of any direct research evidence but this logic might be behind the reason why many companies when negotiating with foreign partners include one or more people on their negotiating team from the partners' home country, usually expatriates. This kind of policy was in place, for instance, in the Scottish subsidiary of an American multinational company in which the present author conducted a case study (Tayeb, 1998). At the time of the research fieldwork in 1997, the Scottish plant was in the process of negotiations with would-be Chinese partners to enter into a joint venture and set up a manufacturing plant in China. The company's negotiating team was made up of five people with expertise in marketing, manufacturing, product, law and business development in China, among others. Two members of the team were also fluent Mandarin speakers.

However, this policy may not necessarily always give a tactical advantage to the companies which use it, especially in dealing with the Chinese, as observed pertinently by Biörkman and Schaap (1994). Members of a negotiation team of Chinese ethnic origin will obviously have the knowledge of the language, although not necessarily local dialects; they may also have a better understanding of the local culture. However, hiring overseas Chinese is no panacea:

> Although there are broad cultural similarities between China and, among others, Taiwan and Hong Kong, it must be noted that they are far from identical. This can lead to misunderstandings when local Chinese wrongly assume that overseas Chinese are familiar with [People's Republic of China's way] of doing things. Overseas Chinese often lack an understanding of how to deal with P.R.C. officials, colleagues and subordinates. They may also fail to observe social protocols. While failures of western expatriates are often overlooked because it is perceived that they are ignorant of correct social behaviours, failures by expatriates of Chinese ethnicity are likely to be counted against them.
>
> (Biörkman and Schaap, 1994: 149)

In fact in the study referred to earlier (Tayeb, 1998), the presence of the two Mandarin-speaking negotiators did not seem to have had any effect either way on the negotiation process, which had started two years earlier and had not yet reached any satisfactory and meaningful state by the time the research fieldwork was completed in 1997.

There are, of course, other aspects of culture which manifest themselves in a negotiation situation. As Hagen (1988) points out, foreign partners not only speak languages other than one's own, but also have a tendency, for cultural reasons, to think in different ways and have different priorities in the ways in which they do business. For example, some people prefer to conduct their business meetings with foreigners, initially at least, in a formal manner, and would be offended to be addressed by their first names; some might believe that the use of an informal style and first name would signal to the partners that they are trusted. Two partners from these different cultural backgrounds could easily misunderstand each other if they engaged in negotiations without a prior knowledge of one another's assumptions and values.

Building Relationships

In some cultures, people involved in business deals would like to build up personal relationships and establish the trustworthiness of their trade counterparts before going on to engage in business contracts and activities with them. In other cultures, business negotiators would prefer to get down to the nitty-gritty of the deals and contracts straightaway, relying heavily on legal rights and obligations clauses included therein to safeguard their interests (see also Howlett, 1991; Lane and DiStefano, 1992; Hung, 1994; Tayeb, 2000).

As Usunier (1996) points out, in some cultures the written agreement is preferred because it provides the structure of the agreement for further discussions and is a symbol of commitment by both parties to the contract. There is no real trust initially and the written agreement provides confidence that the terms of the negotiation will be observed. Trust is then developed gradually. By contrast, cultures that favour oral agreements do so because they trust the other party and expect to be trusted in turn. Trust is therefore a prerequisite to the un-written agreements. Written agreements mainly fulfil legal requirements. As Ang and Teo (1997), following Keegan (1984), rightly point out, differences in agreement preferences can generate misunderstandings:

> To the party that prefers written agreements, his oral preference partner may be perceived to lack commitment. Conversely, an oral preference individual will tend to perceive that his written preference partner does not trust him … In either case, the negotiation success is jeopardized.
>
> (Ang and Teo, 1997: 629)

In this connection, Altany (1989), comparing American business people with their European counterparts, points out that Americans often feel that the European practice of meticulously cultivating personal relationships with business associates slows the expedient conduct of business. They argue that time is money, and the Europeans waste time. But to the Europeans, trust and long-term commitment – not legal contracts and short-term gains – are the heart and soul of a solid business relationship. And the European approach, slower though it is, usually leads to longer and stronger business alliances. The development of these long-term alliances can bring rich rewards for European business partners.

The concept of high-context and low-context, referred to above, is relevant here too. A feature of the high-context, personal style of doing business is that people spend time with clients and partners, become friends and in the process produce reciprocal feelings of obligation. Here there is a greater distinction between insiders and outsiders, between 'us' and 'them' than is found in low-context business cultures. Relaxing with business clients during lunch and after work is crucial to building the close rapport that is absolutely necessary if one is to do business in a high-context business culture; whereas this is not as common or necessary in low-context business (Hall, 1989; Hall and Hall, 1990).

A variation of relationship-building style may be observed in some Arab countries: the use of a third party in building relationships and conducting negotiations. According to Cunningham and Sarayrah (1993), in these countries business negotiations are conducted through mediators, agents and go-betweens, rooted in their time-honoured tribal social system, some of whom might demand, quite legally according to their customs, commissions for the services rendered (Solberg, 1998).

Attitudes to Time

The time needed to conduct negotiations, to get to know one's interlocutor, to complete an agreement and to implement it, although on the face of it a straightforward objective issue, has often quite considerably to do with the perception of the parties concerned, influenced to some extent by their respective cultural backgrounds. The literature on human behaviour within and outside the comparative management discipline deals extensively with the issue of time-orientation and perception of time. A review and analysis of this literature is beyond the scope of the present chapter, but a brief discussion of major relevant points is useful here.

Past, Present, Future Orientation

In some cultures people are forward-looking, in some others 'here and now' is more important than either past or future, and in still others people keep looking to the past even when they plan for the future. This categorization of attitude to time is of course very simplistic, and pigeon-holing people, either as individuals or a cultural group, to fit any of these categories is to distort the complex reality. But one can nevertheless discern a general pattern across nations in term of the emphasis that people place on these three time perspectives.

In India, for instance, the Hindus believe that an individual's life spans over generations from the past to the present and on to the future, as crystallized in an endless reincarnation cycle. For the aborigines of Australia the 'dream time', going back centuries to well before their homeland was invaded by white settlers, is very much alive at present and in their aspirations and hopes for the future.

In an interesting comparison of American and British cultures, Dubin (1970) argues that an American is strongly inclined to believe that present ways of doing things inevitably are to be replaced by even better ways.

For the British, the view of history is essentially to accept the present as the culmination of past developments and, therefore, as representing the highest achievement attainable. A recent attitude survey conducted among a sample of British adolescents, reported on the BBC Radio 4, Today Programme, 16 March 1999, found that British children have a fairly developed past-oriented attitude by the time they are 12 years old.

Time-Keeping

In some cultures 'time is money' and punctuality is therefore of the essence. In others, people tend to take a more relaxed view of time, in both business and non-business activities – meetings might overrun, visitors might be kept waiting in the secretary's room, or the time and date of meetings might be changed at a short notice.

Processing and Use of Time

Hall (1983) identifies two general patterns of time processing: monochronic orientation (M-time) where individuals do one thing at a time and adhere to preset schedules; and polychronic orientation (P-time) where the emphasis is on the importance of the involvement of people in a task, individuals can do several things at the same time and do not necessarily adhere to preset schedules – all can change if need be.

Perception and use of time affects not only day-to-day issues, but also partners' approaches to agreement decisions and, consequently, their perception of time needed to sign an agreement. According to Lichtenberger and Naulleau (1993: 303), for example, German managers' approach to agreement decisions is said to be characterized by a high degree of systemization in planning all the steps leading to the joint venture start-up: business plan, budgets and division of responsibility. The French approach to the agreement decision, by contrast, is said to be characterized by a global appraisal of the opportunity of deciding to start the venture. General figures are used to assess the agreement opportunity, and the planning span is reported to be narrower than the German one. These differences, as the authors point out, may cause tension and misunderstandings which could have serious implications for the partners' relationships during and after the negotiations process.

Long-term, Short-term Orientation

Nations are said to be different from one another in the time span over which they plan their affairs, including business. The Germans, the Japanese and Southeast Asian nations are among those with long-term horizons, and the British and Americans are said to be short-term-oriented. These differing orientations are noticeable especially in company goal-setting and future planning. It must, however, be said that non-cultural factors, such as capital market structures and share-ownership patterns in the USA and the UK, also have a great deal to do with their business people's planning time horizons (Tayeb, 1993, 2000).

Adapting to the Partner's Negotiation Style

A review of the literature on cross-cultural negotiation styles shows that many of the previous studies have focused largely on the influences of one party's culture on its negotiation strategies. Although Thompson (1996) established some theoretical arguments on the cross-cultural impact on negotiation, few studies have empirically investigated the influence of cultural characteristics of a foreign party on another's attitudes and behaviour at negotiations. These characteristics, as Ang and Teo (1997) rightly point out, not only influence one's own negotiation style but may also affect that of the other party. For instance, Shenas (1993) found that differences in negotiating styles are more apparent in cross- than intra-cultural negotiations which leads to more dissonance such as mistrust and less confidence in the foreign partner.

The issue of adaptation in interfirm relationships has been investigated within a broad business context (see for instance, Ford, 1990; Hallén and Seyed-Mohammed, 1991; Håkansson and Snehota, 1995; Brennan and Turnbull, 1998), albeit not in terms of the effects of national culture on such adaptations, and certainly not with regard to cross-cultural negotiations to any significant extent.

Brennan and Turnbull (1995: 182) define interfirm adaptations as 'behavioural modifications at the individual, group, or corporate level carried out by one organisation, which are initially designed to meet specific needs of one other organisation'. Later, the same authors (Brennan and Turnbull, 1996) proposed five metaphors for understanding the process of adaptation in interfirm relationships, especially within the context of industrial marketing and purchasing businesses. They are:

- the 'investment metaphor', where adaptation is viewed as an investment process, involving physical assets;
- the 'decision-making metaphor', where adaptation is considered a decision-making process and suggests a business strategy based on rational thinking;

- the 'political process metaphor' where adaptation is described as a political process and the result of negotiation, power and sacrificing;
- the 'socialization metaphor' where adaptation is seen as a socialization process, where people learn how to behave properly within the context of organizational relationships; and
- the 'evolution metaphor', where adaptation is conceived as an evolutionary process by which the parties involved adjust in order to serve each other better.

Building on this literature, and in a case-study investigation involving six companies, one from China and others from Europe, Fang (2000) explored the extent to which national cultural values influence interfirm adaptations in business relationships and proposed a sixth metaphor, the 'culture metaphor'. The author investigated the process of negotiations which took place over a period of time in 1996 between a Chinese shipyard and three Scandinavian shipping companies (one each from Denmark, Sweden and Norway) and two ship classification societies from the UK and Norway. The study showed that adaptations by the Chinese to the other party in the interfirm relationships may not have been based on any rational thinking but on the Chinese value of reciprocity, rooted in their national culture. In other words, Fang argues, the ways in which the Chinese adapt themselves to the other party depends on how the other party adapts themselves to the Chinese. The author gives a graphic account of how a Norwegian company negotiating team cornered their face-conscious Chinese partners at some point and caused them embarrassment; as a result they jeopardized the business deal at hand and provoked a retaliation by the Chinese in the business that followed. The Chinese negotiators' reciprocity appears to have taken precedence over other principles, such as rational decision-making, in providing a guide for their behaviour in interfirm business relationships.

Ang and Teo's (1997) study of a sample of Singaporean executives similarly investigated the ways in which the cultural traits of a foreign partner might affect one's adaptation during a business negotiation. The authors focused on two aspects of national culture – 'time processing' and 'preference for agreement'. They found that Singaporean executives tended to compartmentalize their time, follow preset schedules, place higher priority on schedules than relationships, and prefer handling one task at a time. They also favoured written over oral agreements. The authors argue that all this goes against the usual expectations on the basis of the participants' cultural values, and attribute the discrepancies to the erosion of Singaporean culture by, among others, the past British rule and westernization of the nation in general.

Which brings us to a discussion of the role of non-cultural factors in negotiation processes. National culture, as the present author has argued elsewhere (Tayeb, 1988, 1995, 1998, 2000), should not be considered as a straitjacket. It is true that people's behaviours and actions are informed by their values and taken-for-granted assumptions, but these values are not purely national culture-based. One's education, age, occupation and life experience in general exert powerful influences on one's values and taken-for-granted assumptions. As a result, an older person might be more tactful in encounters with others, a well-travelled person might be more tolerant of other nationalities, a senior manager might be more time-conscious than a junior office clerk, a well-educated person might have a more intellectually developed mind and sharp problem-solving faculties, than might their opposite numbers.

Besides, national cultures are not homogeneous, and within many nations such as Germany, France, the United Kingdom, India, Russia and the United Sates there exist regional variations and sizeable cultural and religious minorities. Consequently, one might meet, for instance, people who do not keep to an agreed time and schedule in an otherwise 'time and schedule conscious' nation, or people who would prefer written agreements in a 'relationship-based' country. Moreover, the situation in which one finds oneself can also influence one's actions – a friendly atmosphere with trusted foreign partners may not necessarily provoke hostile reactions even if they might cause a Chinese person to lose face.

NATIONAL CULTURE AND HUMAN RESOURCE MANAGEMENT (HRM)

Management of human resources in a single company with operations across different nations is complicated enough; it becomes far more complex and sometimes well nigh impossible when two or more companies join forces (including employees) and embark on a joint venture. As discussed earlier in this book, cross-border partnerships take many forms from broad strategic alliances to multi-parent joint ventures. The extent to which human resource management becomes an issue and the subsequent implications of the national cultures of the parents and the location of the venture obviously depend on the depth of the partnership.

Companies involved in a broad strategic alliance, for example, join together in an exercise of shared strategies and vision, usually in order to be able to handle their environment and markets more effectively, but not shared financial and managerial activities. The companies may own certain proportions of each other's shares, but they do not become a jointly-owned entity and do not lose their independence. They may even exchange senior executives on a reciprocal short-term 'visit' basis, and develop common career management learning and development policies, but they do not merge their employees. Joint ventures move a few steps further than this to shared assets and ownership, pooled skills and knowledge, mixed employees and joint management.

In discussing HRM issues within the context of cross-border partnership, it may be useful to make a distinction between (a) general HRM issues which are relevant to all forms of organizations, single- or multi-parent; (b) those issues which are specific to multi-parent companies; and (c) the cultural dimension of HRM and its implications for the partnership. Of particular relevance to the present chapter are (b) and (c) which are discussed below.

HRM Issues Specific to Cross-Border Partnerships

Lorange (1996) proposes four types of cooperative ventures in his conceptual framework: (1) cooperative ventures with permanent, complementary roles by the parents; (2) a string of negotiated cooperative agreements; (3) project-based cooperative networks; and (4) jointly-owned ventures based on an ongoing business concept. Each of these types, Lorange argues, faces a different set of HRM issues and challenges, with the first type being mostly handled by the respective parent and in the fourth type issues are largely tackled within the venture by its own managers.

Based on preliminary clinical studies conducted by Lorange and Roos (1992), Lorange (1996: 91–2) identifies five critical HRM issues which can be argued to be directly relevant to cross-border cooperative ventures:

- Assignment of human resources to cooperative ventures: who should be assigned where?
- Transferability of human resources: who 'controls' a particular manager?
- The trade-off in time spending between operating and strategic tasks among various managers involved in the cooperative venture.
- Human resource competency: avoidance of judgement biases.
- Management loyalty: to the cooperative venture or to the parent?

Lorange then superimposes these five sets of crucial issues on the four types of cross-border ventures referred to above. Each of the HRM issues is handled differently depending on the type of venture involved. He argues that in a project-based cooperative venture, the HRM function will largely be carried out by each partner in a 'compartmentalized' manner, and largely on behalf of his or her own organizational entity. Similar types of separate HRM arrangements among partners may be made in renegotiated alliances such as in licensing-type cooperative agreements. The HRM function will probably also to some extent be dealt with independently by each parent in the cooperative venture with permanent complementary roles by the parents. In all these three cases coordination, communication and consultation play a significant role in ensuring the smooth running of the venture and its success. For jointly-owned ongoing cooperative venture businesses a strong and fully-fledged HRM function will have to be established within the joint venture itself. Overall, Lorange argues:

> ... the HRM function within all types of cooperative ventures will have to undertake two types of tasks: First, it will have to assign and motivate people in appropriate ways so that the value creation within the cooperative venture will proceed as well as possible. To create such an arrangement requires particular attention to job skills, compatibility of styles, communication compatibility and so on. Second, human resources will not only have to be allocated with a view toward the needs of the cooperative venture activity, but also with a view toward potential repatriation to a parent, to be used later in other contexts for strategic purposes. As such the cooperative venture must be seen as a vehicle to produce not only financial rewards, but also managerial capabilities, which can be used later in other strategic settings.
>
> (Lorange, 1996: 102)

HRM Issues and National Culture

Many of the problems and misunderstandings in international alliances and joint ventures might have their roots in the cultural differences which exist at both national and organizational levels. Examples of the effect of cultural differences on international joint venture performance have been documented by Peterson and Shimada (1978) and Simiar (1980). They found that cultural differences frequently led to failure on the part of parent-company managers to 'understand' one another (see also Faulkner, 1995).

Sensitivity to national culture is of the utmost importance in the management of human resources, including not only specific personnel issues such as training, motivation and remuneration, but also leadership style and organizational design. After all, culture is a social construct and manifests itself when people interact with each other. International joint ventures bring together two or more sets of employees whose national culture, in many cases, gives them fundamentally different views on various work-related issues and problems, such as what constitutes a desirable management style or appropriate organizational hierarchy. Such issues could cause serious problems (Datta, 1988; see also Olie, 1990, for a study of Dutch mergers and acquisitions), but more so in what Salk (1996) calls the encounter phase, the first few months of the joint venture's life. She found in her study of three bi-cultural teams in three joint ventures that serious problems and tensions emanating from cultural misunderstandings subsided considerably once the team members got to know each other and became familiar with their foreign colleagues' ways of doing things.

An important point to note here is that at times stereotypes regarding certain cultures rather than those cultures *per se* seem to cause problems among the multicultural workforce in an IJV (Lichtenberger, 1992; Salk, 1996). Salk, for instance, observed in her extensive qualitative study that all team members were marked by stereotyping and the creation of in-groups and out-groups. Members defined primary social identities and boundaries in terms of the corporate and national origins of members; and in-group/out-group stereotyping was accompanied by attributions to cultural differences that members were reluctant to discuss openly or negotiate about with one another (Salk, 1996: 50). She then gives an interesting example to illustrate this point:

> I attended a meeting of Italian and British managers in which the Italians behaved in a quiet and withdrawn way; immediately after this meeting, British participants described the Italians' 'loud and disruptive' behavior in meetings as a problem in that IJV.
>
> (Salk, 1996: 51)

Similarly, Lichtenberger and Naulleau (1993), make the following observations regarding French and German executives in the Franco-German joint ventures they studied:

> Being asked to characterize their French colleagues, German executives confirmed already known stereotypes of 'French management'. French managers had been described as status- and position-oriented. Authority is being demonstrated through power and distinction. Management in France is considered rather as a 'state of mind' than as a set of techniques. Managerial status is not part of a graded continuum, but rather a change of legal status as well as subtle changes in outlook and self-perception … German managers are being perceived by French colleagues as functional, pragmatic and consensus-oriented on a strategic

level, as time-efficient (use of time is linear) and systematic on the operational level and as very closed in their way of argumentation in external relations.

(1993: 302)

It is, however, worth noting that Schoenberg *et al.* (1995) found the actual behaviours of managers and management styles in four Anglo-French joint ventures to confirm the stereotypes attributed respectively to the two nations and their organizations.

Another major problem regarding the question of national culture and multi-parent companies is the extent to which in certain cases the actors involved appear to be unaware of cultural differences, and hence not able to address the root-causes of some of the tensions and misunderstandings which may have been due to such differences. As Lichtenberger and Naulleau (1993: 300) point out, 'cultural blindness is both perceptual and conceptual: we neither see nor want to see differences' and that, according to research evidence, 'frequently similarity is being assumed even when differences exist'. Burger and Bass (1979), for example, found that managers described their foreign colleagues as more similar to themselves than they actually were.

Then there are the various ways in which different nations deal with the bread-and-butter HRM issues, such as recruitment, selection, training and development, performance appraisal, motivational policies and industrial relations (see for instance Dowling *et al.*, 1999 and Tayeb, 2000, for detailed discussions and illustrations). Other employee management issues such as employees' expectations from their workplace can also be of relevance to IJVs. In some Asian countries, for instance, employees have an emotional relationship with their company and look up to it for help when experiencing difficulties in their private lives, and the organization is usually expected to and does step in to offer help – a loan to purchase a house, guidance on marital problems, even an active role to arrange a marriage for the employee. This is a far cry from the strictly contractual relationship between the employee and his or her workplace in European and Northern American nations – a day's work for a day's pay, nothing more nothing less.

Any joint venture with parents from nations holding widely differing views and preferences regarding these aspects of employee management is a potential hotbed of conflict and tension. An added complication is that the notion of HRM itself, its various models, its role and scope in the company are heavily culture-specific. HRM, an essentially US invention, is neither appreciated nor practicable in many other countries (Clark and

Pugh, 2000; Tayeb, 2000), especially in the developing world with different political, economic and social make-ups and priorities. International joint ventures set up in certain developing countries in Asia with partners from some western developed nations may have a hard time trying to reach a workable solution. As a result, in some cases (see for instance Namazie, 2000) the incoming partners tend to leave HRM/personnel issues to the local partners and concentrate instead on strategic and technical aspects of the joint operation.

Management Style and Organizational Hierarchy

Schoenberg *et al.*'s (1995) study of four major Anglo-French joint ventures from the chemicals and engineering sectors provides an illustration here. The researchers sought to establish major organizational difficulties and opportunities that the partners experienced during the formation and management of the partnership, and the management practices that could overcome most of these differences.

They compared the two nations on two of Hofstede's (1980) dimensions, power distance and uncertainty avoidance, and argued that the former would determine the views of each nationality on such issues as the preferred degree of centralization and the appropriate levels for decision-making whilst the latter would guide the preferences for the number of levels within the organization and the rigidity of the organizational systems. In Hofstede's study the French scored higher on both power distance and uncertainty avoidance indices than did the British. These differences of scores, Schoenberg *et al.* argued, were reflected in the management styles of the managers in the joint ventures studied.

The natural French management style was widely perceived as being more autocratic, with decision-making authority clearly concentrated at top management levels. In contrast, British executives were accustomed to leave more discretion to middle-management levels, with strategic information more widely shared. The two national management styles failed to allocate decision-making discretion at the same organizational level. British managers would assume that the purpose of a meeting was to arrive at a consensus view and then act upon that view. To French managers the purpose of a meeting was simply to clarify the arguments they would later put forward to their bosses for consideration.

The remuneration system and status of employees were other points of difference. For the French, hierarchical position and payment were dependent upon the educational qualifications of the incumbent. For the British they were both based on the content of the job itself. These two different approaches to remuneration caused some serious problems. Following the French approach would mean that for similar jobs in the French parent company significant differences existed between the salary of an *ingénieur* and a *technicien*. In comparison, remuneration in the British partner tended to be based more exclusively upon the job actually done.

In two of the alliances where technical problems had to be solved by bi-national teams, the underlying scientific approaches could be seen to diverge. The French favoured the use of precise theoretical calculations to make sure in advance that a system would work, and would enjoy engineering sophisticated and very general solutions. The British were satisfied with a simpler system that proved empirically to work.

Company Language

The question of adoption of a common language as a means of facilitating communication among employees has been addressed to some extent in the studies which examined the matter within the context of parent–subsidiary relationships, usually concerning expatriates and local employees. Lester (1994), for instance, reports that Siemens, Electrolux and Olivetti, among several major multinational companies (MNCs), have nominated one official language as the basis of communication within the company. In some cases this is the parent company's home-country language, in others another language.

In this connection, Marschan-Piekkari *et al.* (1999), writing within the MNC context, argue that the adoption of a common language has many advantages from a management perspective:

> … It facilitates formal reporting between units in the various foreign locations, thus minimizing the potential for miscommunication and allowing for ease of access to company documents such as technical and product manuals; operating procedures; and record-keeping … It enhances informal communication and information flow between subsidiaries … It assists in fostering a sense of belonging to a global 'family', which has been suggested as an important element in the multinational's use of soft control mechanisms such as corporate culture [Ferner *et al.*, 1995].
>
> (Marschan-Piekkari *et al.*, 1999: 379)

In a multinational company with subsidiaries scattered around the world, the use of such a language, as is shown in the above quote, may be largely confined to documents and other written companywide formal rules and procedures, occasional meetings held by taskforces and teams composed of representatives from different sites, and communication between subsidiaries' senior managers and their colleagues at the HQ. In addition, the decision regarding the choice of common language may ultimately rest with the parent company, which is the dominant figure of the whole enterprise, even if the subsidiaries feel frustrated. In a current investigation conducted by the present author (Tayeb and Thory, 2000) into HRM policies and practices of multinational companies in Scotland, the frustration of a senior Scottish manager of a French company is quite clear:

> We are not a multinational company, we are a French national company who happens to have a factory in Scotland. We are very French... French is the company's language and if you go to France you speak French, and you like to think that when the French come over here they speak a bit of English, well they don't. Even if they can.

However, in joint ventures where sometimes a large number of employees from the partners join forces into a third company, the use of a common language goes well-beyond the above-mentioned cases and becomes an absolute necessity in the detailed day-to-day communication among rank and file as well as senior managers and their colleagues at the HQ of all partners. And frustrations such as those felt by the Scottish manager quoted above can be very destructive. Moreover, in joint ventures where the partners are equal, the choice of the common language can become a more complicated affair than would be the case in MNCs. It is nevertheless important, as Schoenberg *et al.* (1995) point out, to create parity in the joint venture in terms of nationality and language. The founding partners could provide equal opportunties to all the nationalities involved to staff the joint venture. Languages of the partners might be used as the official languages of the venture.

References

Altany, D. (1989) 'Culture Clash', *Industry Week*, 2 October: 13–20.

Ang, S. H. and Teo, G. (1997) 'Effects of Time Processing Orientation, Agreement Preferences and Attitude towards Foreign Businessmen on Negotiation Adaptation', *International Business Review*, vol. 6(6): 625–40.

Biörkman, I. and Schaap, A. (1994) 'Outsiders in the Middle Kingdom: Expatriate Managers in Chinese–Western Joint Ventures', *European Management Journal*, vol. 12(2): 147–53.

Bleeke, J. and Ernst, D. (1995) 'Is Your Strategic Alliance Really a Sale?', *Harvard Business Review*, January–February: 97–105.

Bonvillian, G. and Nowlin, W. A. (1994) 'Cultural Awareness: An Essential Element of Doing Business Abroad', *Business Horizons*, November–December: 44–50.

Brennan, R. and Turnbull, P. W. (1995) 'Adaptations in Buyer–Seller Relationships', in P. W. Turnbull, D. Yorke and P. Naude (eds), *Proceedings of the 11th International Conference on International Marketing and Purchasing* (*IMP*), Manchester Business School, UK: 172–203.

Brennan, R. and Turnbull, P. W. (1996) 'The Process of Adaptation in Inter-Firm Relationships', in H. G. Gemünden, T. Ritter and A. Walter (eds), *Proceedings of the 12th International Conference on International Marketing and Purchasing* (*IMP*), University of Karlsruhe, Germany: 127–48.

Brennan, R. and Turnbull, P. W. (1998) 'Counting the Uncountable? Measuring Inter-Firm Adaptations', in A. Halinen-Kaila and N. Nummela (eds), *Proceedings of the 14th International Conference on International Marketing and Purchasing* (*IMP*), Turku School of Economics and Business Administration, Finland: 133–48.

Burger, P. and Bass, B. M. (1979) *Assessment of Managers: An International Comparison* (New York: Free Press).

Clark, T. and Pugh, D. S. (2000) 'Convergence and Divergence in European HRM: An Exploratory Polycentric Study', in *International Studies of Management and Organization*, vol. 29(4): 83–99.

Cunningham, R. B. and Sarayrah, Y. K. (1993) *Wasta: The Hidden Force in Middle Eastern Society* (Westport Conn.: Praeger).

Datta, D. K. (1988) 'International Joint Ventures: A Framework for Analysis', *Journal of General Management*, vol. 14(2): 78–91.

Dowling, P. J., Welch, D. E. and Schuler, R. S. (1999) *International Human Resource Management: Managing People in a Multinational Context*, 3rd edn (Cincinnati, Ohio: South-Western College Publishing).

Dubin, R. (1970) 'Management in Britain – Impressions of a Visiting Professor', *Journal of Management Studies*, vol. 7(2): 183–98.

Elashmawi, F. (1989) 'Culture Clash in a Multicultural Environment', *International Business Communication*, vol. 1(2): 9–16.

Evans, P. C. (1994) 'Languages and Social Services', unpublished MBA dissertation. Heriot-Watt University.

Fang, T. (2000) 'Culture as a Driving Force for Interfirm Adaptation: A Chinese Case', to appear in *Industrial Marketing Management*.

Faulkner, D. O. (1995) 'The Management of International Strategic Alliances', paper presented to the Annual Conference of AIB, Bradford, UK, April.

Ferner, A., Edwards, P. and Sisson, K. (1995) 'Coming Unstuck? In Search of the "Corporate Glue" in an International Professional Service Firm', *Human Resource Management*, vol. 34(3): 343–61.

Ford, D. (1990) *Understanding Business Markets: Interaction, Relationships and Networks* (London: Academic Press).

Francis, J. N. P. (1991) 'When in Rome? The Effects of Cultural Adaptation on Intercultural Business Negotiations', *Journal of International Business*, vol. 22(3): 403–28.

Graham, J. L., Mintu, A. T. and Rodgers, R. (1994) 'Explorations of Negotiation Behaviors in Ten Foreign Cultures using a Model Developed in the United States', *Management Science*, vol. 40(1): 72–95.

Gulbro, R. and Herbig, P. (1996) 'Negotiating Successfully in Cross-Cultural Situations', *Industrial Marketing Management*, vol. 25(3): 235–41.

Hagen, S. (1988) *Languages in British Business* (Newcastle: Newcastle upon Tyne Polytechnic).

Håkansson, H. and Snehota, I. (1995) *Developing Relationships in Business Networks* (London: International Thomson Business Press).

Hall, E. T. (1983) *The Dance of Life* (New York: Doubleday).

Hall, E. T. (1989) *The Dance of Life: The Other Dimension of Time* (New York: Doubleday).

Hall, E. T. and Hall, M. R. (1990) *Understanding Cultural Differences* (Yarmouth, Maine: Intercultural Press).

Hallén, L. and Seyed-Mohammed, N. (1991) 'Interfirm Adaptation in Business Relationships', *Journal of Marketing*, vol. 55: 29–37.

Harrigan, K. R. (1986) *Managing for Joint Venture Success* (Boston: Lexington Books).

Hofstede, G. (1980) *Culture's Consequences* (California: Sage).

Howell, W. S. (1982) *The Empathic Communicator* (Prospect Heights: Waveland Press).

Howlett, T. (1991) *Negotiating in Asia: A Buyers Manual for Successful Negotiations in Selected Asian Markets* (Hong Kong: Trade Media).

Hung, C. L. (1994) 'Business Mindsets and Styles of the Chinese in the People's Republic of China, Hong Kong and Taiwan', *International Executive*, vol. 36(2): 203–21.

Jankowicz, A. D. (1994) 'The New Journey to Jerusalem: Mission and Meaning in the Managerial Crusade to Eastern Europe', *Organization Studies*, vol. 15: 479–507.

Keegan, W. J. (1984) *Multinational Marketing Management* (Englewood Cliffs, NJ: Prentice Hall).

Konieczny, S. (1994) 'Project Managing: International Joint Projects', *Journal of General Management*, vol. 19: 60–75.

Lane, H. and DiStefano, J. J. (1992) *International Management Behavior: From Policy to Practice* 2nd end (Boston: PWS-KENT).

Lester, T. (1994) 'Pulling Down the Language Barrier', *International Management*, July–August: 42–4.

Lichtenberger, B. and Naulleau, G. (1993) 'French–German Joint Ventures: Cultural Conflicts and Synergies', *International Business Review*, vol. 2(3): 297–307.

Lichtenberger, B. (1992) *Interkulturelle Mitarbeiterführung: Überlegungen und Konsequenzen für das Internationale Personalmanagement* (Stuttgart: M&P), cited in Lichtenberger and Naulleau (1993).

Lorange, P. (1996) 'A Strategic Human Resource Perspective Applied to Multinational Cooperative Ventures', *International Studies of Management and Organization*, vol. 26(1): 87–103.

Lorange, P. and Roos, J. (1992) *Strategic Alliances – Formation, Implementation and Evolution* (Cambridge, Mass.: Blackwell).

Macquin, A. and Rouzies, D. (1998) 'Selling Across the Culture Gap', *Financial Times*, 13 March, survey p. 10.

Marschan-Piekkari, R., Welch, D. and Welch, L. (1999) 'Adopting a Common Corporate Language: IHRM Implications', *International Journal of Human Resource Management*, vol. 10(3): 377–90.

Meyer, H.-D. (1993) 'The Cultural Gap in Long-term International Work Groups: A German–American Case Study', *European Management Journal*, vol. 11: 93–101.

Namazie, P. (2000) 'A Preliminary Review of Factors Affecting International Joint Ventures in Iran', paper presented at the 27th Annual Conference of the Academy of International Business (UK Chapter) Strathclyde University, April.

Niederkofler, M. (1991) 'The Evolution of Strategic Alliances: Opportunities for Management Influence', *Journal of Business Venturing*, vol. 6: 237–57.

Olie, R. L. (1990) 'Culture and Integration Problems in International Mergers and Acquisitions', *European Management Journal*, vol. 8(2): 206–15.

Peterson, R. B. and Shimada, J. Y. (1978) 'Sources of Management Problems in Japanese–American Joint Ventures', *Academy of Management Review*, October: 796–804.

Ronen, S. (1986) *Comparative and Multinational Management* (New York: Wiley).

Salk, S. (1996) 'Partners and Other Strangers: Cultural Boundaries and Cross-Cultural Encounters in International Joint Venture Teams', *International Studies of Management and Organization*, vol. 26(4): 48–72.

Schoenberg, R., Denuelle, N. and Norburn, D. (1995) 'National Conflict within Anglo-French Joint Ventures', *European Business Journal*, vol. 7(1): 8–16.

Shenas, D. G. (1993) 'A Comparative Study of Ethical Issues in International Business: The Case of American and Japanese Business Transactions', *International Journal of Management*, vol. 10(1): 39–46.

Simiar, F. (1980) 'Major Causes of Joint Venture Failures in the Middle East: The Case of War', *Management International Review*, vol. 23: 58–68.

Solberg, C. A. (1998) 'Buyer Behaviour in Arab Organisations', paper presented to the Conference on Globalization, the International Firm and Emerging Economies, 27 May–1 June, Izmir, Turkey.

Tayeb, M. H. (1988) *Organizations and National Culture*: *A Comparative Analysis* (London: Sage).

Tayeb, M. H. (1993) 'English Culture and Business Organisations', in D. J. Hickson (ed.), *Management in Western Europe* (Berlin: Walter de Gruyter): 47–64.

Tayeb, M. H. (1995) 'The Competitive Advantage of Nations: The Role of HRM and its Socio-Cultural Context', *International Journal of Human Resource Management*, vol. 6: 588–605.

Tayeb, M. H. (1996) *The Management of a Multicultural Workforce* (Chichester: Wiley).

Tayeb, M. H. (1998) 'Transfer of HRM Policies and Practices across Cultures: An American Company in Scotland', *International Journal of Human Resource Management*, vol. 9(2): 332–58.

Tayeb, M. H. (2000) *The Management of International Enterprises*: *A Socio-Political View* (Basingstoke: Macmillan).

Tayeb, M. H. and Thory, K. (2000) 'Human Resource Management within the Context of Parent-Subsidiary Relationships: A Scottish Experience', paper presented at the 27th Annual Conference of the Academy of International Business (UK Chapter), Strathclyde University, Glasgow, April.

Thompson, A. G. (1996) 'Compliance with Agreements in Cross-Cultural Transactions: Some Analytical Issues', *Journal of International Business Studies*, vol. 27(2): 375–90.

Ting-Toomey, S. (1992) 'Cross-Cultural Face Negotiation: An Analytical Overview', paper presented at the Pacific Region Forum, Simon Fraser University, Canada, April.

Tse, D. K., Francis, J. and Walls, J. (1994) 'Cultural Differences in Conducting Intra- and Inter-Cultural Negotiations: A Sino-Canadian Comparison', *Journal of International Business Studies*, vol. 24(3): 537–55.

Tung, R. L. (1993) 'Managing Cross-National and Intra-National Diversity, *Human Resource Management*, vol. 32(4): 461–77.

Usunier, J.-C. (1996) 'Cultural Aspects of International Business Negotiation', in P. N. Ghauri and J.-C. Usunier (eds), *International Business Negotiations* (Oxford: Pergamon): 91–118.

Part IV
Issues of Concern for International Collaboration: Size Matters

7 Interorganizational Relationships and Firm Size

Sarah Cooper

INTRODUCTION

Contributions within this volume have considered a number of generic issues of relevance to firms of all sizes. A variety of international collaborative relationships, such as those between Rover and Honda, and Seat and VW, have been considered in the literature and elsewhere in this text to highlight the types of 'trading' which go on between large multinational organizations seeking to extend their international coverage and knowledge base (see for example, Carr, 1999; Gil and de la Fé, 1999; Johnson and Scholes, 1999). Due to their increasingly important role within the economy, this chapter considers specifically the context of the small firm and examines ways in which they may both benefit from and contribute to the success of a wide range of alliances.

Small firms are often constrained in terms of resources but are generators of a sizeable proportion of the most innovative ideas; partnership, if well-planned, can enable smaller enterprises to realize their full potential within dynamic markets. Additionally, particular attention is paid to firms in technology-based sectors as high-technology industries are perceived as major sources of future economic prosperity and, importantly, employment growth. Small firms play an important role in the emergence and development of new technologies (Rothwell and Dodgson, 1993) and participate in inter-organizational relationships in order to enable them to compete and maximize their technological and financial performance (Rothwell and Dodgson, 1991).

ECONOMIC CHANGE

The economies of many western nations have experienced fundamental structural changes over the last 20 to 30 years; local and national enterprise agencies, keen to support the development of robust regional economies, have been confronted by such changes. Some traditional sectors, for example

153

steel-making and coal-mining, have declined resulting in dramatic man-power reductions while others have reduced their labour requirements following the widespread application of new technology. During the 1960s and 1970s there was a trend towards the formation of large firms; this was stimulated by the belief that economies of scale would be forthcoming. The result was the development of large, often vertically integrated firms, and the creation of sizeable numbers of diversified organizations. The experience of some such organizations was not the realization of economies of scale, but a loss of strategic focus leading to a decline in performance.

The dominant trend of the 1980s and 1990s has been the breaking-up of large organizations. This has been stimulated by the belief that focus is the key and it is better for firms to concentrate on a narrower range of activities and to perform them well. A key driving force behind the restructuring and divestment activities of organizations has been a push for increased efficiency and improved financial performance. In the case of publicly-owned companies the imperative to maximize shareholder value to satisfy investors has been a prime motivator. The economy has, thus, seen restructuring and downsizing amongst a large number of firms; the result for many employees has been the loss of their job and for younger generations the disappearance of an opportunity to build a long-term corporate career. New opportunities have emerged, however, as the need remains for many of the tasks performed by the 'delayered' employees; thus, while in-house jobs have been lost opportunities for 'service' providers have emerged.

In some cases, restructuring and breaking-up of large organizations has led to the formation of corporate spin-outs where activities suitable for separation are identified; 'many activities which were once thought essential to have in house' have 'become much more attractive to buy in from an associated specialist supplier' (National Economic Development Office, 1986). This has resulted in the development of complex interorganizational networks within which many small firms play key roles. While some established sectors of the economy have experienced negative structural changes, those comprising organizations engaged in the exploitation of products and services based upon new and emerging technologies have seen significant growth.

SMALL FIRMS AND NEW TECHNOLOGIES

In the 1960s 'the prevailing orthodoxy, in Britain at least, was that small firms no longer had much relevance to economic progress' (Stanworth and Gray, 1991). Over the last 30 to 40 years, however, there has been a shift in emphasis which has seen the support of the small firm become a central plank of economic development policy. This has occurred as a result of a growing realization that encouragement of small firms is desirable on a number of fronts:

> a vigorous and successful small firm sector ... keeps open channels of entry into business and provides a continuing incentive to the ambitious and enterprising to start up in business on their own account ... the economy requires the birth of new enterprises in substantial number and the growth of some to a position from which they are able to challenge and supplant the existing leaders of industry.
>
> (HMSO, 1971)

Small firms are important due to their flexible and adaptive nature, and due to the competition which they provide for large firms (Storey *et al.*, 1987; Oakey and Cooper, 1991). From the perspective of job satisfaction, small firms are seen as offering a working environment in which some people are more highly motivated and function better (HMSO, 1971; Cooper, 1973).

A large proportion of firms within the economy are small (Storey, 1994). The employment contribution made by UK small firms has fluctuated during the twentieth century and the recent increase is bringing figures back into line with those seen in the late 1930s when small firms with less than 200 employees accounted for 31.2 per cent of employment. The contribution by small firms then fell which resulted in their relative decline to a position in 1963 where they accounted for just 19.7 per cent of employment. The trend began to even out and subsequent growth has seen the small-firm sector's contribution increase to its current level of around 32 per cent. Micro-businesses with zero to nine employees account for by far the largest proportion of firms, and Storey (1994) indicates that in 1991 92 per cent of all UK businesses came within the micro-business category, contributing 28 per cent of total employment. While many firms are small in terms of the 'raw' number of employees, most function within complex interorganizational networks, collaborating with a wide variety of public and private sector bodies.

The small size of the firm gives it flexibility, responsiveness and dynamism, key advantages in the fast-moving world of technology development, where the ability to be and remain innovative (Porter, 1990) is central to organizational survival. Small firms make a valuable contribution to economic growth as a result of their capabilities in innovation (Rothwell and Zegveld, 1982; Rothwell and Dodgson, 1993). Schumpeter (1934) hailed them as the source of innovations capable of causing 'economic gales of destruction', while Rothwell (1984) has identified the variable advantages of small and large firms at different stages of the innovation process. They play a key role in the development of some sectors, for example semiconductors, while in others they adopt a niche strategy, differentiating their product or process offerings to gain market share. Pavitt *et al.* (1987) conclude that small firms create more innovations than their large firm counterparts due to them being less bound by convention. Their activities complement those of large firms through the provision of sub-contract services, allowing large firms to focus on their core competences, maximizing use of their resources by contracting out activities.

Rothwell (1984) considers that small and large firms have distinct and complimentary advantages and disadvantages when it comes to innovation (Table 7.1). With regard to aspects such as marketing, due to their size, small firms are able to respond quickly; however, they are not well-placed when it comes to making a significant impact in the marketplace, as they lack the power and are unable to support the development of a complex

Table 7.1   Innovation management in small firms

Small firms	Large firms
Marketing	*Marketing*
quick reactions (+)	develop distribution infrastructure (+)
exports costly (−)	market power (+)
Management	*Management*
dynamic (+)	can lack dynamism (−)
risk-taking (+)	accounting-led (−)
little bureaucracy (+)	bureaucracy (−)
	professional managers (+)
Internal communications	*Internal communications*
informal and efficient (+)	long channels (−)
rapid decision-making (+)	slow (−)
adaptable to change (+)	less flexible (−)
Manpower	*Manpower*
less funding for specialists (−)	better able to attract skilled staff (+)
External communications	*External communications*
lack time/finance for help (−)	'plug-in' to networks (+)
Finance	*Finance*
problems attracting backing (−)	able to borrow funds (+)
fewer projects (−)	spread risk across several projects (+)
	fund diversification (+)

Source: Adapted from Rothwell (1984).

distribution infrastructure. Small firms are in a weak position to exploit markets far beyond their current base, and particularly in overseas markets where their products may be highly attractive to potential customers. By contrast, large firms are hindered by their size from responding quickly to changes within the market. They have the resource base, however, to exploit both domestic and overseas markets using more highly developed distribution systems, and market power to make their products and services known to a wide range of potential customers. It can be seen from Table 7.1 that in the areas of management, internal communications, manpower, external communications and finance, small firms and large firms have their own inherent advantages and disadvantages.

Such comparisons of the respective strengths and weaknesses of small and large firms suggest that significant advantages are to be gained from firms collaborating to further their innovative efforts; weaknesses can be compensated for and strengths exploited through cooperation.

THE SMALL TECHNOLOGY-BASED FIRM AND ALLIANCES

It is clear from the literature on alliances that the business relationships so classified may take one of a variety of forms (Nueno, 1999). Some relationships are developed on a formal basis, controlled by cooperative agreements and contracts, while others are the result of informal arrangements between organizations. Technology-based firms develop alliances with a wide range of organizations within their domestic market and in overseas locations. The most likely alliance partners are other commercial organizations which may or may not be customers and suppliers of the firm, and universities and research establishments active in areas of technology relevant to the firm. Some alliances develop as a result of entrepreneurs spinning out to establish their own firm and maintaining formal or informal links with their former employer. Most spin-out firms are established in the locality of the incubator firm, but a minority are set up in different countries by highly mobile individuals who may be emigrating or returning to their homeland after a period of time spent living and working abroad (Cooper, 1998). Few new technology based firms (NTBFs) operate in isolation, most are embedded within complex networks in the local national and international environment. Some links are maintained over relatively short distances while others are sustained over many hundreds or thousands of miles.

The large majority of technology-firm founders establish firms in the same sector in which they worked immediately prior to start-up (Cooper, 1998), and a large proportion of spin-outs are established in the same locality as the incubator organization (Markusen *et al.*, 1986; Cooper, 1996, 1998). The localized spin-out pattern reinforces a region's technology profile and is important to the formation and growth of technology clusters (Cooper, 1996). *In situ* expansion of indigenous firms leads subsequently to regional growth. These processes combine to result in the development of technology-based clusters like those in the USA along Route 128 and in Silicon Valley, and in the UK in Scotland's Silicon Glen and East Anglia's Silicon Fen. Relationships are frequently maintained with the former employer and some of these links endure for many years with firms carrying out collaborative or joint development work. Small firms tend to possess entrepreneurial drive and dynamism, while lacking the organizational and financial resources to be able to go international on their own; certain types of relationship may enable them to overcome their shortcomings.

Commentators have developed different perceptions of alliances and the benefits which accrue to those who form them. Jorde and Teece (1992) consider that a 'strategic alliance can be defined as a bilateral or multilateral relationship characterised by the commitment of two or more partner firms to reach a common goal'. The important aspects here are that alliances may have any number of partners, and it important that they share goals which are perceived and fully appreciated by all. Nueno (1999) believes that in most cases 'those entering an alliance have a secret agenda that they do not want to share with their partners in the combination', suggesting that many of the goals are covert rather than overt. If learning takes place through the alliance, a potential problem is that collaborators will become competitors when the alliance ends or breaks down, so that 'alliances are a means of lulling competitors into a false sense of security before you stab them in the back' (Clarke and Brennan, 1988). Perhaps Hamel *et al.*'s (1989) view encapsulates the dangers in a less-contentious way, such that 'collaboration is competition in a different form'. The rate of alliance formation has gathered pace, and the rate of growth is increasing as more and more firms strive to improve their competitive position through collaborative means. Given that alliances appear to be potentially threatening as well as bringing benefits, firms of all sizes, and in particular small firms, need to appreciate potential dangers.

Strength used to be assumed to result from independence in the marketplace, and relationships with competitors were avoided. Due to the pressures noted above firms are seeking to form relationships with organizations within and external to their sector, able to provide the best access to resources and contribute the most expertise and competences, and these are frequently found in competitors within the marketplace. Therefore, it is not uncommon to find competitors becoming involved in collaborative arrangements where each contributes differing competences to the alliance, or resources required for an activity are pooled. Indeed, Hergert and Morris (1988) found that the vast majority (over 71 per cent) of the 839 international collaborative agreements which they studied were established between rivals. Even when rivals collaborate with regard to certain aspects of their activities in other areas of business they continue to be competitors. The small firm can benefit from alliance participation which allows it to improve its competitive position and enables it to advance to a position beyond that which it could have achieved on its own. It is important that alliances are conceived in terms of the contribution which they will make to the realization of organizational objectives, and how they will alter the competitive position of the firm. Alliance participation, therefore, needs to be incorporated into the strategic planning process and be considered explicitly in the resulting plan. Many small firms, however, do not have the time and resources to engage in much formal forward planning and strategic thinking. While a well-planned alliance may be most beneficial, a poorly planned one can prove disastrous.

Many small firms have distinct competences, and it is these which give them their competitive advantage. A potential threat to the small firm is that it risks losing its competitive edge if too much of the information about its core competences is passed to the partner during the lifetime of the alliance. It is important, therefore, if a firm is to be in a position to survive as the alliance develops and when the alliance is concluded, that the firm is aware of the dangers of hollowing-out of its core skills. It needs to put in place some mechanism to ensure protection of its intellectual property. The most appropriate form of protection will depend upon the nature of the alliance. Informal relationships may be more difficult to protect and control than those that are based upon formal contracts. Small firms may lack the necessary expertise to know how best to protect themselves from abuse by their partners. They may also not fully comprehend all of the potential dangers from inadvertently providing too much information to their collaborators, and definitely more than is required for performance of the alliance activities.

CONCEPTUALIZING ALLIANCES: THEIR APPROPRIATENESS FOR THE SMALL FIRM

Alliances may be classified according to the degree of dependency and control exerted between partners; therefore, the term covers a wide variety of configurations ranging from informal cooperative ventures through participation in a full-blown joint-venture company to merger or acquisition (Lorange and Roos, 1993; Nueno, 1999). A useful framework for understanding alliances is the 'value-chain' perspective (Porter, 1985). The value-chain concept is useful since it helps with the identification of synergies and with highlighting some of the strategic reasons why particular organizations choose to collaborate. Breaking down organizations into their constituent activities and comparing the strengths and weaknesses of alliance partners through analysis of the value chain enables alliances to be scrutinized and their rationale identified. Where organizations are highly vertically integrated and perform the majority of activities to a high level of proficiency, they may be unlikely to benefit significantly from alliance formation. Where, however, the range of activities within organizations is relatively limited, as is the case with many small firms, there are many more opportunities for benefits to accrue from alliance participation. The addition of firm A's strengths to those of firm B should enable collective progress, but additional benefits may be realized through synergies derived from the unique combination of activities, where the resulting output from the alliance is greater than the collective contributions of the parties involved, the $2+2=5$ effect. Delaney (1993) points out that not all technology is easily transferred, some is firm-specific, so collaboration is less likely to occur or to be successful in such circumstances. Collaboration may help a firm to reduce the financial risk associated with R&D (Rothwell, 1991) and may allow a firm access to specialist equipment owned by others which it could not afford to purchase (Nueno, 1999). The forms and likelihood of information interchange are determined by the needs of the organization and the people within it (Sweeny, 1987).

Three types of economies may be identified, scale, complementary and scope (Lorange and Roos, 1993). The small firm is able to benefit from forging links based upon any of these three forms. The relentless nature of technological progress has been discussed, and the consequent demand for investment in upper-value-chain activities, such as R&D, procurement and production can place significant strains on the small firm. Collaboration over joint programmes of R&D is an attractive option for firms with the expertise to contribute ideas which it is unable to pursue on its own due to a lack of human or financial resources and time. Some countries are more advanced than others and collaboration with a firm in a more developed country, and the transfer of technology which ensues, may enable a small firm to develop competences ahead of other firms within its domestic marketplace. Research-based alliances, in sectors such as biotechnology, are proving popular where small firms offer specialist expertise and large firms contribute financial resources for development and the back-up of a broadly based research department. In the software and electronics sectors, Cooper (1996) identified a number of firms which developed R&D alliances with commercial firms and specific departments within universities and research establishments, mainly in the UK, but some were maintained with organizations overseas. A difficulty which small firms encounter is maintaining external links when their personnel are stretched in meeting the many commitments of their everyday jobs. Frequently staff juggle several functional hats, which is commonly the case with R&D staff who perform other activities when not applying their minds to new product and service developments. Cooper (1996) revealed that only 46 per cent of small software and electronics firms had full-time R&D staff, others had employees who combined a part-time role in R&D with time spent on other activities.

Relationship maintenance can prove a challenge for small firms that have relatively limited resources to keep open lines of communication with partners. While it is common for staff in small organizations to be multifunctional, multiskilled and multitasking, larger firms by contrast frequently have staff who have one responsibility and may dedicate time to keeping open strong lines of communication. Maintaining communication channels with international collaborators can place small firms under significant pressure. Sweeny (1987) considers that, since links or networks are based upon 'person-to-person' contacts, proximity is relatively important, hence the desire 'to be located within the half-hour contact potential'. He does acknowledge, however, that once having met, the telephone and other remote means provide an alternative, punctuated by the occasional personal meeting.

In a survey of 94 small software and electronics firms, Cooper (1996) asked respondents to rate the importance attributed to close proximity to technical information suppliers when the location of the firm was chosen. At odds with the opinion of Sweeny (1987), there was a widespread feeling that proximity was unimportant. Only 4 per cent of respondents considered it 'very important', 18 per cent 'quite important', 13 per cent were 'neutral', another 18 per cent thought it 'not very important' and the majority (46 per cent) thought it 'not at all important'; the pattern varied little between sectors. Respondents considered that communication with colleagues was achieved effectively by telephone, fax and e-mail and visits made to key information suppliers when necessary. Nearly 80 per cent of respondents considered that their R&D links were not influenced by location. Those who felt they had played a part mainly cited the fact that proximity aided communication, although most respondents felt that modern communications technology meant that distance no longer had to pose a barrier to high-quality information exchange. Thus, it appears that the widespread adoption of IT has eased some of the difficulties formally associated with relationship maintenance and is making it increasingly possible for small firms to work with international collaborators. If a source of information is important distance becomes relatively immaterial.

Complementary benefits are realized from the second broad type of alliance, where firms with differing but complementary strengths contribute differing skills and resources to the alliance. Thus, strength in the upper part of the value chain is traded for access to strength/competence in the lower part (Lorange and Roos, 1993). Given that many small firms are not able to be strong in all areas of activity, this type of relationship is likely to prove highly attractive. The anticipated result is that all partners improve their competitive position. While the benefits of a successful alliance are clear, a number of potential dangers threaten to weaken the unsuspecting small firm. It may be difficult for a small firm to work out what it should contribute to the alliance and what it is reasonable to expect in return. Arguably, the greatest opportunities for learning exist in complementary alliances. Where a small firm has specific technical expertise it may have to share some of that knowledge with its alliance partners. It is important that it only gives its partner(s) access to the essential information, since providing too much may result in the partner becoming competent to such an extent that it is able to squeeze the small firm out of the market. Alternatively, the firm may find itself outpaced by its alliance partner. Small firms, given their narrower human resource base, may be less well-placed to capitalize on the information which they acquire; however, they should ensure that they maximize their learning, as they can guarantee that their large firm partners will be doing just that.

Small firms also look to gain from the scope benefits resulting from collaboration over activities in the lower part of the value chain. Here, combining product ranges, establishing joint sales forces or creating joint distribution systems can permit access to a much broader range of customers in a much more extensive geographical area (Lorange and Roos, 1993). 'The central aim of any organization is to define the needs of a target market and to adapt products and services to satisfy these needs more effectively than competitors' (Hutt and Speh, 1985). A key aspect concerning firms in high-technology sectors is that many customers for their sophisticated products come from overseas markets. It can be difficult for a small firm to obtain much information on that overseas marketplace, or indeed from a range of marketplaces, where prospective customers may be located. Links established with organizations in overseas markets allows information on the particular local context to be fed back and incorporated into the design and development process.

Many small technology-based firms have rudimentary sales and marketing activities which are frequently the result of part-time efforts by the founder or other senior executives (Oakey *et al.*, 1988, 1993) reacting to enquiries but with little proactive effort to seek out potential customers and promote the goods and services on offer. Cooper (1996) reveals that only 43 per cent of small electronics and software firms had full-time sales staff. The ability of firms to achieve a geographical spread of sales is significantly related to the presence of full-time sales and marketing staff to carry out the commitment to overseas activities (Cooper, 1996). Where a firm is unable to afford its own staff, tapping into those of others will help bridge the gap. Lack of a well-developed sales and marketing function can leave a firm with little or no market feedback with suggestions on new development opportunities identified by customers (Shanklin and Ryans, 1984). There may be a danger that a firm will engage in technology-push innovation, in the absence of a market for the potential outcome.

Von Hippel (1988, 1989) identifies the importance of 'lead users' in the product development process. He considers that links with market leaders allow firms access to information that will allow them to develop products which the market will want for the foreseeable future. He stresses the importance of market leaders; 'users steeped in the present are unlikely to generate novel product concepts that conflict with the familiar' (1989). Collaboration provides access to greater levels of expertise, and can help the small firm enter a new market more rapidly and gain a stronger market position. Investment is shared, risk is shared, so too are profits. Intelligence gained through the improved marketing and distribution infrastructure enables firms to tailor their products and services to meet particular needs, thereby increasing the attractiveness of their offering to firms in familiar and unfamiliar markets.

SMALL TECHNOLOGY-BASED FIRMS AND THE PRESSURE TOWARDS ALLIANCE FORMATION

A range of factors influences the tendency towards the formulation of multi-faceted relationships. Tidd, Bessant and Pavitt (1997) highlight four over-arching reasons why firms collaborate; 'to reduce the cost of technological development or market entry, to reduce the risk of development or market entry, to achieve scale economies in production, to reduce the time taken to develop and commercialise new products'. It is likely, then, that most firms will have a combination of reasons for collaborating, which can be divided into technological, market and organizational motives. Also, the rapid rate of technological change poses an increasing challenge for firms attempting to remain at the cutting-edge of technology development. In the following we describe a number of the forces driving alliance formation which are of particular relevance to the small firm.

Technological Change

A major challenge for small firms in technology-based sectors is the rapid rate of technological change and the speed at which competitors continue to develop new products. It is becoming more and more difficult to maintain the lead in a field where shortening product life-cycles gives less and less time and advantage over competitors (Duysters *et al.*, 1999). This, allied with the increasing amount of investment required, makes it more and more difficult for small companies to compete in dynamic, fast-growing marketplaces. Firms no longer have a significant period in which to recoup the returns on investment in R&D, and they need to invest in ongoing innovation in new product development in order to remain ahead of competitors or in the leading group within their sector. Small firms in particular find that the requirement to invest continually in new product development is often greater than they can meet and sustain on their own. Consequently, many will seek to join forces with other organizations that may possess a strong cash-base and expertise in the same R&D field. Pooling resources enables firms to meet the relentless requirement for new product development. The outcome of any research programme is uncertain and the ability to spread risk and share uncertainty with others is attractive to many firms.

Research and Development Cycles

As a result of increasing stress to engage in more and more research and development and consequent problems of funds and skills required, a solution commonly adopted by firms is to have in-house the skills required most frequently and to out-source those required much less often. It is very difficult for small firms to maintain the high levels of R&D investment required to sustain an ongoing programme of new product and service development (Oakey *et al.*, 1993). A major problem is that sometimes very high levels of R&D investment are required well in advance of financial returns through sales. Oakey *et al.* (1993) highlight the difficulties faced by many small firms in the scientific instruments and electronics sectors, but similar problems are experienced in many other sectors where resource requirements are high, such as biotechnology (Oakey *et al.*, 1990).

Few firms are able to sustain a lead within a marketplace when they have only one product in their portfolio; thus, firms need to invest to develop further products following their first major breakthrough. Many, however, find it exceedingly difficult to raise adequate funds from external sources such as banks and venture capitalists, so have to depend upon the profits generated within the firm. This can dramatically slow down the rate of development work within the technology-based firm. For this reason a large number of firms are started as service providers where revenue generated is invested in product development work. In time, firms are able to make the transition from being service providers to product developers. For these firms, the business relationships that they develop with those firms to which they offer services are important to the launch and growth of the enterprise. Relationships with others can enable firms to generate capital, and alliances may be formed based upon trading one firm's capital in return for expertise that can facilitate the product development process.

Increasing Technological Complexity

For a long time firms involved in development of technically sophisticated products have developed relationships with suppliers able to produce components and perform contract work to assist in the design, production and assembly of items. The nature of these relationships is frequently more than an exchange of money for services provided. Firms develop long-term relationships with contractors that are able to provide advice and support to assist in the firm's development efforts. The formation of alliances for the development of products requiring distinct competences is one way for firms to mitigate against a lack of in-house expertise. It is increasingly common for products and services to combine strands of knowledge drawn from a number of different areas of science and technology, and while large firms may be able to afford the luxury of employing specialists in a range of fields to enable them to develop such products, it is likely that most small firms will be able to employee only a modest number of highly-paid specialists. The more that technology development requires the use of strands of differing expertise the more likely to it is that firms will form alliances with public or private sector bodies offering know-how to help them remain competitive.

Even large firms are looking more closely at which skills they require to have available in-house and which may be more suitably sourced from out of the organization, as and when the need arises. Such an approach offers opportunities for small firms that tend to be focused and possess specialist know-how. The new collaborative model means that large firms are more inclined to look to specialist providers, many of which are small firms.

Global Competition

Ohmae (1989) views international strategic alliances as an appropriate response to globalization; organizations no longer look to the immediate local environment as the sole market for their products and services. New forms of technology are making it possible to identify customers nationally and internationally, and technologies such as the Internet mean that small firms are able to make their products and services known to a much larger potential customer base. It is thus becoming easier for companies across regional national and international boundaries to sell their products over a much broader geographical area. This is stimulating firms which find competitors in their locality to seek in turn customers across a much broader geographical area. Competitors are, therefore, seen not only as originating within the same domestic marketplace, but as coming from the global marketplace. Small firms find competitors coming onto their 'patch' and are forced to react to protect themselves.

Barriers to Entry

In some countries, local ownership requirements may prevent or severely limit foreign investment except through strategic alliances with local firms. Large inward investors may therefore identify small local companies with which to develop relationships to overcome legal restrictions. Small firms, though, encounter significant difficulties in attempting to overcome barriers to entry; the lack of a profile and power within the marketplace renders it difficult for them to make headway in markets that are foreign to them. Alliances established with an overseas partner are a good method for a small firm to overcome such barriers to entry. They allow firms to get into markets that would otherwise be closed to them, and firms are able to gather local intelligence from their partners. Market expansion is possible and with a lower level of risk.

'Government' Encouragement

The benefits of alliances to enterprise development and innovation is recognized by some government programmes. The European Union has developed a number of collaborative programmes to encourage relationships between firms in member states, some of which are intended to assist small firms in particular. The Bureau de Rapprochement des Entreprises (BRE) has achieved some success amongst small firms. 'The BRE is a non-confidential and easy-to-use system based on the dissemination of co-operation requests and it has been developed by DG23 to promote transnational and international co-operation between SMEs' (Europa website, 2000). The network's successes include an Irish company in the food and drink sector which has negotiated agency and distribution agreements in Germany and Switzerland, and one in the multimedia sector which has agreed a technology transfer deal with a firm from northern Europe (Europa website, 2000). Other programmes require corporate and academic partnerships where the idea is that research, technology and knowledge is transferred between partners within member countries. Dahl (1994) highlights the identification of alliances as being able to play a strategic role in the international expansion of many Norwegian companies. The Norwegian Ministry of Foreign Affairs formulated an official exporting strategy for the 1990s; the government provided financial assistance to firms wishing to cooperate with international partners to facilitate exporting.

Market Factors

Delivery of total product/service packages is becoming increasingly required by customers, who do not wish to deal with several suppliers but wish to acquire a total package. For example, in the information and telecommunications sector a customer may not wish to buy different components of the system from different suppliers and manufacturers. It is, therefore, increasingly common for firms to identify other organizations with complementary products and services; the consortium is then able to offer an attractive, comprehensive product portfolio, providing potential and actual customers with access to a total customer package. This approach may allow a small firm to get its products distributed to a much broader range of customers and over a much wider geographical area, both within its domestic marketplace and abroad.

Where a firm's local or domestic marketplace is relatively small, but the products and services of the company are attractive to a much broader range of national and international customers, an alliance based upon market development with another organization with an extensive network and resource base may facilitate the firm's growth. Norway, for example, is a relatively small economy and for organizations in many manufacturing industries the domestic market is too small to absorb the quantities necessary for a firm to achieve economies of scale (Dahl, 1994). For a firm to exploit economies of scale it needs to produce in greater quantities and export products into overseas markets.

The 'Price' of Organizational Restructuring

The financial cost of a merger is high, and success is not guaranteed. Costs can be incurred in both financial terms but also in relation to time and hassle resulting from difficulties in managing corporate cultures and activities. Alliances are also perceived as preferable to acquisition or merger because they allow access to strengths without being 'lumbered' with organizational weaknesses. An alliance may provide a satisfactory way of getting around these problems and in an international context is a way of avoiding difficulties in merging different working styles, and of overcoming barriers to the acquisition and integration of an organization in a different society. This is not to say that the relationship will not eventually develop to such an extent that merger takes place; but in the shorter term alliances are less risky and more flexible. If merger is the eventual choice it will take place with much more information available to all parties.

In the case of a small firm it may be uncertain about the advantages of becoming part of a large foreign, corporate network, where different national and corporate cultures may bring about destructive conflict. The first step of a strategic relationship may persuade both parties that merger is in the best interests of all concerned, but equally it provides the opportunity for either side to walk away if it is not seen to be of mutual benefit. An alliance may help inform on the wisdom of such a significant move, allowing firms to access the strengths of an organization while at the same time avoiding having to take on board the negative corporate baggage. A small firm will often wish to maintain its independence, flexibility and small and friendly culture. In fact a number of firms are set up by entrepreneurs precisely to escape from the large-firm corporate environment, and accessing resources will enable the small firm to tap into the wheat while avoiding the chaff.

MAKING ALLIANCES WORK

While the number of alliances may be growing the failure rate is high, with the Conference Board reporting success rates of only 34 per cent (Conference Board Associates, 1993) and other studies presenting a success rate of alliances at less than 50 per cent (Nueno, 1999). It is important that goals are shared, as a lack of convergence of perspectives can prove highly destructive. Information needs to be shared, but certain factors may prevent the sharing of know-how; it may be feared, for example, that a competitor might be created. As has been mentioned, some executives have moved into small firms to escape the large-firm environment; rigid systems, hierarchies and committees are an encumbrance to innovation and where a small firm collaborates with a large firm it may become embroiled in the large-firm decision-making processes. For successful alliances to develop, the large firm has to create a team which mirrors the positive aspect of innovation within the small firm.

The main disadvantage of strategic alliances is that the firm may have to give up control over some aspect of its resources. Lei and Slocum (1992: 81–2) maintain that

> partners hope to learn and acquire from each other technologies, products, skills, and knowledge that are otherwise available to their competitors. Yet, without understanding and identifying the risk inherent in alliances, collaboration may unintentionally open up a firm's entire spectrum of core competencies, technologies, and skills to encroachment and learning by its partners.

Whilst it is clear that this may cause problems for the firm which loses control over its resources, Hamel *et al.* (1989) consider that alliances should be seen as an opportunity to learn, that is part of the idea behind them.

A firm's core secrets may be some of the only assets that it has to give it a lead over its rivals, and there may be a fear that transfer of know-how may increase levels of competition. Also, difficulties may be experienced transferring know-how as small firms may lack the in-house expertise to make the most of the information that is received. In international transfers, language may pose a problem and small firms have a narrower human resource base from which to draw those with language skills. In addition, some knowledge is tacit which is not easily transferred between parties. Where specialist skills are lost through a lack of awareness of what should have been transferred, core knowledge may be lost; this is termed 'technological bleedthrough' (Harrigan, 1987), in which skills of central importance to the small firm may leak out during the lifetime of the alliance. Small firms are notoriously lax at protecting their intellectual property with legal safeguards as the cost of patenting can be high and few are able to effectively police the patents which they hold; however, a firm can stand to lose significantly if it fails to secure protection. It is important that firms identify which are their core activities and put in place mechanisms such as licensing agreements that allow them to control the deals which they make.

In attempting to work together, different organizational cultures, time-frames and systems may have the effect of placing barriers in the way of efficient interaction. Small firms tend to have more informal ways of working which help to facilitate innovation, flexibility and dynamism. Large firms, by contrast, will more generally have in place sets of procedures, guidelines and systems which influence the ways in which work is performed. Hence, there may be antagonistic tendencies between the ways in which alliance partners work. De Meyer (1999) highlights the ways in which partnerships are established at the strategic level within an organization and implemented at an operational level. Within the small firm these levels are likely to be synonymous given their modest organizational structure, while in the large firm these activities are carried out at different levels with different personnel involved. Where conflict in an alliance occurs, it is likely that conflict will be resolved quickly within the small firm but may take some time in the large firm causing frustration. Another important aspect in considering relationships between small and large firms is the concept of power and its link with culture. Davis (1968) considered that successful relationships depend upon degrees of compatibility, particularly with regard to business styles. Business styles are linked to organizational culture, which in turn is linked to aspects of power. Power cultures are often characterized by the possession of power in the hands of a single individual in small businesses (Cartwright and Cooper, 1996), whilst power and control are more widely diffused across the majority of large organizations. Therefore, in relationships between large and small firms the potential problems resulting from the different loci of power need to be considered.

Where organizations are from different 'backgrounds', as for example when commercial organizations collaborate with those from the public sector, such as universities, significant problems can be experienced as a result of the small commercial firm having a different approach to key dimensions of the alliance. One area which has been a cause of tension is timeframes, where commercial organizations have experienced a 'lack of urgency' in the approach adopted by staff within university settings (Oakey, 1985). This has the potential to create tensions between alliance partners in private–public sector relationships. Given that universities are under increasing financial stress, and are looking to collaborative contracts with industry as an important source of income, approaches have changed quite markedly within universities. Research staff are now much more in tune with the needs of the commercial sector, bringing about a decline in problems. However, where the addition of differences in national culture are introduced, as in the case of international alliances, they serve to complicate the picture still further.

Garnsey and Wilkinson (1994) detail perhaps one of the most salutary tales for small firms, highlighting the dangers of alliances in their discussion of Anamartic Ltd, a spin-out from Sinclair Research. Based in Cambridge, UK, the firm developed the new technology of the solid-state disk. The firm required £3 million pounds and found it difficult to secure a financial backer. It therefore considered two strategic routes, that of licensing the design or entering a joint venture. Eventually the organization identified two collaborators; the first was Tandem Computers of California, which became its R&D partner, and a second was Fujitsu of Japan, which became its manufacturing partner. There were various advantages of the alliance, Tandem was paid for R&D and became a major customer for the products developed by Anamartic. Anamartic gave exclusive marketing rights to Tandem with the ability to specify specific options in manufacture. Fujitsu manufactured the solid-state disks and became an investment partner, and in addition became the sole supplier to Anamartic. Disadvantages of the alliance were that Tandem imposed its own candidate as Chief Executive (CE) of Anamartic, and it also refused the standard disk in favour of specialist disks for its own products. It also prevented Anamartic dealing with other firms. Fujitsu, as the sole supplier, was in a strong position to charge Anamartic whatever it liked for the products which it manufactured on its behalf, despite maintaining that it was charging competitive prices. As a result of focusing on technology for Tandem, the standard technology which would have been available to other customers was late in getting to the market, and was expensive. Eventually the CE was removed and a new one installed, but in spite of attracting Siemens as an R&D provider and BT as a highly interested new customer these developments came too late. The company was already in serious difficulties with its cash flow, and as a result went bankrupt in 1992. Fujitsu acquired the intellectual property rights, which were connected with pioneering technology, and was able to capitalize on it.

The story illustrates a number of interesting dimensions. It provides an example of what happens when a firm with good technology finds itself unable to finance its development and faces the dilemma of whether to license and enjoy fee income, or to attempt to continue its development through a joint venture or other type of relationship. The culture of conservatism within the venture capital market in Britain placed Anamartic in the difficult position of requiring funding over a longer period of time than financiers were prepared to entertain. The Japanese take a longer-term view of technology development and the potential returns that can be enjoyed. Anamartic found itself in a weak bargaining position and working with some astute and powerful large-firm partners. The requirement to customize products for Tandem and the bargains struck over price with Fujitsu locked Anamartic into an almost impossible position with a CE not working in its best interests. The extent to which the partners in the alliance shared common goals is questionable, and this story is an example of how complementary capabilities, which on the face of it the partners shared, are not sufficient to ensure the success of any alliance. The two large-firm partners had significant experience of working with other firms and arguably their different ways of doing business gave Anamartic sizeable problems.

ALLIANCES IN BIOTECHNOLOGY

The biotechnology industry is an example of a sector where the development of synergistic relationships between large companies and small specialist firms, sometimes described as research boutiques, has become a common occurrence (Fisher, 1996). The term biotechnology covers a range of research-based methods for drug discovery, including gene therapy and combinatorial chemistry. Oakey *et al.* (1990: 46–7) note that

> long lead times make it difficult to raise sufficient capital to cover the costs of protracted new product development. Moreover, many NBFs [new biotechnology firms] lack the production and marketing capability necessary to exploit fully a new product development. Relations between the large and small firms may progress from R&D contracting to licensing and joint ventures ... Beyond their financial vulnerability, NBFs appear to lack expertise in crucial areas of business management such as marketing.

The biotechnology industry has seen a large number of alliances established between large, medium and small firms (Oakey *et al.*, 1990; Fisher, 1996), particularly between large and small specialist firms. Viewed at their most simple, such partnerships are established with small biotechnology firms, acting as the product innovators, coming forward with new ideas. Some of the ideas they are able to exploit on their own, but others require resources far in excess of those possessed by the firm, whether human or financial. The small firms benefit from the entrepreneurial drive and determination to succeed in newly-emerging marketplaces. Large firms, such as those in the pharmaceutical industry, can be perceived as market deliverers, whose advantages lie in their deep pockets and access to comprehensive distribution networks. While arguably lacking in entrepreneurial spirit, these large firms have the market know-how and reputation to push products out into the public domain in a way in which small firms can only dream of.

The creation of relationships between small specialist firms and larger, more diversified organizations can provide large firms with a window into an industry in which they currently have only a minority interest. The view that they gain through collaboration can provide them with valuable knowledge to shape their own development strategies towards markets in which they are currently unfamiliar, or which are newly-emerging and are, therefore, new to everyone. Based on what they discover, the large firm may decide either to reduce its activities with respect to the market or, if opportunities are seen to be significant, to expand further into the market. Small firms may develop new combinations and yet there is a long road to be travelled before a compound will find its way to market. Large companies are able to fund the testing and trial stages required to ensure that products launched into the marketplace are safe and will result in no unforeseen side effects. Large firms also have access to laboratories and test scientists who will work with trial groups to test products, and prepare products to pass rigorous regulatory tests.

A TWENTY-FIRST CENTURY VIEW

An organizational model may be proposed for the twenty-first century which identifies networks as the most favoured structure. Under such a model firms trade what they are best at for access to other strengths possessed by other members of the network. By adopting this approach firms will reduce the range of activities undertaken by staff within the organization and maximize the use of outsourcing services in their broadest terms. From a resource-efficiency viewpoint this reduces overall wastage within the system as the most efficient provider within the system performs activities. It also has the effect of reducing the amount of duplication within a network, which may be efficient in resource terms but means that increasing power falls into the hands of a smaller number of providers. Modern communications technology will enable firms, both large and small, to participate in interorganizational relationships within national and across international borders.

From a policy point of view any moves which help increase the progress towards competitiveness of firms will be viewed in positive terms. The more that relationships are established which transcend international boundaries the harder it becomes to quantify the economic impact of multipliers within the regional economy in which firms are located. Governments encouraging firms to become involved in international collaborative arrangements must realize that while firms can benefit, they have to walk the tightrope between opening up sufficiently so that all can be part of a win–win situation, while at the same time not exposing unintentionally a firm's whole spectrum of competences. Small firms are potentially vulnerable given their weaker position and more limited resources, and their reliance upon a narrower range of competences which if lost are more likely to bring about the downfall of the firm. Firms will have to learn appropriate alliance-management strategies if the President of Chiron Corporation, Edward Penhoet's vision of the future is to come true – that the 'company of the future will have fewer employees and more relationships' (Fisher, 1996).

References

Carr, C. (1999) 'Globalisation, Strategic Alliances, Acquisitions and Technology Transfer. Lessons from ICL/Fujitsu and Rover/Honda and BMW', *R&D Management*, vol. 29(4): 405–21.

Cartwright, S. and Cooper, C. L. (1996) *Managing Mergers, Acquisitions and Strategic Alliances: Integrating People and Cultures* (Oxford, Butterworth-Heinemann).

Clarke, C. and Brennan, K. (1988) 'Allied Forces', *Management Today*, November: 128–31.

Conference Board Europe Associates (1993) 'Strategic Alliances: Guidelines for Successful Management', Report no. 1028, New York.

Cooper, A. C. (1973) 'Technical Entrepreneurship: What do we Know?', *R&D Management*, vol. 3(2): 59–64.

Cooper, S. Y. (1996) 'Small High Technology Firms: A Theoretical and Empirical Study of Location Issues', unpublished PhD thesis, Department of Business Organization, Heriot-Watt University, Edinburgh.

Cooper, S. Y. (1998) 'Entrepreneurship and the Location of High Technology Small Firms; Implications for Regional Development', in R. P. Oakey and W. During (eds), *New Technology Based Firms in the 1990s*, vol. V (London: Paul Chapman): 247–67.

Dahl, T. (1994) 'Norwegian Firms in International Strategic Alliances: Long-term or Short-term Objectives?', BA (Hons) dissertation, Department of Business Organization, Heriot-Watt University, Edinburgh.

Davis, R. B. (1968) 'Compatibility in Corporate Marriages', *Harvard Business Review*, vol. 46: 86–93.

De Meyer, A. (1999) 'Using Strategic Partnerships to Create a Sustainable Competitive Position for High-tech Startup Firms', *R&D Management*, vol. 29(4): 323–8.

Delaney, E. J. (1993) 'Technology Search and Firm Bounds in Biotechnology: New Firms as Agents of Change', *Growth and Change*, vol. 24(2): 206–28.

Duysters, G., Kok, G. and Vaandranger, M. (1999) 'Crafting Successful Strategic Technology Partnerships', *R&D Management*, vol. 29(4): 343–51.

Europa website (2000) 'BRE in Ireland: Companies Going Global (Bureau de Rapprochement des Entreprises)', http://europa.eu.int/comm/dg23/success/ss-bre_ireland/ss-bre_ireland.html.

Fisher, L. M. (1996) 'How Strategic Alliances Work in Biotech', *Business and Strategy*, first quarter, p. 7, http://www.strategy-business.com/technology/96108/page1.html.

Garnsey, E. and Wilkinson, M. (1994) 'Global Alliance in High Technology: A Trap for the Unwary', *Long Range Planning*, vol. 27(6): 137–46.

Gil, M. J. A. and de la Fé, P. G. (1999) 'Strategic Alliances, Organizational Learning and New Product Development: The Cases of Rover and Seat', *R&D Management*, vol. 29(4): 391–404.

Hamel, G., Doz, Y. and Prahalad, C. K. (1989) 'Collaborate with your Competitors and Wayne', *Harvard Business Review*, vol. 67(1): 133–9.

Harrigan, K. R. (1987) *Managing for Joint Venture Success* (Lexington, Mass.: Lexington Books).

Hergert, D. and Morris, D. (1988) 'Trends in International Collaborative Agreements', in F. Contractor and P. Lorange (eds), *Cooperative Strategies in International Business* (Lexington, Mass.: Lexington Books): 99–110.

HMSO (1971) *Small Firms: Report of the Committee of Inquiry on Small Firms* (The Bolton Report), Cmnd. 4811 (London: HMSO).

Hutt, M. D. and Speh, T. W. (1985) *Industrial Marketing Management: A Strategic View of Business Markets* (Chicago: The Dryden Press).

Inkpen, A. C. (1998) 'Learning, Knowledge Acquisition, and Strategic Alliances', *European Management Journal*, vol. 16(2): 223–9.

Johnson, G. and Scholes, K. (1999) *Exploring Corporate Strategy* (London: Prentice-Hall Europe).

Jorde, T. M. and Teece, D. J. (1992) *Antitrust, Innovation and Competitiveness* (Oxford: Oxford University Press).

Lei, D. and Slocum, J. W. (1992) 'Global Strategy, Competence Building and Strategic Alliances', *California Management Review*, Fall: 81–97.

Lorange, P. and Roos, J. (1993) *Strategic Alliances: Formation, Implementation and Evolution* (Oxford: Blackwell).

Markusen, A., Hall, P. and Glasmeier, A. (1986) *High Tech America* (Boston: Allen & Unwin).

National Economic Development Office (1986) *Corporate Venturing: A Strategy for Innovation and Growth* (London: National Economic Development Office).

Nueno, R. (1999) 'Alliances and Other Things', *R&D Management*, vol. 29 (4): 319–22.

Oakey, R. P. (1985) 'British University Science Parks and High Technology Small Firms: A Comment on the Potential for Sustained Industrial Growth', *International Small Business Journal*, vol. 4(1): 58–67.

Oakey, R. P., Cooper, S. Y. and Biggar, J. (1993) 'Product Marketing and Sales in High-Technology Small Firms', in P. Swann (ed.), *New Technologies and the Firm* (London: Routledge): 201–22.

Oakey, R. P., Faulkner, W., Cooper, S. Y. and Walsh, V. (1990) *New Firms in the Biotechnology Industry* (London: Pinter).

Ohmae, K. (1989) 'The Global Logic of Strategic Alliances', *Harvard Business Review*, vol. 67(2): 143–54.

Pavitt, K., Robson, M. and Townsend, J. (1987) 'The Size Distribution of Innovating Firms in the UK – 1945–83', *Journal of Industrial Economics*, vol. 35(3): 297–316.

Peters, T. (1990) 'Get Innovative or Get Dead', *California Management Review*, vol. 33(1): 9–26.

Porter, M. E. (1985) *Competitive Advantage* (New York, The Free Press).

Rothwell, R. (1984) 'The Role of Small Firms in the Emergence of New Technologies', *OMEGA The International Journal of Management Science*, vol. 12(1): 19–29.

Rothwell, R. (1991) 'External Networking and Innovation in Small and Medium-Sized Manufacturing Firms in Europe', *Technovation*, vol. 11(2): 93–112.

Rothwell, R. and Dodgson, M. (1991) 'External Linkages and Innovation in Small and Medium-Sized Enterprises', *R&D Management*, vol. 21: 125–37.

Rothwell, R. and Dodgson, M. (1993) 'Technology-Based SMEs: Their Role in Industrial and Economic Change', in R. Rothwell and M. Dodgson (eds), *International Journal of Technology Management, Special Publication on Small Firms and Innovation*: 8–22.

Rothwell, R. and Zegveld, W. (1982) *Innovation and the Small and Medium-Sized Firm* (London, Frances Pinter).

Schumpeter, J. A. (1934) *The Theory of Economic Development* (Cambridge, Mass., Harvard University Press).

Shanklin, W. L. and Ryans, J. K. (1984) *Marketing High Technology* (Lexington, Mass.: Lexington Books).

Stanworth, J. and Gray, C. (eds) (1991) *Bolton 20 Years On: The Small Firm in the 1990s* (London: Paul Chapman).

Storey, D. J. (1994) *Understanding the Small Business Sector* (London: Routledge).

Storey, D. J., Keasey, K., Watson, R. and Wynarczyk, P. (1987) *The Performance of Small Firms* (London: Croom Helm).

Sweeny, G. P. (1987) *Innovation, Entrepreneurs and Regional Development* (London: Frances Pinter).

Tidd, J., Bessant, J. and Pavitt, K. (1997) *Managing Innovation* (Chichester: Wiley).

von Hippel, E. (1988) *The Sources of Innovation* (Oxford: Oxford University Press).

von Hippel, E. (1990) 'New Product Ideas from "Lead Users"', *Engineering Management Review*, vol. 18(3): 60–63.

Part V
Business Partnership Across the Fence in Europe

8 Interfirm Linkages: The European Experience

Sabine Urban, Ulrike Mayrhofer and Philippe Nanopoulos

INTRODUCTION

Interfirm linkages, ranging in type (cooperation agreements, equity invest-ments, joint ventures, mergers and acquisitions, and so on) and intensity, have become increasingly common in the last 20 years around the world. Beyond a portfolio of products (a concept dear to strategic analysts), today the portfolio of linkages determines to a large extent a firm's developmen-tal directions, competitiveness and financial performance. These 'blurred' groupings (Davis and Meyer, 1998), or fuzzy sets, have undeniably flour-ished within the context of globalization and the spread of new informa-tion and communication technologies. There are other specific factors which have led to the abundance of interfirm linkages within Europe which should be considered as well (Urban and Vendemini, 1992).

Not only is Europe a *de facto* pole of the 'Triad' (USA, EU, Japan), but also an institutional ensemble with a political will and instruments for eco-nomic integration. Strategic alliances as well as mergers/acquisitions con-stitute both a vector for and indicator of this integration, much in the same way as the exchange of goods or foreign direct investments. Europe is, then, a reality constructed by public authorities (countries and acting between supranational and subsidiary principles) and other economic actors: compa-nies, financial institutions, research laboratories, labour forces, consumers.

Is this European ensemble then united and homogenous? Of course not: cultures remain varied, each marked by history and diverse social philoso-phies. The strategic role (in economic terms) of the government has been, since the industrial revolution, completely different in Great Britain, France, Germany and Italy. For example, the 'social' market economy is extolled in Germany, while this concept is practically unknown in other European Union countries. From this perspective it is easy to understand the lasting importance of domestic, or *intra-national*, cooperation agreements.

Perhaps paradoxically, the reality of European diversity (on the one hand a source of richness and on the other of conflict and weakness) explains the increasing number of agreements between companies on the *European level*. Europe is, in fact, a space that allows companies to acquire both a critical mass for research and production and a powerful negotiating position.

But the European fibre, or the rationale of European development, is clearly not shared by all of the socioeconomic actors, notably by companies with specific commercial or technological constraints, and these vary by sector. Once the world becomes a 'global village', the company loses its national identity. Why should the 'borderless' company be concerned specifically with one or another 'local' reality? The increase in number, and especially in the value of agreements between European companies and the *rest of the world* illustrates this growing ambiguity. The 'mechanistic', materialist and financial perspective on the economy tends to dominate in today's climate, benefiting from the propulsive power of the United States. The importance of the European tradition of ethics and political philosophy (which goes back to Aristotle) has weakened along with modern evolution (Amartya, 1991). Europe thus feels the need to recapture a certain lost direction; but, nonetheless, Europe is following the dominant model of making financial value the highest priority.

Along with money comes the implementation of technical standards and practices, such as accounting, management and so forth, that little by little are standardizing the global world. European companies are following the trail blazed in the larger global market and are developing operations in collaboration with industrial groups in the *rest of the world*. Mercantilism in the tradition of Colbert or Bismark (that is, capitalism *à la française* or following the German model) is being abandoned. European enterprises now need more than ever to adapt to change by developing new competencies, new areas of activity, new targeted specialization, and complementarities of information and knowledge networks. In reality, we are not only seeing linkages intended to facilitate short-term adaptation by playing on the flexibility provided by joining several enterprises (Tarondeau, 1999), but, more importantly, we now see anticipation and innovation initiatives within converging, competitive arenas. In the long run, the factors of performance and competitiveness lie with strategic proximity as well as industrial and technological complementarity – and the way these are organized by participating companies. Numerous are the linkages developed with the goal of producing new knowledge and organizational routines (thus acquiring new competencies) in an attempt to 'control' the future (Hamel and Prahalad, 1994).

The phenomenon of interfirm linkages, and more specifically their now commonplace nature, should be studied (and then interpreted) from at least two points of view: that of the concept's definition and that of its observation (or access to information). Interfirm linkages take a wide variety of forms of cooperation between firms, ranging from purely contractual agreements to the total integration of participating companies. Figure 8.1 shows the diversity of these links. The typology suggested by Yoshino and Rangan (1995) divides linkages into two primary categories: formal contractual agreements and those that involve an investment of capital, either in the collaborating firm or in a new jointly created firm. The analytical chart proposed identifies five types of linkages: the contractual agreement, the acquisition of a minority equity investment, a joint venture, acquisition and merger.

The *contractual agreement* is a flexible type of collaboration. The relationship can include one or several elements of the value chain. The *acquisition of a minority interest* in the capital of another player may accompany a collaborative initiative, but it may also be intended to plan for a future acquisition. The *joint venture* establishes strong links between the players and is subject to the control of its parent companies. *Acquisition*, which includes any acquisition of a controlling interest or of a 100 per cent stake in the equity of another company, is an irreversible maneuver. Following such an action, the acquiring company exercises control over the acquired entity. Finally, in the case of *merger*, two or more companies join their assets to form a single company.

Only capital investments over a set monetary value are required to register with governmental authorities. So the phenomenon of interfirm linkages is difficult to comprehend in its entirety, particularly since its growth in recent years. While official statistics only reflect a part of the real situation, the economic and specialized press provide us with a relatively complete overview of the operations which occur. Using this information, a few organizations have performed an exhaustive analysis of one or several publications (Braxton Associates *et al.*, 1995; Hergert and Morris, 1987; Ghemawat *et al.*, 1986). These surveys contribute to a better understanding of the cooperation agreements which exist, but they do not take into account merger-acquisition operations, nor do they include the most recent data. To fill this deficit of information, the CESAG (Center for Applied and Theoretical Research in Business Administration at Robert Schuman University, Strasbourg) has established a database of information relating European interfirm linkages. The period of observation extends from 1993 (corresponding to the realization of the single European Market) to 1998. Data has been obtained from an exhaustive review of the daily information bulletin *Europe* (edited by a private agency affiliated with the European Community) which carefully relates the strategic maneuvers of European

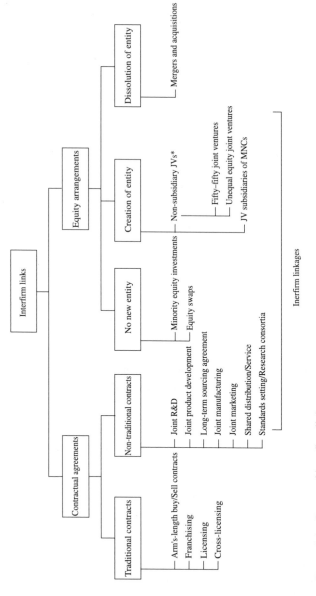

Figure 8.1 Range of interfirm links

Source: Adapted from Yoshino and Rangam (1995: 8).

Table 8.1   Contents of the CESAG database

YEAR OF THE ALLIANCE:	1993, 1994, 1995, 1996, 1997, 1998
NATIONALITY OF THE ACTORS:	Domestic alliances European Union Central and Eastern Europe North America Asia-Pacific Rest of the world
SECTOR OF ACTIVITY:	Nace 2 Code (Statistical nomenclature of the economic activities in the European Union)
LEGAL FORM OF THE ALLIANCE:	Contractual agreement Acquisition of minority interest Joint venture Acquisition-Merger

Source: CESAG, Strasbourg 1999.

companies. In all, 6996 linkages have been identified (across all sectors). The nature of the information gathered is presented in Table 8.1.

The *nationality* of the actors is defined by the location of the group's headquarters, since this is where the major decisions regarding a collaborative agreement are made. The *sector of activity* of the agreement is registered according to the statistical nomenclature of economic activities within the European Community ('Nace 2'). Finally, the *legal classification* of the agreement is surveyed according to the work of Yoshino and Rangan (1995).

To study linkage strategies put into place by European companies, we first consider their principal characteristics in section 1, and then explore the dynamics of the phenomenon in section 2.

SECTION 1   PRIMARY CHARACTERISTICS OF INTERFIRM LINKAGES

Interfirm linkages now constitute a global economic phenomenon, impacting everyone regardless of country of origin or economic sector. These linkages take place under a variety of legal configurations which correspond to stronger or weaker forms of integration and which reflect diverse strategic or operational approaches.

Geographic Layout: Going Global

Figure 8.2 presents the geographic repartition of linkages developed during the period 1993–98. It shows that European companies most often linked with European counterparts; in 36.5 per cent of the agreements, the partner is located in another European country. Domestic alliances, involving players from the same country, represent 13.8 per cent of the agreements signed. The interest expressed by European firms for linkages with partners in Central and Eastern Europe[1] is limited: only 5.6 per cent of the agreements involve a partner from one of these countries. On the other hand, linkages developed with North American companies are numerous and represent, in all, 23.6 per cent of the agreements. Companies in Asia-Pacific countries were involved in 10 per cent of the agreements, and 10.5 per cent of the agreements were signed with players from other countries.

The geographic distribution of the agreements reflects the fact that the European enterprises have to a large extent integrated the concept of economic globalization and European integration into their strategies for development. While the companies show a preference for alliances within Europe, they are also allying themselves with other poles of the Triad, demonstrating desire on the part of companies to diversify their portfolios of partners. The size of the North American and Asian markets probably explains the interest in European firms for developing linkages in these

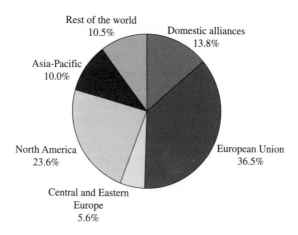

Figure 8.2   Geographic distribution of linkages developed by European enterprises, 1993–98 (*n* = 6613)

Source: CESAG, Strastbourg database.

geographic zones. The importance of the markets might explain why few agreements were signed in the countries of Central and Eastern Europe, despite the geographic and cultural proximity of these countries.

During the 1990s, the choice of alliances has appeared to be dictated by the trend towards globalization. While European companies have demonstrated a preference for linkages with their European homologues in order to offer mutual reinforcement, they are also seeking to build links with North American and Asian forms in order to ensure their international expansion.

Distribution among Sectors: Constant Reconfigurations

During the 1970s and 1980s, interfirm linkages essentially concerned the manufacturing sectors. The beginning of the 1990s marks the rapid development of alliances in the service industries (Braxton Associates, Horack Adler & Associates and Morris, 1995; KPMG Corporate Finance, 1999). Within the European Union, the implementation of the single market, leading to the free circulation of goods and capital, reinforced the level of competition within the tertiary sectors. In more traditional industries, globalization has triggered a real race for size. Finally, we should note the impact of deregulation of sectors such as telecommunications. Figure 8.3 shows the ten most active sectors in terms of interfirm linkages.

The distribution of sectors in interfirm linkages reveals a dominance in agreements in the traditional manufacturing sector and in the service sectors. The ten most active sectors represented below include, in all,

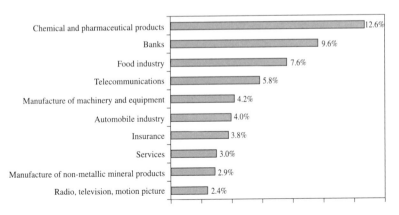

Figure 8.3   The ten most active sectors for interfirm linkages, 1993–98 (*n* = 3915)
Source: CESAG, Strasbourg database.

55.9 per cent of the agreements. The most active manufacturing sectors have a global reach and also contribute significantly to global commerce (Globus, 1999b). The chemical/pharmaceutical sectors are first, a phenomenon which can be explained by the importance of technological investment which calls for an effort to engage in complementary research and cost-sharing. In the area of services, the free circulation of services and capital as well as measures of deregulation have undeniably stimulated linkages. Linkages between banks and insurance companies can be interpreted as a response to the deregulation of financial activities within Europe, which has dramatically modified the competitive environment of the financial players (Mayrhofer and Roth, 1999).

The nomenclature used for the sectors of activity for this analysis ('Nace 2') is aggregated, but we mention the content of each sector using some examples:

- *Food industry*: this relatively homogeneous sector includes all of the industries related to human alimentation (meat, fish, produce, dairy, beverages, etc.) as well as activities related to animal alimentation.
- *Chemical-pharmaceutical*: basic and specialized chemical activities are regrouped with pharmaceutical and cosmetic industries. We also include in this sector activities relating to the fabrication of artificial and synthetic fibres.
- *Fabrication of mineral and metal products*: this sector is relatively vast because it combines all activities of production and transformation of mineral-based products (glass, ceramics, cement, plaster, stone, etc.).
- *Fabrication of machines and equipment*: this sector is doubtless the most heterogeneous. It includes in fact all activities relating to the production of machines and equipment for industry and agriculture as well as the fabrication of arms and munitions. The production of domestic appliances is also part of this sector.
- *Automobile industry*: this sector includes all activities on the chain of production of automobiles (for individuals and for transport) including both the primary builders and their parts suppliers.
- *Post and telecommunications*: the sector includes essentially all telecommunications activities (telephone, EDI, etc.).
- *Banks*: this sector includes all financial intermediation activities (monetary intermediation, leasing, credit supply, portfolio management, etc.).
- *Insurance*: here we find all insurance-related activities (life insurance, property and casualty, capitalization, retirement funds, etc.).
- *Services*: this category also includes a wide variety of activities which all relate to the concept of services provided primarily to companies

(legal, accounting, consulting, auditing and financial analysis, publicity, personnel recruiting and training, etc.).

Legal Classification: Risk-Management Strategies

Engagement and involvement on the part of the players varies according to the type of link. If *cooperation agreements* and *minority equity investments* represent only a tentative commitment, *merger-acquisitions* correspond to a more strongly determined affirmation. In the case of cooperative alliances, the engagement of the partners is not definitive and the length of the cooperation is often of a determined period; these links can be qualified as *weak* (or *transitory*) links. By contrast, the merger-acquisitions are irreversible maneuvers that imply a loss of independence for at least one of the players; these represent a *strong* link between companies. The *joint venture* falls in the middle. Figure 8.4 shows the distribution of linkages according to legal classification.

The commitment from European enterprises appears strong since the large majority of linkages involve an investment of capital (92.6 per cent). With 60.9 per cent, acquisition is the dominant legal form. Joint ventures represent 17.0 per cent of the agreements and acquisitions of minority interest 11.1 per cent. Only 7.5 per cent of the agreements are simply contractual formalities. Finally, it is important to point out the marginal nature

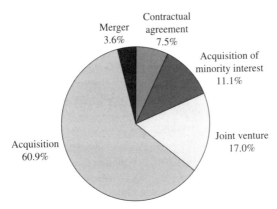

Figure 8.4   Legal forms of linkages undertaken by European enterprises, 1993–98 (*n* = 6861)

Source: CESAG, Strasbourg, database.

of mergers (3.6 per cent). The predominance of acquisitions shows the structural effect of the linkages: this type of arrangement leads to a substantial reduction in the number of actors. As Urban and Vendemini (1992) point out, *the opening of the borders in Europe leads to more competition, but with fewer competitors.*

It is interesting to note that the legal classification of linkage varies according to the sector of activity, and more precisely with the degree of maturity and the contextual environment (institutions, privatization, extent to which markets are open, and so on). These distinctions are presented in further detail in Figure 8.5. Examining the evolutions from the perspective of activity sector confirms the predominance of *strong* linkages. But this assessment must be qualified when we look at the dynamics of the evolution of the legal forms of linkage. In fact, technological, commercial or regulatory constraints vary by activity sector and have evolved differently over the course of the last two decades. The variability of these constraints explains to a large extent the differing evolution of forms of engagement selected by the partner companies. But the diversity of conditions proper to each sector has had an impact on choice relating to strategic alliances.

The traditional manufacturing industries of the European economy are today global sectors with an important share of worldwide trade (food products, machines and equipment). In these mature sectors we see a reduction in the number of players, amplified as markets become more global. As growing competitive pressures having pushed prices down, the reduction of profit margins has led the companies to reduce their costs. This rationalization of expenses is often translated by a race for critical size to achieve economies of scale (basic chemical production, for example). At the same time, the explosion of costs relating to research and development favours complementary research efforts and cost-sharing; witness the relative importance of joint ventures in the automobile and pharmaceutical industries or in the sector of specialized chemical production. Figure 8.5 clearly shows the trends observed in these important European industries.

The realization of the single market in Europe and progressive deregulation in certain sectors (banking, insurance, telecommunications) have reinforced competition within the service industries in Europe leading to waves of restructuring. Increasing numbers of mergers-acquisitions in the banking and insurance sectors characterize the end of the exploratory period, leading the large European groups to set their sites more globally (cf. Figure 8.5).

Services provided to enterprises constitute a sector that is growing rapidly thanks to a better understanding of the advantages of outsourcing. The supply is made up of a large number of small, very specialized

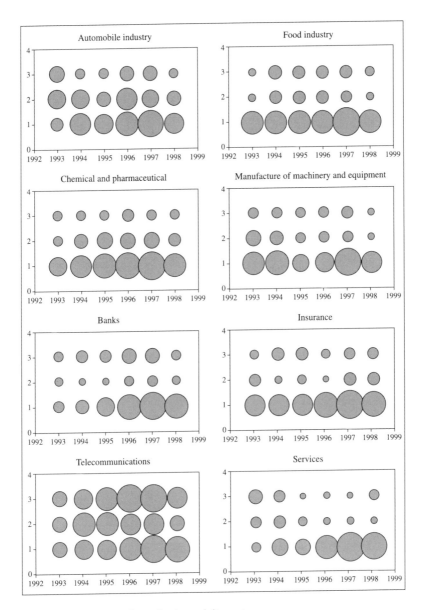

Figure 8.5   Legal configuration by activity sector

Source: CESAG, Strasbourg, database.

Note: The *Y*-axis represents the legal form of the linkage: 1 = *strong forms* (mergers–acquisitions), 2 = *joint venture*, 3 = *weak or transitory forms* (contractual agreement, acquisition of minority interest). The size of the circle is proportional to the number of alliances counted for the corresponding legal form of the linkage.

companies; and the creation of a larger portfolio of competencies supports merger-acquisition activities.

The telecommunications networks are less and less dominated by large national groups. The development of digital technology, price reduction and the growing need to communicate and exchange information are at the origin of very large growth in the sector. But this revolution is fairly recent. As users become more diverse and demanding, companies are pushed to diversify their portfolios of partners by multiplying the types of agreements they undertake: acquisitions (integration and enlargement of the supply), joint ventures (partnership with information enterprises) and contractual agreements (commercial partnerships, network enlargement).

These few examples are only a partial representation of the complexity and diversity of the economic realities that govern the choices in terms of type of interfirm linkages sought in the different sectors of activity. But the individual description of the specific situations is more than can be addressed within this chapter.

An entity's legal and financial control is also determined by ownership and distribution of social capital, and the data that follows concerns joint ventures from this viewpoint. We observe first of all that European companies hold a majority control of common capital in zones which are

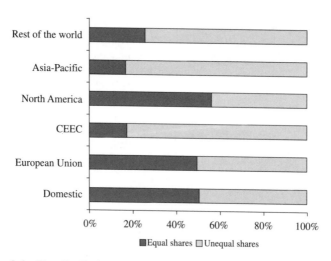

Figure 8.6   The distribution of capital in joint ventures by geographical zone (% of total), 1993–98 (*n* = 754)

Source: CESAG, Strasbourg database.

Note: CEEC stands for Central and Eastern European Countries.

high-risk or far-away (and therefore less well-known) or because of lack of local capital; on the other hand, in zones which are geographically or culturally close, a preoccupation for control of capital is less strong and is more balanced: cf. Figure 8.6.

Underlying Strategic and Operational Schemes: From Congeniality to Force

These schemes can be approached at different levels since each decision is influenced by two series of trends: on the one hand we have the *bottom-up* pressures, which take into consideration the preoccupations of the players at the base of an organization; on the other hand we have the *top-down* pressures, which express the desires of the organizational leaders or top management. These pressures exist whether the organizations are public (national or European agencies, for example) or private (companies, groups, and so forth).

Logical Foundations

On the macroeconomic level it is understandable that even in the case of a free economy, which stimulates and gives a sense of responsibility, the government authorities cannot be completely disinterested in entrepreneurial dynamics since they affect overall growth and employment. In fact, in modern history, governments have always paid attention to this factor, whether to stimulate a competitive international dynamic or to gain power or influence (Perroux, 1954, 1961, 1969, 1973, 1982; Urban, 1998), or to ensure a minimum level of self-sufficiency in strategic areas of defense or communications. Terms have been coined to illustrate these preoccupations: policies of 'national champion', alliances for aid (with Russia, for example), alliances for prospective development (such as China or Brazil), and so on. On a European level, 'Euro-strategies' have been implemented, imposed by broader competition or by a more sophisticated demand, or by the necessary diversification of managerial competencies (Urban and Vendemini, 1992; Jacquemin and Pench, 1997; Commissariat Général du Plan, 1997).

At the microeconomic level, four deep-reaching trends explain the importance of interfirm linkages during the last two decades:

- The dynamic of change in a global environment calling for rapid adaptation and an anticipation of new trends, and therefore internal restructuring;

- Competition in the area of know-how, obliging companies to join with their homologues to optimize areas of competence (technological, commercial, etc.) and resources, and/or to develop new joint competencies;
- The need to reduce research and development, production and marketing costs and to share the risks and costs linked to the development of new products; and
- The ambivalent balance between outsourcing certain functions in order to refocus activities on a core business and the development of new activities in order to maintain control over the entire production process.

Strategic Expression

In terms of strategic content, the underlying logic of interfirm linkages can be located along three axes (see Figure 8.7) – Activities, Technologies,

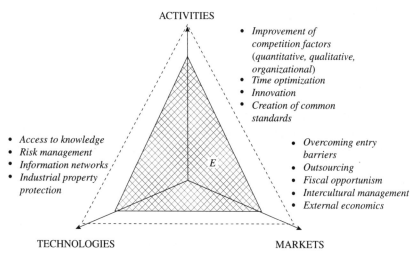

The development of an enterprise can be carried out via 3 principal lines of action: *A, M* and *T*. For example, enterprise *E*, uniquely with its resources, can cover a field of activities indicated by the shaded zone. In cooperation with other enterprises, the fields and rhythms of activities could be tended or re-enforced in a profitable manner (this extended zone being within the dotted lines) by playing on the potential advantages of the cooperation (various and non-exclusive strategic or operational variables listed by the bullet points).

Notes: - - - - -   Partnership advantages (systemic analysis)
Italics: Motivations for partnership decisions
△   Strategic field of the firm

Figure 8.7   Axes of a development policy coordinated among several actors

Markets – each of which support the creation of value, relative to their capacity for adaptation and the expectations of the individual firm (or group of firms). It is clear that every autonomous company or industrial group must combat each of the problems mentioned, but interfirm linkages allow for the acceleration or deepening of a solution (at least in principal – the application of agreements can, of course, lead to a variety of surprises).

SECTION 2   THE DYNAMICS OF LINKAGES: STRATEGY FOR ADAPTING OR ANTICIPATING?

In a context where environmental changes are accelerating and multiplying (Hafsi and Demers, 1997), the ability to adapt and anticipate will condition to a large extent how competitive a firm is. Adaptation refers to an organization's capacity to respond to change; anticipation relates to a prospective vision or to an ability to predict future needs and trends (Baumard, 1996; Hamel and Prahalad, 1994). What is the primary rationale of these linkages? Are companies developing alliances in order to adapt to new conditions in the environment or are they, on the contrary, anticipating future events?

The Evolution of Linkages, 1993–98

If during the 1980s, interfirm linkages saw a growing development, the beginning of the 1990s marked a relative stabilization, or even a decrease, in agreements (Braxton Associates *et al.*, 1995; Mertens-Santamaria, 1997). Figure 8.8 shows the evolution in the number of agreements undertaken by European companies between 1993 and 1998.

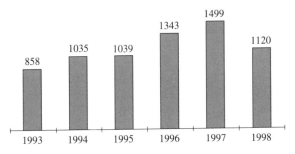

Figure 8.8   The evolution in number of interfirm linkages undertaken by European companies, 1993–98 (*n* = 6894)

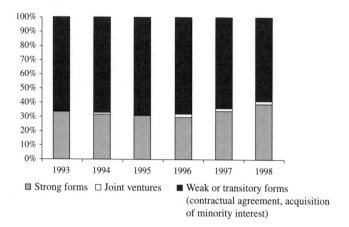

Figure 8.9   The evolution of agreements undertaken by European companies by form of integration in % of total per year, 1993–98 (*n* = 6613)
Source: CESAG, Strasbourg database.

The numbers presented reveal that interfirm linkages increased in popularity between 1993 and 1997 before decreasing in 1998. But, we need to note that the value of the operations has considerably increased. Between 1991 and 1997, the value of merger-acquisitions even quadrupled (Globus, 1999a). Similarly, cooperative forms of linkages have deepened (Urban and Mayrhofer, 1999) and cover an increasingly broad field in the value chain (research and development, production, distribution and so forth). Since 1996, the stronger forms of linkage have been developing clearly to the detriment of the weaker forms: cf. Figure 8.9.

Towards a Reconfiguration of Actors in Interfirm Linkages?

Table 8.2 and Figure 8.10 show the evolution and the geographic repartition of the alliances undertaken. The spatial dynamics of the linkages reveals a relative stability in the European-based alliances; Europe is really becoming a unified entity (Urban and Mayrhofer, 1999). Moreover, we see that Europe is becoming more global little by little. The progression of linkages with North American partners confirms the figures recently presented for foreign direct investments (FDI): the FDIs effected by European companies in North America have, in fact, seen a strong expansion in recent years (Les Notes Bleues de Bercy, No. 164, 1999).

Table 8.3 emphasizes the dynamics of interfirm linkages by sector. For each year of observation, the ten most active sectors are indicated. The

Table 8.2   Geographic dynamics of linkages undertaken by
European companies, 1993–98 (*n* = 6613)

Nationality of the partner	1993	1994	1995	1996	1997	1998
Domestic alliances	64	90	112	231	242	176
European Union	350	427	372	420	459	384
Central and Eastern Europe	67	64	60	70	62	50
North America	176	215	230	276	371	290
Asia-Pacific	84	106	117	151	126	75
Rest of the world	97	93	98	136	174	98
Total	838	995	989	1284	1434	1073

Source: CESAG, Strasbourg database.

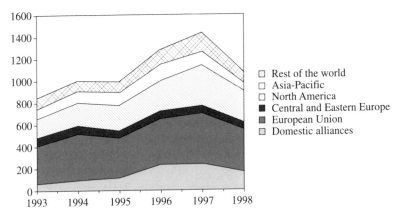

Figure 8.10   Geographic dynamics of linkages undertaken by European companies, 1993–98 (*n* = 6613)

table shows that while the five top sectors remain very active during the entire observation period, the repartition of sectors nonetheless fluctuates between 1993 and 1998. Thus, the weight of the agreements undertaken in the service industries tended to increase. This confirms the figures recently presented by the United Nations: in 1991, 41 per cent of the international merger-acquisitions were made in the tertiary sectors, yet these represent 59 per cent of the agreements in 1997 (Globus, 1999a). This trend seems to be accentuated since in 1998 two new tertiary sectors make the list – information technology and retail business.

Table 8.3   Dynamics by sector of linkages undertaken by European companies, 1993–98

Sector	1993	1994	1995	1996	1997	1998
Chemical and pharmaceutical products	x	x	x	x	x	x
Banks	x	x	x	x	x	x
Food industry	x	x	x	x	x	x
Telecommunications	x	x	x	x	x	x
Manufacture of machinery and equipment	x	x	x	x	x	x
Automobile industry	x	x	x	x	x	
Insurance	x	x	x	x	x	x
Services		x			x	x
Manufacture of non-metallic mineral products	x	x	x	x		
Manufacture of basic metals		x			x	
Electricity, gas and water supply				x	x	
Radio, television and motion picture	x			x		
Computer and related activities						x
Retail trade						x
Manufacture of railway, aircraft, spacecraft and ships	x					
Publishing, printing and reproduction of recorded media						x
Manufacture of pulp, paper and paper products			x			
Manufacture of electrical equipment			x			

In summary, observation of the evolution of geographic distribution and distribution by sector indicates a reconfiguration of the actors participating in interfirm linkages. The phenomenon extends now to a larger group of countries and sectors of activity. Furthermore, a recent study by the authors also indicates a growing participation of companies of more modest size (Urban and Mayrhofer, 1999).

Strategic Alliances and Value Migration

The creation of value is, ever more so, linked to know-how and to the integration of new technologies in the production of goods and services. This reality is seen in the growing contribution of intangible assets and of services in international trade as well as in FDIs. This observation is equally true for linkage operations.[2] It appears that interfirm linkages aim to provide a technological *push* in several cases:

- In sectors which have reached maturity and are in need of rejuvenating, as mentioned in the preceding paragraph;
- In sectors with intense capital needs and rapidly changing technology;
- In sectors seeing a particularly rapid globalization of their markets; and
- In developing sectors where the actors need to impose new joint norms on the market in order to gain authority.

Beyond technological mastery, know-how and a pertinent business design (Sliwotzky, 1996) are fundamental for an organization's expansion and profitability. So learning of every kind (intellectual, operational, relational – Urban, 1999) is a major objective (explicit or implicit) in interfirm linkages. And the ability to learn needs to be organized. The advantage of implementing flexible structures, a network rather than a centralized structure of the 'chateau' type, for example, is generally recommended (Butera, 1990; Barlett and Ghoshal, 1989; Baudry, 1995). From this point of view, the diversity of European managerial cultures can be seen both as a handicap and as an asset; but, with influential consulting and auditing firms working to homogenize standards internationally, this diversity is decreasing.

TOWARDS 'CO-OPETITION':[3] TRUST OR TREACHERY?

The term co-opetition calls up two antithetical concepts, that of competition and that of cooperation (or partnership, agreement). It is both war and peace, associated by a game theory, or precisely by the schematic representation of a 'value network'. The value network situates the 'players' in relation to one another and shows their interdependence. Etymologically, partners are parts of a set. In fact, we want to point out a paradoxical logic (Aliouat, 1996) in the development of enterprises, conceptualized by François Perroux in a premonitory fashion in 1960 with the original analysis of the bivalent relation between 'competition-cooperation', a persistent underlying economic factor. The principle itself of co-opetition is based on the idea that a common action, associating several players, allows for the creation of added value, profitability, time savings, productive and organizational flexibility, international influence, negotiating power and so on, which are stronger than that which could be gained from a solitary action. This generalized theory is not, however, evident in practice; in order to be led in a judicious manner, a collaboration calls for clear procedures, a common system and trust among partners. Without these explicit guidelines, an adequate legal structure and trust, the sharing of resources, power and influence will in the end be illusive and value-destructive. The traps and possible sources of conflict are numerous (Urban and Vendemini, 1992):

- Interfirm linkages may ruin the entrepreneurial and innovative dynamics of previous companies through poor reorganization of human resources.
- The assets and know-how previously attained risk being diluted or dilapidated in a 'melting pot': eliminating the creation of value.
- Savings (in terms of cost reduction) and new synergy also increase costs relating to managing the complex organization: relations of cause and effect are blurred, there is a multiplication of relations between the different parts of the new system leading to loss of time and money.
- Complementarity of competence imagined at the outset is sometimes poorly evaluated or proves unstable, leading to a zero-sum game or even a loss of value.
- The reduced level of incertitude imagined *ex ante* proves illusive in the end in many cases: competition is simply displaced, with competitive battles taking place on a larger scale (more competition with fewer competitors) and in more extreme conditions. For example, we can cite the case of the American group Alcan, which proposed buying Reynolds (in August 1999) in order to remain first in the world in aluminum, this in response to a plan for merger between Alcan (Canada), Péchiney (France) and Algroup (Switzerland).

Both academic literature and more confidential studies done by consulting firms evaluate the failure rate at about 50 per cent for interfirm linkages. But in each study, the samples are limited to a single sector, country, short time-frame or portfolio of clients. Despite this bias, the results are, nonetheless, severe. Given the investigative methods used (reports from participating companies, analysis of captive situations) the evaluation is approximative since failures are not likely to be revealed by the concerned actors. A larger field of investigation for future research would be that of the dynamic of agreements, or their evolution from the initial agreements. Until we have these systematic studies, we will have to be content with conjectures and suppositions. For now, the forward race of giants launched in a war among giants leaves the observer perplexed. The social sacrifices that figure into the cost of linkages are a subject for concern because they question the principle of social democracy which Europe has, up to now, embraced.

CONCLUSIONS

In conclusion, we need to ask the following fundamental question: are interfirm linkages a means for adding value, relevant for companies as well as for society as a whole (considered as a global organization)? From two different perspectives, the answer is far from evident.

On the individual level of companies, Collis and Montgomery (1998) (among others) present an analysis in a case published in the *Harvard Business Review* (May–June 1998) in which they propose a sort of golden triangle (see Figure 8.11). From this outline, we see that in order to be effective competitive advantages must be rigorously managed. It is precisely here that the partners (especially international partners) present many problems! Furthermore, it is not sure that the resources of a newly-constituted group are multiplied and not merely an addition of the initial resources of the individual players. The progressive integration of Eastern Europe into Western Europe cruelly illustrated this point during the 1990s (Gemünden and Ritter, 1998; Engelhard and Blei, 1998; Schliesser, 1998; Stewart, 1998).

On the societal level, the response is equally ambiguous (Ricciardelli, 1998). What is sure on the other hand is that European companies have seen a real frenzy in linkages: cooperation agreements, alliances, mergers, acquisitions and joint ventures are all in vogue.[4] Without a doubt, Europe is on the move, and not only on the defensive!

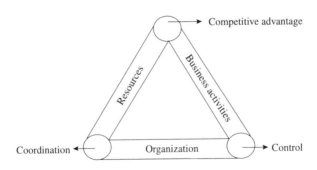

Figure 8.11   The triangle of corporate strategy
Source: Based on Collis and Montgomery (1998): 72.

Notes

1. Bulgaria, CEI, Hungary, Poland, Czech Republic, Romania, Slovakia, Ukraine, Slovenia, Uzbekistan, Turkey, Estonia, Croatia, Azerbaijan.
2. Beyond data from the CESAG database presented above, we refer to the works of the European Commission published in *Panorama de l'Industrie Communautaire*, particularly 1993: 101–8 and 1994: 23–36, Luxemburg, Eurostat, as well as to the annual reports of the DG IV on competition politics (the most recent report, no. 27, concerns the year 1997), Brussels, EU. See also references under Commission des Communautés Européennes.
3. The term is from Nalebuff and Brandenburger (1996).
4. Linkages among 'stars' in 1999 are in fact most common during the past year: infrastructures (Vivendi RWE, Vivendi-US Filter), production and distribution of energy (Alsthom-ABB, EDF-Louis Dreyfus, Scottish Power-Pacicorp), nuclear activities (Cogema-CEA-Siemens), arms manufacturing (GIAT Indus-tries-Vickers-Alcatel-Thomson CSF), oil, chemical and pharmaceutical activities (Hoeschst-Rhône Poulenc, Elf-Total-Fina, Air Liquide-BOC, Zeneca-Astra, Sanofi-Synthélabo), automotive (Ford-Volvo, Renault-Nissan, Volvo-Scania), aeronautics (Dasa-Casa, British Aerospace Marconi Electronic Systems, Aero-Spatiale-Matra), information technology and telecommunications (Vodafone-AirTouch, Olivetti-Telecom Italia, Alcatel-Xylan, GEC-Reltec, Deutsche Telekom-One Zone, Microsoft-Deutsche Telekom and Bertelsmann, Deutsche Telekom-France Telecom, Erricsonn Qualcomm, Siemens and Fujitsu), luxury industry (Pineau/Printemps/Redoute-Gucci), audiovisual (Vivendi-Pathé) and banking (Banco de Santander-Banco Central, San Paolo/IMI-Banca di Roma, Comit-Banca Intesa, BNP-Paribas, etc.).

References

Aliouat, B. (1996) *Les stratégies de coopération industrielle* (Paris: Economica).
Amartya, S. (1991) in *Ethique et économie* (Paris: PUF): 5–29.
Baumard, Ph. (1996) *Prospective à l'usage du manager* (Paris, Editions Litec).
Bartlett, C. A. and Ghoshal, S. (1989) *Managing Across Borders; The Transnational Solution* (Boston, Mass.: Harvard Business School Press).
Baudry, B. (1995) *L'économie des relations interentreprises* (Paris: La Découverte).
Braxton Associates, Horack Adler & Associates, and Morris, D. (1995) *A European Approach to Strategic Alliances*, vol. I, *Synthesis of Main Findings* (London: Internal document, sold by the consultants).
Butera, F. (1990) *Il castello e la rete. Impresa, organizzazioni e professioni nell'Europa degli anni'90* (Milan: Franco Angeli Libri).
Collis, D. and Montgomery, C. A. (1998), 'Creating Corporate Advantage', *Harvard Business Review* (May–June): 70–83.
Commission des Communautés Européennes (1993) *Panorama de l'Industrie Communautaire* (Luxembourg: Eurostat).
Commission des Communautés Européennes (1994) *Panorama de l'Industrie Communautaire* (Luxembourg: Eurostat).
Commission des Communautés Européennes (1997) *Rapports annuels de la DG IV sur la politique de la concurrence*, Report no. 27 (Brussels: European Union).

Commissariat Général du Plan (1997) *Europe: l'impératif de coopération et de conquête industrielle* (Paris: Economica).

Davis, S. and Meyer, C. (1998) *Blur* (Reading, Mass.: Addison-Wesley), translated into French under the title *Le paradigme du flou; vitesse, connectivité, immatérialité* (Paris: Edition Village Mondial).

Engelhard, J. and Blei, C. (1998) 'German–Hungarian Joint Ventures: Unstable from the Beginning?' in S. Urban (ed.), *From Alliance Practices to Alliance Capitalism* (Wiesbaden: Gabler): 131–66.

Gemünden, H. G. and Ritter, T. (1998) 'The Impact of Radical Environmental Change on a Company's Network Activities: An Empirical Study in East and West Germany', in S. Urban (ed.), *From Alliance Practices to Alliance Capitalism* (Wiesbaden: Gabler): 95–130.

Ghemawat, P., Porter, M. E. and Rawlinson, R. A. (1986) 'Patterns of International Coalition Activity', in M. E. Porter (ed.), *Competition in Global Industries* (Boston, Mass.: Harvard Business School Press): 345–65.

Globus (1999a) *Firmen-Hochzeiten International* (Hamburg: Globus Infografik): 18 January 1999.

Globus (1999b) *Waren des Welthandels* (Hamburg: Globus Infografik): 1 February 1999.

Hafsi, T. and Demers, C. (1997) *Comprendre et mesurer la capacité de changement dans les organisations* (Montréal: Les Editions Transcontinental).

Hamel, G. and Prahalad, C. K. (1994) *Competing for the Future. Breakthrough Strategies for Seizing Control of Your Industry and Creating the Markets of Tomorrow* (Boston, Mass.: Harvard Business School Press).

Hergert, M. and Morris, D. (1987) 'Trends in International Collaborative Agreements', *Columbia Journal of World Business*, vol. 22(2): 15–21.

Jacquemin, A. and Pench, L. R. (1997) *Pour une compétitivité européenne: Rapports du Groupe Consultatif sur la Compétitivité* (Brussels: De Boeck-Université).

KPMG Corporate Finance (1999) *Le marché des mergers et acquisitions transfrontalières en 1998* (Paris: Internal document, sold by the consultants).

Mayrhofer, U. and Roth, F. (1999) 'Modèles de développement et stratégies de rapprochement: une comparaison France–Allemagne dans le secteur financier', *Gestión Internacional*, vol. 3(2): 1–11.

Mertens-Santamaria, D. (1997) 'Entreprises européennes et mondialisation (1978–1996): Etat des lieux et stratégies', in *Notes et études documentaires*, no. 5051 (Paris, La Documentation Française).

Nalebuff, N. B. and Brandenburger, A. (1996) *Co-opetition* (Doubleday Dall Publishing Group).

Les Notes Bleues de Bercy (1999) *Les investissements directs étrangers*, no. 164, 1–15 August 1999. 8p.

Perroux, F. (1954) *L'Europe sans Rivages* (Paris: Presses Universitaires de France).

Perroux, F. (1961) *L'Economie du XXe Siècle* (Paris: Presses Universitaires de France).

Perroux, F. (1969) *'Indépendance' de la Nation* (Paris: Aubier-Montaigne).

Perroux, F. (1973) *Pouvoir et Économie* (Paris: Bordas).

Perroux, F. (1982) *Dialogue des Monopoles et des Nations: Equilibre ou Dynamique des Unités Actives* (Grenoble: Presses Universitaires de Grenoble).

Ricciardelli, M. (1998) 'Europe's Troubled Path towards an Employment Policy', in S. Urban (ed.), *From Alliance Practices to Alliance Capitalism* (Wiesbaden: Gabler): 301–32.

Schliesser, W. (1998) 'International Insurance Networks in Europe', in S. Urban (ed.), *From Alliance Practices to Alliance Capitalism* (Wiesbaden: Gabler): 167–200.

Sliwotzky, A. J. (1996) *Value Migration*; *How to Think Several Moves Ahead of the Competition* (Boston, Mass.: Harvard Business School Press).

Stewart, J. (1998) 'Financial Institutions, Networking and Industrial Development', in S. Urban (ed.), *From Alliance Practices to Alliance Capitalism* (Wiesbaden: Gabler): 201–24.

Tarondeau, J.-C. (1999) *La Flexibilité dans les Entreprises* (Paris: Presses Universitaires de France), 'Que sais-je?' edition.

Urban, S. (1998) 'Quelques réflexions sur la modernité de François Perroux au regard de la pensée stratégique', *Economies et Sociétés*, *Sciences de Gestion*, vol. 98(8–9): 119–26.

Urban, S. (1999) *Relations of Complex Organizational Systems*: *A Key to Global Competitivity – Problems, Strategies, Visions* (Wiesbaden: Gabler).

Urban, S. and Mayrhofer, U. (1999) *Les Stratégies de Rapprochement des Entreprises Françaises et Allemandes en Europe*: *Tendances et Perspectives* (Paris: Commissariat Général du Plan).

Urban, S. and Vendemini, S. (1992) *European Strategic Alliances*: *Co-operative Corporate Strategies in the New Europe* (Oxford: Blackwell Business).

Yoshino, M. Y. and Rangan, U. S. (1995) *Strategic Alliances*: *An Entrepreneurial Approach to Globalization* (Boston, Mass.: Harvard Business School Press).

Part VI
The Fate of the Offspring

9 The Endgame

Monir H. Tayeb

INTRODUCTION

Joint ventures, and indeed other forms of strategic alliances, have had a mixed record. The median lifespan for alliances is only about seven years, and nearly 80 per cent of joint ventures – one of the most common alliance structures – ultimately end in a sale by one of the partners (see for instance, Bleeke and Ernst, 1991, 1995). Many reasons such as strategic misfit, pre-occupation with short-termism, and incompatible organizational and human resource management policies have been offered by researchers as the causes of the relatively high failure rate of alliances. This chapter discusses major causes of such failures.

FAILURE AND SUCCESS – DEFINITIONS AND CRITERIA

International alliances, especially joint ventures, are in principle similar to single-parent, profit-oriented companies when it comes to definitions and criteria of their performance: making profits, increasing market share, beating competition and meeting other strategic and operational objectives. But the nature of the 'beast' is somewhat different and, as a result, what might be perceived as failure or success in a straightforward manner in single-parent firms might be a complex matter in IJVs.

Take the much debated issue of IJVs' termination for example. A single-parent company's termination signals its ultimate failure, but for some IJVs it may even be considered as success, that is if they were meant to be disbanded having successfully achieved their objectives set by the parents.

A judicious take-over of a company by another one in most cases is hailed as an exciting, shrewd move by a successful bidder, usually resulting in an overnight increase in the share prices of both companies involved. But a joint venture which is taken over by one of the partners and turned into a wholly-owned subsidiary may be considered as a failure in certain quarters, both academic and professional.

In many single-parent companies, instability, symbolized for instance by continuous reorganization, restructuring, changes of strategies, in proactive or passive response to the changes in the environment, are considered by all researchers (for instance the followers of the contingency theory originated in the late 1950s and early 1960s) as a sign of success and good management. But in the case of IJVs these internal 'upheavals' conjure up the spectre of failure as far as many, not all, researchers are concerned. While adapting to external environments is applauded by some researchers (for example Killing, 1983; Doz, 1996), Badaracco (1991) and Yan and Zeng (1999) positively view such instability as a healthy state of affairs in IJVs.

There are a number of research projects whose authors have measured the performance of IJVs in their various forms and shapes. In most studies, success has been defined and assessed in terms of financial profitability, but quite a few have used other, usually subjective, criteria. Beamish and Banks (1987), for example, measured success by managerial assessment of long-term viability of the partnership.

Lyles and Salk (1997: 333–4) question the wisdom of using objective criteria such as market share, profitability and return on investment, or other assessments of these by top management, and consider them problematic within the context of any organization, including IJVs. Echoing Geringer and Hébert (1989), Hill and Hellriegel (1994) and Parkhe (1993) the authors argue that 'it is difficult to make meaningful comparisons across IJVs that rule out differences in products, markets served and other factors'. As mentioned earlier, it is generally accepted that business performance includes measures such as business volume growth, achieving planned goals, making profits, achieving acceptable levels of employee productivity, lowering unit costs and lowering overhead costs. However, Lyles and Salk (1997) point out that firms 'do not always enter into IJVs exclusively or primarily for potential business performance of the JV as a stand-alone entity (Yan and Gray, 1994)'. And they go on to emphasize the relevance and appropriateness of another criterion for performance: 'the degree to which the IJV builds competencies by developing its workforce, accumulating management skills, and creating the organisational capabilities for strategy implementation'. 'Human resource performance', they further argue, is an important mechanism and measure of the adaptive or competency-building capabilities of the IJV organization (Brown and Duguid, 1991; Lyles, 1988; Szulanski, 1993).

In their own project, Lyles and Salk identified and analysed three distinct types of performance criteria (Hill and Hellriegel, 1994): economic and business criteria (Harrigan, 1986), accumulation of know-how and capabilities within the IJV (Kogut, 1988), and overall performance in relation to effort and expected outcomes (Geringer and Hébert, 1991).

Sarkar *et al.*'s (1997) study, conducted through personal in-depth semi-structured interviews with 12 construction experts from industry associations and firms, indicated that the performance of project ventures can be measured via three constructs which, according to the authors, intuitively also make sense in a managerial perspective:

> First, the project needs to be executed efficiently, and resources need to be utilized well. This leads in turn to positive outcomes from the project, where the firm feels that profitability has been high and the client feels happy about the services offered. This in turn leads to a perception that the collaboration has worked well, the firms have learned from each other, and that overall there have been strategic gains from the partnership.
>
> (Sarkar *et al.*, 1997: 278)

Hébert and Beamish (1997) elected to evaluate the performance and success of a sample of Canada-based IJVs through two perceptual measures of success: the satisfaction of the parent firms and the business performance of the IJVs:

> The former was selected because it is one of the most frequently used performance variables in the JV literature; it has been found to be an effective predictor of parent firms' future actions in partnerships and a necessary precursor to long-term performance (Beamish, 1984; Anderson and Weitz, 1989; Anderson and Narus, 1990). Satisfaction of the parent firms was assessed with respect to the IJV in general, its performance, and the relationship between the parent firms. The second variable, business performance of the IJV, can be defined as the extent to which an IJV has achieved the expectations the parent firm had of it when the IJV was formed (Geringer and Hébert, 1991). It was measured along ten performance dimensions, ranging from sales to product technology and overall performance.
>
> (1997: 4A)

FACTORS CONTRIBUTING TO SUCCESS OR FAILURE

As Tallman *et al.* pertinently observe,

> full understanding of IJVs is still far away. These are complex relationships, depending on interpersonal and intercultural understandings,

strategic harmony, resource fit, and economic success to survive and prosper.

(1997: 185)

But this of course has not prevented academics and practitioners alike from trying to understand IJVs, especially with regard to the causes of their success and failure.

The high level of international joint venture failure (Beamish, 1985) has naturally motivated many researchers to investigate the reasons behind these firms' success or failure. These factors are legion and could be grouped under three broad categories: the nature of the venture (multi-parented), external environment and internal organization and management.

The fact that IJVs and other forms of cross-border collaborative firms are owned and in most cases managed by two or more parents makes them inherently risky and doomed to failure, according to many researchers (Beamish and Inkpen, 1995). Killing (1982), for example, argues that the

problems in managing joint ventures stem from one cause: there is more than one parent. The owners, unlike the shareholders of a large, publicly owned corporation, are visible and powerful. They can – and will – disagree on just about anything.

(1982: 121)

In this connection, Porter (1990), noting that alliances involve significant costs in terms of coordination, reconciling goals with an independent entity and creating competitiveness, argues that these costs make many alliances transitional rather unstable arrangements and, therefore, alliances are rarely a sustainable means for creating competitive advantage.

There is evidence that IJVs are particularly more risky and prone to failure if they are located in less-developed countries, owing to the size of the gap in the developed-country partner's knowledge of local political, economic and cultural systems (Lee and Beamish, 1995). In this connection Tallman *et al.* (1997) argue that multinational firms look to joint ventures with local companies more in areas where they have the least knowledge of local conditions (Kogut and Singh, 1988), yet the vast differences in the partners in such situations make these ventures most difficult to manage.

The characteristics of both the parents' countries and especially the country in which IJVs are located could impact upon their performance, as indeed on single-parent firms, but the situation might just be that much more complicated and exaggerated in the case of IJVs. These characteristics, which are almost always out of the IJVs' and their parents' control, include changes in foreign country investment or ownership regulations, shifts in political regimes, labour rates, cost of capital, raw material and the like (Inkpen and Beamish, 1997).

Niederkofler (1991) argues that a major cause for cooperative failure is managerial behaviour. In nature, cooperation differs fundamentally from competition. Whereas competitive processes are well-understood and practised daily, the key success factors in cooperative processes are widely ignored. However, it is fair to say that internal organization and management of IJVs, including also their ownership patterns, have attracted and generated many studies and been investigated from various angles. Analysing international joint venture success in developing countries in relation to equity composition, Lecraw (1984), for instance, finds that low success occurs when ownership is equally divided between an MNC and its local partner.

Dymsza (1988) suggests that achievement of major goals, complementary contributions by partners, synergies of combined resources, and comprehensive joint venture agreements are key factors leading to success. Beamish and Delios (1997) note that congruency and specification of objectives at the outset have a positive influence on joint venture performance. Harrigan (1986) places the blame for IJVs failures squarely at the door of their managers and asserts that alliances fail because operating managers do not make them work, not because contracts are poorly written.

Harrington (1988), on the basis of his study, suggested that common areas of joint venture failures included:

- Partners would not get along.
- Market disappeared.
- Managers from disparate partners in the venture could not work together, what was thought to be good housekeeping by one partner did not prove to be as good as expected.
- Partners who were to contribute information or resources could not deliver through their personnel.
- Partners reneged on their promise.

Harrington's suggestion demonstrates that common management activities, business undertakings, programming goals and profits and common risks and opportunities require the attention of managers and other employees of the partner organizations, not only at the negotiation stage in the alliance partnership (Datta, 1988) but also throughout its lifespan.

As Faulkner (1995) puts it, long-term success, whilst obviously reliant upon the economic benefits, is also particularly strongly dependent upon the attitudes of the partners towards each other, how they manage the joint enterprise, and on the degree to which the partners adopt a positive learning philosophy thus enabling the alliance to evolve.

A series of seminal studies, spanning two decades from the early 1960s, investigated the relationship between a firm's strategy and performance in single-parent companies (see for example Chandler, 1962; Child, 1972; Rumelt, 1974; Caves, 1980). Later studies, conducted within the context of IJVs, found that the strategy–structure linkages led to successful performance, consistent with the paradigm developed by the above-mentioned pioneers. As Hébert and Beamish (1997) point out, IJVs

> can assume distinct strategic roles depending on their competitive environment, their parent firms' strategy and their competencies (Child, Yan and Lu, 1997). In addition, these roles have different organisational requirements (Bartlett and Ghoshal, 1986, 1989; Anand *et al.*, 1997). The performance of IJVs could thus be a function of the fit achieved between their strategic roles and the structure of their relationships with parent firms.
>
> (1997: 421)

A relevant issue regarding the management of IJVs is the way in which the parents might share out the management of their offspring. Killing (1982), for example, makes a distinction between dominant parent and shared-management IJVs and argues that the former tends to lead to a better performance and, ultimately, a higher rate of success. Whereas in shared-management ventures both parents manage the enterprise, the dominant parent IJVs are managed by one parent like wholly-owned subsidiaries. The dominant parent selects all the functional managers for the enterprise. According to Killing, certain industries, such as the land development and construction business, oil and gas exploration, tend to depend, successfully, on dominant parent joint ventures. Shared management ventures, although they can arise in any industry, are more common in manufacturing situations in which one parent is supplying technology and the other knowledge of the local market.

Killing goes on to say that, in his study, dominant ventures tended to outperform shared-management ventures – half of the shared-management ventures in the study had to be liquidated or reorganized, the others worked well. As Killing points out, the difference in failure rates between dominant parent ventures and shared-management ventures in his study is particularly striking, since 'shared management ventures are not consistently used for riskier business tasks, their higher failure rate is a strong indication that they are more difficult to operate than dominant parent ventures' (1982: 121).

Moreover, the deteriorating performance in a shared-management venture would appear to trigger off a vicious circle leading to the ultimate annihilation of the venture: It

> obliges each parent to become more involved in the details of the venture. This reduction in the manager's autonomy slows and confuses the decision-making process, and performance worsens. Such a small fluctuation thus triggers a series of events that can throw the system out of equilibrium, leading to the destruction of the venture.
>
> (1982: 122)

However, the relationship between control and performance appears to be inconclusive (Beamish, 1993). As Hébert and Beamish (1997) point out, not all subsequent studies support Killing's (1982) pioneering study and the results of the few available published reports reviewed by Geringer and Hébert (1989) and Hébert (1994) are most often contradictory. Hébert and Beamish's (1997) own work, discussed briefly earlier in this chapter, supports Blodgett's (1992) findings that fifty–fifty equity JVs typically exhibit higher performance. In addition, the authors' study showed that

> the relationships linking the dimensions of control sharing and autonomy with performance are less direct and more complex than expected ... Essentially, the sharing of operational and strategic control is positively related to the overall performance of IJVs. Strategic autonomy is also a significant factor of satisfaction and business performance, while technological autonomy is negatively related to both overall and business performance.
>
> (Hébert and Beamish, 1997: 419)

CULTURE AND PERFORMANCE

International joint ventures appear to be particularly susceptible to failure on management and other behavioural fronts because, arguably, of their higher potential for cultural misunderstandings. Chapters 5 and 6 discussed, respectively, the implications of organizational and national cultures for the management of human resources in merged companies and IJVs. Here the impact of these two sets of culture on the performance of IJVs are briefly discussed drawing on some available evidence.

Organizational culture, a company's ways of doing things, refers to basic assumptions and beliefs that are shared by members of an organization. These operate unconsciously and define, in a basic 'taken-for-granted' fashion, an organization's view of itself and its environment. These assumptions and views are based on shared experiences and have worked for a long enough time to have come to be taken for granted (Schein, 1985). As we saw in Chapter 5, organizational culture can cause problems where companies with distinctive cultures merge or form a third venture jointly. Employees from the parent firms tend to carry with them their home-company cultural baggage which may not be easy to shrug off, in the short term at least. This baggage, if not directly responsible for poor performance, or indeed high performance if complementary, can have implications for the day-to-day running of the venture, in the form of tension and frustration for example. The words of the president of one Canadian venture with functional managers from three companies provides an interesting illustration here:

> The differences in corporate background show up in a number of ways. In one division, I discovered I had insulted a senior manager by going directly to a subordinate to get some information. In his previous company, the hierarchy was very strictly observed, and if you wanted information you asked at the top and the request was relayed down until some one could answer. Then the answer came all the way back up. I'm used to an operation where you go directly to the man who can answer the question. Employees of another division are disgruntled with the bureaucracy they find here. They are used to a small entrepreneurial organization. What we regard as the facts of life, like the time taken to get an approval, they look at with surprise and dismay.
>
> (Killing, 1982: 124)

Johnson *et al.* (1997) draw attention to, among other things, trust as a cultural factor which has significant implications for the smooth running of international joint ventures and other cross-border collaborations. Cooperation works when the partnership 'generates the largest possible amount of mutual trust' (Buckley and Casson, 1988: 24). Studies such as those conducted by Madhok (1995), Badaracco (1991) and Wallace (1993) recognize trust to be a critical factor for a successful collaboration. Wallace, for example, found that trust is a necessary success factor in knowledge-driven alliances, and as trust develops partners start to rely more on each other. Trust has also been noted as one of the main constructs in alliance formation (Sheth and Parvatiyar, 1992) and as the biggest stumbling block to a successful alliance (Sherman, 1992).

Moreover, the creation (and perpetuation) of trust is one of the most important factors which permeates the whole life-cycle of collaborative partnerships, from partner selection and preparation (Geringer, 1988) to exchange (Blau, 1964) and formation (Madhok, 1995) and to the development of enduring strategic partnerships (Morgan and Hunt, 1994; Williamson, 1985). As Johnson *et al.* (1997) rightly point out, trust and trust-building are firmly rooted in the national culture of the partners involved and their cultural sensitivity to one another. The authors elaborate further:

> When a firm understands and bridges cultural differences in [international collaborative alliances], the ability to communicate effectively increases substantially. With effective communication, problems are solved, decision making is shared, and expectations are clarified. Good communication contributes to trust building and neutralizes the deleterious effects of conflict and misunderstandings. The firm's sensitivity to its partner's culture removes a significant barrier to communication and, therefore, to trust building.
>
> (1997: 231)

In this connection, Datta and Rasheed (1993) point out that a lack of cultural sensitivity can easily lead to misunderstandings in cross-border partnerships. This, in turn, could result in failure. Pucik (1988), for example, found the failure to break from culture-bound views of business had led to trouble in Japanese–Western alliances.

Most experts attribute the success of cooperative arrangements to how well the partners get along (see for example, Beamish, 1984; Cullen *et al.*, 1995). Killing's (1982) seminal study, referred to above, demonstrates how national cultural differences can interfere with this 'getting along' process:

> The board of directors of one American–British joint venture continually disagreed about the amount of data required before a decision could be made. The British could not understand why the Americans wanted all those numbers. The Americans, on the other hand, believed the British were flying blind.
>
> One very successful joint venture manager, who had taken his American venture from $4 million to $60 million in annual sales, had to decide where to locate a new plant. The manager and his American board members felt that the plant should not be put in the same European

country as the existing one since they would then both fall under the same union jurisdiction, thus risking simultaneous strike action. The European board members, however, wanted the plant built near one of the existing plants in order to absorb laid-off workers.

(1982: 121)

Killing further found that cross-border collaborations between partners from developed and developing countries are particularly troublesome. An American–Iranian venture in Killing's study had serious problems until a new general manager sent most of the Americans back home. They could not adapt to dealing with a workforce that had, on average, grade-three education. The Americans were replaced by Iranians who were first sent for short training periods in the US parent. Performance improved considerably.

As the author points out, such cultural differences can delay the creation of an effective, cohesive management team. The ability of managers to interpret one another's estimates – the forecasts of a sales manager, the delivery promises of a production manager, the cost estimates of an engineer – can develop more rapidly in a group that shares many basic assumptions, in which everyone is seen as working towards the same objective (Killing, 1982: 124).

References

Anand, J., Ainuddin, A. and Makino, S. (1997) 'An Empirical Analysis of Multinational Strategy and International Joint Venture Characteristics in Japanese MNCs', in P. W. Beamish and J. P. Killing (eds), *Cooperative Strategies: Asia Pacific Perspective* (San Francisco: New Lexington Press).

Anderson, E. and Weitz, B. (1989) 'Determinants of Continuity in Conventional Industrial Channel Dyads', *Marketing Science*, vol. 8(4): 310–23.

Anderson, J. C. and Narus, J. A. (1990) 'A Model of Distributor Firm and Manufacturing Firm Working Partnerships', *Journal of Marketing*, 54(January): 42–58.

Badaracco, J. L. (1991) *The Knowledge Link: How Firms Compete Through Strategic Alliances* (Boston, Mass.: Harvard Business School Press).

Bartlett, C. A. and Ghoshal, S. (1986) 'Tap your Subsidiary for Global Reach', *Harvard Business Review*, November–December: 87–94.

Bartlett, C. A. and Ghoshal, S. (1989) *Managing across Borders: The Transnational Solution* (Boston, Mass.: Harvard Business School Press).

Beamish, P. W. and Banks, J. C. (1987) 'Equity Joint Ventures in the People's Republic of China', *Journal of International Marketing*, vol. 1(2): 29–48.

Beamish, P. W. and Delios, A. (1997) 'Improving Joint Venture Performance through Congruent Measures of Success', in P. W. Beamish and J. P. Killing (eds) *Cooperative Strategies: European Perspective* (San Francisco: New Lexington Press).

Beamish, P. W. and Inkpen, A. C. (1995) 'Keeping International Joint Ventures Stable and Profitable', *Long Range Planning*, vol. 28(3): 26–36.

Beamish, P. W. (1984) 'Joint Venture Performance in Developing Countries', unpublished doctoral dissertation, University of Western Ontario, London, Canada.

Beamish, P. W. (1985) 'The Characteristics of Joint Ventures in Developed and Developing Countries', *Columbia Journal of World Business*, vol. 20(3): 13–19.

Beamish, P. W. (1993) 'The Characteristics of Joint Ventures in the People's Republic of China', *Journal of International Marketing*, vol. 1(2): 29–49.

Blau, P. M. (1964) *Exchange and Power in Social Life* (New York: Wiley).

Bleeke, J. and Ernst D. (1991) 'The Way to Win in Cross-Border Alliances', *Harvard Business Review*, November–December: 127–35.

Bleeke, J. and Ernst, D. (1995) 'Is Your Strategic Alliance Really a Sale?', *Harvard Business Review*, January–February: 97–105.

Blodgett, L. L. (1992) 'Factors in the Instability of International Joint Ventures: An Event History Analysis', *Strategic Management Journal*, vol. 13(6): 475–81.

Brown, J. S. and Duguid, P. (1991) 'Organizational Learning and Communities-of-Practice', *Organization Science*, vol. 21(1): 40–57.

Buckley, P. J. and Casson, M. (1988) 'The Concept of Cooperation', *Management International Review*, vol. 28: 19–38.

Caves, R. E. (1980) 'Industrial Organization, Corporate Strategy and Structure', *Journal of Economic Literature*, vol. 18: 64–92.

Chandler Jr., A. D. (1962) *Strategy and Structure* (Cambridge, Mass.: MIT Press).

Child, J. (1972) 'Organizational Structure, Environment and Performance: The Role of Strategic Choice', *Sociology*, vol. 6: 1–20.

Child, J., Yan, Y. and Lu, Y. (1997) 'Ownership and Control in Sino-Foreign Joint Ventures', in P. W. Beamish and J. P. Killing (eds), *Cooperative Strategies: Asia Pacific Perspective* (San Francisco: New Lexington Press).

Cullen, J. B., Johnson, J. L. and Sakano, T. (1995) 'Japanese and Local Partner Commitment to IJVs: Psychological Consequences of Outcomes and Investments in the IJV Relationship', *Journal of International Business Studies*, vol. 26(1): 91–116.

Datta, D. K. and Rasheed, A. M. A. (1993) 'Planning International Joint Ventures: The Role of Human Resource Management', in R. Culpan (ed.), *Multinational Strategic Alliances* (New York: International Business Press): 251–72.

Datta, D. K. (1988) 'International Joint Ventures: A Framework for Analysis', *Journal of General Management*, vol. 14(2): 78–91.

Doz, Y. L. (1996) 'The Evolution of Cooperation in Strategic Alliances: Initial Conditions or Learning Processes?', *Strategic Management Journal*, vol. 17 (Summer): 55–85.

Dymsza, W. A. (1988) 'Successes and Failures of Joint Ventures in Developing Countries: Lessons from Experience', in F. J. Contractor and P. Lorange (eds), *Cooperative Strategies in International Business* (San Francisco: New Lexington Press).

Faulkner, D. O. (1995) 'The Management of International Strategic Alliances', paper presented to the Annual Conference of AIB, Bradford (UK), April.

Geringer, J. M. and Hébert, L. (1989) 'Control and Performance of International Joint Ventures', *Journal of International Business Studies*, vol. 20: 235–54.

Geringer, J. M. and Hébert, L. (1991) 'Measuring Performance of International Joint Ventures', *Journal of International Business Studies*, vol. 22: 249–63.

Geringer, J. M. (1988) *Joint Venture Partner Selection: Strategies for Developed Countries* (Westport, Conn.: Quorum Books).

Harrigan, K. R. (1986) *Managing for Joint Venture Success* (Boston, Mass.: Lexington Books).

Harrington, W. (1988) 'Focused Joint Ventures in Transforming Economies', *Academy of Management Executive*, vol. 6: 67–75.

Hébert, L. (1994) 'Division of Control, Relationship Dynamics and Joint Venture Performance', unpublished doctoral dissertation, University of Western Ontario, London, Canada.

Hébert, L. and Beamish, P. W. (1997) 'The Characteristics of Canada-based International Joint Ventures', in P. W. Beamish and J. P. Killing (eds), *Cooperative Strategies: North American Perspective* (San Francisco: New Lexington Press): chapter 15.

Hill, R. C. and Hellriegel, D. (1994) 'Critical Contingencies in Joint Venture Management: Some Lessons from Managers', *Organization Science*, vol. 5(4): 594–607.

Inkpen, A. C. and Beamish, P. W. (1997) 'Knowledge, Bargaining Power and the Instability of International Joint Ventures', *Academy of Management Review*, vol. 22(1): 177–202.

Johnson, J. L., Cullen, J. B., Sakano, T. and Takenouchi, H. (1997) 'Setting the Stage for Trust and Strategic Integration in Japanese–US Cooperative Alliances', in P. W. Beamish and J. P. Killing (eds), *Cooperative Strategies: North American Perspective* (San Francisco: New Lexington Press): chapter 9.

Killing, J. P. (1982) 'How to Make a Global Joint Venture Work', *Harvard Business Review*, May–June: 120–7.

Killing, J. P. (1983) *Strategies for Joint Venture Success* (New York: Praeger).

Kogut, B. (1988) 'Joint Ventures: Theoretical and Empirical Perspectives', *Strategic Management Journal*, vol. 9: 319–32.

Kogut, B. and Singh, H. (1988) 'The Effect of National Culture on the Choice of Entry Mode', *Journal of International Business Studies*, vol. 49: 411–32.

Lecraw, D. J. (1984) 'Bargaining Power, Ownership, and Performance of Transnational Corporations in Developing Countries', *Journal of International Business Studies*, vol. 24(3): 637–54.

Lee, C. and Beamish, P. W. (1995) 'The Characteristics and Performance of Korean Joint Ventures in LDCs', *Journal of International Business Studies*, vol. 26(3): 637–54.

Lyles, M. A. (1988) 'Learning Among Joint Venture Sophisticated Firms', *Management International Review*, vol. 28: 85–98.

Lyles, M. A. and Salk, J. E. (1997) 'Knowledge Acquisition from Foreign Parents in International Joint Ventures: An Empirical Examination in the Hungarian Context', in P. W. Beamish and J. P. Killing (eds), *Cooperative Strategies: European Perspective* (San Francisco: New Lexington Press): chapter 13.

Madhok, A. (1995) 'Revisiting Multinational Firms' Tolerance for Joint Ventures: A Trust-based Approach', *Journal of International Business Studies*, vol. 26(1): 117–37.

Morgan, R. M. and Hunt, S. D. (1994) 'The Commitment–Trust Theory of Relationship Marketing', *Journal of Marketing*, vol. 58(July): 20–38.

Niederkofler, M. (1991) 'The Evolution of Strategic Alliances: Opportunities for Management Influence', *Journal of Business Venturing*, vol. 6: 237–57.

Parkhe, A. (1993) 'Strategic Alliance Structuring: A Game Theoretic and Transaction Cost Examination of Interfirm Cooperation', *Academy of Management Journal*, vol. 36(4): 794–829.

Porter, M. E. (1990) *The Competitive Advantage of Nations* (Basingstoke: Macmillan).

Pucik, V. (1988) 'Strategic Alliances with the Japanese: Implications for Human Resource Management', in F. J. Contractor and P. Lorange (eds), *Cooperative Strategies in International Business* (Lexington; Lexington Books): 487–98.

Rumelt, R. P. (1974) *Strategy, Structure and Economic Performance* (Boston, Mass.: Harvard Business School).

Sarkar, M., Cavusgil, S. T. and Evirgen, C. (1997) 'A Commitment–Trust Mediated Framework of International Collaborative Venture Performance', in P. W. Beamish and J. P. Killing (eds), *Cooperative Strategies: North American Perspective* (San Francisco: New Lexington Press): chapter 10.

Schein, E. H. (1985) *Organizational Culture and Leadership: A Dynamic View* (San Francisco: Jossey-Bass).

Sherman, S. (1992) 'Are Strategic Alliances Working?', *Fortune*, September: 77–8.

Sheth, J. N. and Parvatiyar, A. (1992) 'Towards a Theory of Business Alliance Formation', *Scandinavian International Business Review*, vol. 1(3): 71–87.

Szulanski, G. (1993) 'Intra-Firm Transfer of Best Practice, Appropriate Capabilities, and Organizational Barriers to Appropriation', in D. P. Moore (ed.), *Academy of Management Best Papers Proceedings, 1993*, 53rd annual meeting, Atlanta, Ga, 8–11 August.

Tallman, S., Sutcliffe, A. G. and Antonian, B. A. (1997) 'Strategic Organizational Issues in International Joint Ventures in Moscow', in P. W. Beamish and J. P. Killing (eds), *Cooperative Strategies: European Perspective* (San Francisco: New Lexington Press): chapter 8.

Wallace, A. (1993) 'American and Japanese Perspectives on the Determinants of Successful Joint Ventures', paper presented at the Annual Meeting of the Academy of International Business, Maui, Hawaii.

Williamson, O. E. (1985) *The Economic Institutions of Capitalism* (New York: Free Press).

Yan, A. and Gray, B. (1994) 'Bargaining Power, Management Control and Performance in United States-China Joint Ventures: A Comparative Case Study', *Academy of Management Journal*, vol. 37(6): 1478–517.

Yan, A. and Zeng, M. (1999) 'International Joint Venture Instability: A Critique of Previous Research, a Reconceptualization, and Directions for Future Research', *Journal of International Business Studies*, vol. 30(2): 397–414.

Index

acculturation   4–5, 103–5, 116–18, 121, 123, 124
  and acquisitions   107–8
  and discrepancies   120–1
  group   108, 121–3
  and Social Science Research Council   105–7
Ackerman, L.D.   57, 59
acquisitions   106–8, 179, 181, 187–8, 190, 194–5, 199
  see also acquisitions from cultural perspective
acquisitions from cultural perspective   108–23
  acculturation and discrepancies   120–1
  compatibility and discrepancies   118–20
  consumer wholesale   109–11
  group acculturation   116–18, 121–3
  manufacturing   113–14
  production   111–13
  service industry   114–16
activity sector   188, 192
adaptive state   117, 122, 123, 125, 136, 137
adjustment   117, 121, 123, 125
Adler, N.J.   58
age   55, 138
agents   134
agreements   135, 137, 190
  collaborative   159
  contractual   181, 190
  cooperation   179, 181, 187, 199
  global   10, 18–19
  joint venture   209
  licensing   140, 169
  oral   133, 137
  regional   10, 18–19
airlines industry   41
Akehurst, G.   32
Alcan   198
Algroup   198

Aliouat, B.   197
Allaire, Y.   101
alliances   157–63, 165, 166, 167, 168–72, 179, 199
  in biotechnology   172–3
  strategic   1, 9, 196–7
  and technology-based firms   163–8
Allio, R.   31
Altany, D.   133
Altendorf, D.M.   104
Amartya, S.   180
Anamartic Ltd   171–2
Anand, J.   210
Anderson, E.   62, 207
Anderson, J.C.   207
Ang, S.H.   133, 136, 137
Annis, R.C.   107
anthropology theories   103–5
Antoniou, P.   58
Appell, A.   60
Arab Free-Trade Area   19
arrogance   92
artefacts   109, 110, 112, 114, 115, 118, 119
Asahi, M.   72, 76
Asia   2, 142, 143, 185
  Southeast   13, 136
  see also Asia-Pacific
Asia-Pacific   184, 190, 195
assets   198
assimilation   104, 107, 116, 120, 122, 123, 124
  forced   118, 125
Association of South East Asian Nations   19
attitudes   92
Australia   105, 134
automobile industry   185, 186, 188, 189, 196
autonomy   67, 68, 123
  managerial   3–4
  strategic   67
Azjac, E.J.   57

Badaracco, J.L.   28, 206, 212
Baird, I.S.   59, 60
Baker, T.   34
banking sector   185, 186, 188, 189, 196
Banks, J.C.   206
Barney, J.B.   29
Barsoux, J.-L.   58
Bartlett, C.A.   197, 210
basic assumptions   120, 124, 138
Bass, B.M.   142
Bastien, D.T.   107
Baudry, B.   197
Baumard, Ph.   193
Beamish, P.W.   1, 2, 94, 206, 207,
    208, 209, 210, 211, 213
  on context of cross-border
      partnerships   10, 12–13, 14
  on equity international joint ventures
      58, 62
behavioural norms   92, 109, 110, 112,
    114, 115, 118, 119
benefits   162
Berg, S.V.   24
Berry, J.W.   103–4, 105, 106, 107,
    108, 116, 122
Bessant, J.   163
Biörkman, I.   132
biotechnology   160–1, 165, 172–3
Blau, P.M.   213
Bleackley, M.   25
Bleeke, J.   1, 23, 24, 57, 60, 205
Blei, C.   199
Blodgett, L.L.   211
board membership, joint   42
Bonvillian, G.   129
bottom-up pressures   191
Bourcier, C.   102
Bowditch, J.L.   107
brands   109, 111
Brazil   191
Brennan, K.   158
Brennan, R.   136
Bresman, H.   81, 82
Britain   2, 4, 55, 56, 91, 179, 213
  context of cross-border partnerships
      13, 16, 17, 18, 19
  interorganizational relationships and
      firm size   154, 155, 161, 167,
      171
  national culture   131, 134–5, 136,
      137, 138, 141, 142, 143, 144,
      145
  Silicon Fen   158
  Silicon Glen   158
British Telecom   171
Bronn, P.S.   25
Brown, J.S.   206
Bruton, G.   59
Buckley, P.J.   86, 212
Buono, A.F.   107
Bureau de Rapprochment des
    Enterprises   167
Burger, P.   142
business
  design   197
  performance   207
  plans   55
  policy implementation   57–8
  strategy development   56–7
  styles   170
Butera, F.   197
buy-outs   38

Canada   105, 207
capabilities   206
capital   190–1
  cost   209
  investment   181, 187
  market structures   136
  social   190
capitalism   12
Carr, C.   153
Carter, N.M.   61
Cartwright, S.   104, 107, 170
Casson, M.   86, 212
Caves, R.E.   210
Center for Applied and Theoretical
    Research in Business
    Administration   181, 183, 184
Central and Eastern Europe   16, 184,
    185, 190, 195, 199
centralization   143
Chance, N.A.   105
Chandler Jr, A.D.   56, 210
change   124, 191
chemical and pharmaceutical products
    sector   143, 172, 185, 186, 188,
    189, 196

Chief Executive Officers 55, 61, 67–8, 89
Child, J. 210
Chile 12
China 4, 41, 49, 191
    context of cross-border partnerships 11, 12, 13, 14, 16
    equity international joint ventures 55, 56, 58, 60
    learning in international joint ventures 73, 82, 88, 89–90, 95
    national culture 131–2, 137, 138
Chiron Corporation 174
Clark, T. 142–3
Clarke, C. 158
coal-mining 154
collaboration 73, 82, 93, 160, 163
Collis, D. 199
commercial constraints 188
commitment 95, 129
    long-term 133
committees 169
communication 41, 45, 89, 93, 113, 129–30, 140, 161, 213
    external 157
    internal 157
compatibility 48, 118–20, 170
competence 37–9, 44, 46, 72, 139, 159, 160, 206
    complementarity 198
competition 25, 26, 42, 81, 169, 188, 192, 198, 209
    global 166
competitive advantage 26, 72, 159
competitive approach 30, 31, 40, 208
    see also cooperation/competitive approach
competitive defence 39
competitive dynamics 41
complementary
    benefits 162
    contributions 209
    economy 160
    research 188
complexity 31, 42–3
computer sector 196
Conference Board 168
conflict 121, 170
congeniality 191

congruence 107
Conjunctive Relations 106
consultation 140
consumer wholesale 109–11
Contact Situation 105
contingency theory 206
Contractor, F.J. 1, 59
contractual agreements/formalities 187, 190
control 61–2, 170
Cooper, C.L. 104, 107, 170
Cooper, S.Y. 153–74
cooperation 181, 212
    agreements 179, 187, 199
cooperative
    approach 28, 30, 31, 36, 40, 41, 139
    /competitive approach 24–5, 26–8, 29, 36–7, 39, 43–8, 197–8
    failure 209
    linkages 194
coordination 140, 208
Cordery, J. 59
corporate culture 43, 124
cost/benefit 40
cost-sharing 188
costs 37, 208
creativity 74
cross-cultural issues 82–3
Crossan, M.M. 73, 75, 77, 78, 79–80, 81, 87, 88
Cullen, J.B. 213
cultural
    characteristics 17–18
    compatibility 43–4
    conflict 124–5
    distance 82
    divide 92
    effects 83
    identity 117
    processes 106
    systems 105, 208
    understanding 38
culture 5, 10, 31, 58, 76, 128–45, 170
    corporate 43, 124
    cross-cultural issues 82–3
    high-context 129, 130, 133
    host 119

culture – *continued*
  and human resource management
    138–45
  industrial relations   10
  levels   102–3
  low-context   129, 133–4
  national   124
  and negotiations   128–38
  organizational   45
  and performance   211–14
  political   10
  regional   124
  role   113
  shock   84
  see also acquisitions from cultural
    perspective; cultural
Cunningham, R.B.   134
Czech Republic   13, 73, 90

Dahl, T.   167
Datta, D.K.   141, 209, 213
Davis, R.B.   170
Davis, S.   179
de la Fé, P.G.   153
De Meyer, A.   170
Deal, T.E.   102
decision-making   137, 143, 169
deculturation   105, 116, 121, 122, 125
Delaney, E.J.   160
Delios, A.   209
Demers, C.   193
Denmark   137
dependent variables   61–2
deployment   84
  expatriate   83–5
deregulation   185, 186, 188
Dess, G.G.   62
Devlin, G.   25
DG23   167
Dinur, A.   83, 88
discrepancies   124, 125
DiStefano, J.J.   133
distribution among sectors:
  reconfiguration   185–7
Ditta, D.K.   72
Dobkin, J.A.   62
Dodgson, M.   153, 155
Dolwing, P.J.   142
domestic cooperation agreements   179

dominant parent   55, 60, 68
double-loop learning   78, 80
Dowling, M.J.   26
downsizing   154
Doz, Y.L.   22, 23, 87, 95, 206
Dubin, R.   134
Duguid, P.   206
Duysters, G.   164
Dyer, W.G.   102
Dymsza, W.A.   209
dynamism   155, 170
  environmental   36, 37

East India Company   13
economic
  advancement   10, 19–20
  and business criteria   206
  change   153–4
  institutions   3
education   138
Elashmawi, F.   130
electrical equipment sector   196
electricity, gas and water supply sector
  196
Electrolux   144
electronics sector   161, 163, 164
encounter phase   141
endgame   205–14
  culture and performance   211–14
  failure and success   205–7
Engelhard, J.   199
engineering sector   143
entry barriers   166
environment/environmental
  dynamism   36, 37
  external   208
  technological   46
  uncertainty   41
equity international joint ventures
  3–4, 55–69
  business policy implementation   57–8
  business strategy development   56–7
  dominant parent   60
  executive participation in parent
    company policy-making
    meetings   58–9
  future research   67–9
  human resource management
    practices, locally based   58

equity international joint ventures –
  continued
  independent, dependent and control
    variables   61–2
  questionnaires   61
  regression analyses   64–7
  resource dependence   59–60
  summary statistics   63–4
  test procedures   63
equity investment   40–1, 42
Ernst, D.   1, 23, 24, 57, 60, 205
ethnocide   105, 122
Europe   2, 5, 13, 22, 133, 137, 142,
    167, 181, 183
  see also Central and Eastern Europe;
    European; linkages: Europe
European Community   183
European Union   5, 18–19, 166–7,
    179, 185, 190, 195
Evans, P.C.   130
evolution   73
executive participation in parent
    company policy-making meetings
    58–9
expatriate deployment   83–5
experience   31, 45, 48
external environment   208

f-statistic   64
failure   205–7
  contributory factors   207–11
family difficulties   84
Fang, T.   137
Far East   22, 49
Faulkner, D.O.   140, 210
Ferner, A.   144
finance   157
financially focused drivers   35
Firsirotu, M.E.   101
Fisher, L.M.   172, 174
flexibility   155, 170
Florkowski, G.W.   15
food and drink sector   167, 185, 186,
    188, 189, 196
force   191
Ford, D.   136
foreign direct investment   10, 11, 12,
    14, 194, 197
former Soviet Union   14, 16, 138, 191

France   2, 13, 14, 16, 17, 135, 138,
    141–5, 179
Francis, J.N.P.   129
Freeman, J.H.   61
Friendship, Commerce and Navigation
    treaties   18
Frost, P.J.   102
Fujitsu   171–2
Fuller, M.B.   14, 23
functionalism   102

game theory   27, 28, 197
Garcia-Canal, E.   59
Garnsey, E.   171
Gates, S.   55, 59
Gemünden, H.G.   199
geographic layout   *see* location
Geringer, J.M.   62, 72, 206, 207, 211,
    213
Germany   15, 44, 90, 128, 135, 138,
    141–2, 167, 179
Ghamawat, P.   181
Ghoshal, S.   197, 210
Gil, M.J.A.   153
global agreements   10, 18–19
globalization   179
go-betweens   134
goals   41, 55, 208, 209
Gomes-Casseres, B.   11
Goodman, R.L.   32
government   191
  encouragement   166–7
  political economic ideology and
    policies   10–14
Graf, G.   57
Graham, J.L.   129
Grant, R.M.   24, 28, 29, 30, 37
Gray, B.   26, 27, 206
Gray, C.   154
Greenpeace   15
growth   111
Gugler, P.   1
guidelines   170
Gulbro, R.   129
Gutmann, B.   91–2
Gyndwali, D.R.   78, 88

Hafsi, T.   193
Hagen, S.   132

Håkansson, H. 136
Hall, E.T. 129, 134, 135
Hall, M.R. 129, 134
Hallén, L. 136
Hamel, G. 75, 77, 80, 158, 169, 180, 193
  on partner selection 22, 23, 24, 25, 28, 29, 30
Hamill, J. 57
Hannan, M.T. 61
Harrigan, K.R. 14, 26, 31, 57, 59, 169, 206, 209
Harris, P.R. 107
Hay, M. 27
Heath, P.S. 86
Hébert, L. 14, 62, 72, 96, 206, 207, 210, 211
Hedlund, G. 81
Hellriegel, D. 206
Hennart, J.F. 24, 28, 30
Herbig, P. 129
Hergert, D. 159
Hergert, M. 181
heterogeneity 29
hierarchies 169
Hill, R.C. 206
Hitachi 16
Hofstede, G. 143
Holden, N. 75
home country 9–10
Honda 153
Hong Kong 132
Hoon-Halbauer, S.K. 60
host country 10–20
  cultural characteristics 17–18
  economic advancement, level of 19–20
  global and regional agreements 18–19
  government political economic ideology and policies 10–14
  legal requirements 14–15
  pressure groups 15
  trade unions 15–17
Howell, W.S. 129, 130
Howlett, T. 133
Huber, G.P. 78
human resource management 5, 14, 17, 55, 67, 89, 128, 138–45, 211

company language 144–5
management style and organizational hierarchy 143–4
practices, locally based 58
restructuring 92
human resource performance 206
Hung, C.L. 133
Hungary 4, 13, 55, 56
Hunt, G. 57
Hunt, S.D. 86, 213
Hutt, M.D. 162

identity 82
imitability 29, 36–7, 46
in-groups 141
independent variables 61–2
India 9–10, 12, 16, 134, 138
individual level of companies 199
induction courses 111
industrial relations 142
information
  and communication technologies 179, 195
  exchange 4, 129
  flow 93
  sector 167
  technology 162
Inkpen, A.C. 58, 208, 209
  on learning in international joint ventures 73, 75, 76, 77, 78, 79–80, 81, 83, 87, 88, 94, 95
innovation 74, 155–6, 157, 164, 170
institutions 3, 10
insurance sector 41, 185, 186, 188, 189, 196
integration 104, 107, 116, 118, 123
  physical 108, 121, 122, 123, 124, 125
intellectual property 169, 171
interlinkages 48
internal organization 208, 209
international business theory 27
international joint ventures 2, 205, 206, 208, 209, 210, 211–12
  Canada 207
  context of cross-border partnerships 9, 10, 12, 13, 14, 15, 17, 20
  human resource management 128

international joint ventures – *continued*
  national culture 131, 140, 142
  see also equity; learning
International Labour Organization
  18
International Monetary Fund 13
Internet 166
interorganizational relationships and
    firm size 83, 153–74
  alliances 157–63, 168–72
  alliances in biotechnology 172–3
  economic change 153–4
  new technology 154–7
  technology-based firms and alliances
    163–8
intra-national cooperation agreements
  179
investment 164, 209
  equity 40–1, 42
  minority equity 181, 187
  see also foreign direct investment
Iran 13, 14, 17, 214
Israel 2, 4, 55, 56
Italy 141, 179

Jacquemin, A. 191
Jankowicz, A.D. 131
Japan 11–12, 13, 16, 18, 74, 83, 129,
    130, 135, 179, 213
Jarillo, J.C. 23
Jemison, D.B. 57
job satisfaction 155
Johanson, J. 75
Johnson, G. 153
Johnson, J.L. 212, 213
joint venture agreements 209
joint ventures 1, 3, 4, 11, 139, 143,
    145, 205
  interfirm linkages in Europe 181,
    187, 188, 190, 199
  see also equity international joint
    ventures; international joint
    ventures
Jones, P. 32
Jorde, T.M. 158
Joshi, M.P. 88

Keegan, W.J. 133
Kennedy, A.A. 102

Killing, J.P. 1, 2, 57, 60, 62, 206,
    208, 210–11, 212, 213–14
Kilmann, R.H. 102
Kitching, J. 111
know-how 196, 198, 206
  transfer 92, 169
knowledge 4, 40, 59, 72, 75, 88, 90,
    93, 94, 167
  development 73–4, 77–82
  emergent 74
  explicit 74, 78, 83, 93, 95
  operational 74
  stored 74
  tacit 74, 78, 79, 83, 93, 95, 169
  transfer 36
Kogut, B. 24, 26, 27, 28, 72, 77, 80,
    206, 208
Konieczny, S. 128
Koot, W.T.M. 60
Korbin, S.J. 11

labour rates 209
land development and construction
    business 210
Lane, H.W. 58, 133
language 130–2, 144–5, 169
large firms 154, 156, 157, 168, 169,
    170, 172, 173
Larsson, R. 59
lead users 163
leadership style 140
leapfrogging 39
Learned, E.P. 56
learning in international joint ventures
    72–96
  cases 89–92
  cross-cultural issues 82–3
  evolution of venture 86–7
  expatriate deployment 83–5
  internationalization 75
  learning and knowledge
    development 73–4, 77–82;
    group level 79; individual
    level 78–9; organizational
    level 79–82
  managers 92–4
  networks 87–9
  technology transfer 85–6
  trust 86

Lecraw, D.J. 11, 209
Lee, C. 208
legal classification 10, 14–15, 183
   risk-management strategies 187–91
Lei, D. 24, 25, 169
Lester, T. 144
Levinson, N.S. 72, 76
Li, J. 59
Li, K.-Q. 58
licence 10
licensing agreements 169
licensing-type cooperative agreements
   140
Lichtenberger, B. 135, 141, 142
life experience 138
life-cycle approach 73, 88
Likert scale 61
linkages 161
linkages: Europe 179–200
   competition/cooperation 197–8
   distribution among sectors:
      reconfiguration 185–7
   evolution (1993–8) 193–4
   geographic layout 184–5
   legal classification: risk-management
      strategies 187–91
   logical foundations 191–2
   reconfiguration 194–6
   strategic alliances and value
      migration 196–7
   strategic expression 192–3
   strategic and operational schemes
      191
Llaneza, A.V. 59
location 38, 161, 184–5
Lorange, P. 1, 24, 25, 59, 139, 140,
   160, 162
Louis, M.R. 107
loyalty 139
Lu, Y. 210
Lundberg, C.C. 102
Lyles, M.A. 4, 57, 59, 60, 80, 206
Lynch, R.P. 24, 25
Lyons, M.P. 25

McGee, J.E. 26
machinery and equipment sector 185,
   186, 188, 189, 196

Macquin, A. 131
macroeconomic level 191
Madhok, A. 212, 213
Mahoney, J.T. 24, 28
Malekzadeh, A.R. 104, 107, 108,
   116, 120, 123
management 92–4, 157, 208, 209
   culture 92
   style 76, 143–4
   see also human resource
      management; managerial
managerial
   autonomy 3–4
   behaviour 209
   styles 58
manpower 157
manufacturing sector 113–14, 185,
   186, 188, 210
marginality 105, 122
market 193
   economy, social 179
   expansion 166
   factors 167–8
   -focused drivers 34, 35
   motives 164
   presence 39
   size 39, 40
   see also marketing
marketing 111, 156, 163
   joint 42
Markusen, A. 158
Marschan-Piekkari, R. 144
Martin, J. 102
Mayrhofer, U. 179–200
mediators 134
meetings 41
Megginson, W.L. 26
melting pot assimiliation 104, 122,
   198
mergers 168, 179, 181, 187–8, 190,
   194–5, 199, 211
merging organizational cultures
   101–25
   acculturation: anthropology theories
      103–5
   acculturation and acquisitions
      107–8
   acculturation and Social Science
      Research Council 105–7

merging organizational cultures –
  continued
  acquisitions from cultural
    perspective 108–23
  culture levels 102–3
  views and paradigms 101–2
Mertens-Santamaria, D. 193
metaphors 102, 136, 137
Mexico 12
Meyer, C. 179
Meyer, H.-D. 128
microeconomic level 191
Middle East 16
mineral and metal products sector
  186, 196
minority equity investments 181, 187
Mirvis, P.H. 107
mobile groups 106
mobility 29, 35–6, 37, 46
Mohr, J. 24, 31
monochronic orientation 135
Montgomery, C.A. 199
Moran, R.T. 107
Morgan, G. 102
Morgan, R.M. 86, 213
Morris, D. 159, 181
motivation 140, 142
Mowery, D.C. 31
multiculturalism 104, 118, 122, 123
multimedia sector 167
multinational corporations 55, 57, 68,
  144, 145, 153, 208, 209

Nahavandi, A. 104, 107, 108, 116,
  120, 123
Namazie, P. 14, 143
Nanopoulos, P. 179–200
Narus, J.A. 207
Nath, R. 15
national culture 124
National Union of Mineworkers 16
National Union of Teachers 16
nationality 145, 183
nature of the venture 208
Naulleau, G. 135, 141, 142
negotiations 2, 10, 128–38
  adaptation to partner's negotiation
    style 136–8
  communication 129–30

language 130–2
relationships, building 132–4
time, attitudes to 134–6
Netherlands 141
networking 32, 38, 42, 46–7, 87–9,
  94, 161
Nevin, J.R. 24
new biotechnology firms 172
new product development 164
new technology-based firms 157,
  196
Newburry, W. 4, 55–69
Newson, L. 105
Niederkofler, M. 209
Nikko Securities 12
Nissan 16
non-metallic mineral products 185,
  196
Nonaka, I. 73, 74, 78, 83
North America 142, 184, 185, 190,
  194, 195
  see also Canada; United States
North American Free Trade Agreement
  19
Norway 89–90, 137
  Ministry of Foreign Affairs 167
Nowlin, W.A. 129
Nueno, R. 157, 158, 160, 168

Oakey, R.P. 155, 163, 164–5, 170,
  172
objectives 209
occupation 138
Ohmae, K. 166
oil and gas exploration sector 210
Oklie, R.L. 141
Olivetti 144
openness 48
operational schemes 191
operational structure 41
Opium War 13
oral agreements 133, 137
organizational
  culture 4–5, 84, 212
  design 140
  hierarchy 143–4
  motives 164
  restructuring 168
Ottati, G.D. 86

out-groups   141
outsourcing   188
ownership patterns   209
ownership regulations   209
Oxley, J.E.   31

p-value   64
Padilla, M.A.   103
Pan, Y.   82
Pandian, J.R.   24, 28
Parker, B.   57, 58, 62
Parkhe, A.   34, 72, 76, 78, 82, 206
partner independence   76
partner selection: motivation and
     objectives   2, 10, 22–49
  complexity   42–3
  cooperative/competitive dichotomy
     24–5
  cultural compatibility   43–4
  definition   23
  experience   45
  focus for study   32–3
  game theory   27
  imitability   36–7
  international business theory   27
  mobility   35–6
  research aims   25–6
  research method   33–4
  research questions   28–31
  resource-based view   28
  service-sector partnerships   34–5
  transaction-cost theory   27
  transparency   40–2
  uniqueness   37–9
  value   39–40
Parvatiyar, A.   213
patenting   169
Pavitt, K.   156, 163
Pearson correlations   63, 64, 66, 67
Péchiney   198
Pekar, P.   31
Pench, L.R.   191
Peng, M.W.   86, 88
Penhoet, E.   174
Penrose, E.T.   29
performance   206, 211–14
  appraisal   92, 142
permanence   40
permission regulations   11

Perroux, F.   191, 197
personnel
  exchange   41
  status   143
  transfers   83
Peteraf, M.A.   28, 29, 30
Peterson, R.B.   140
Pettigrew, A.M.   102
pharmaceutical sector   *see* chemical
     and pharmaceutical
pluralism   104, 118, 123
Poland   13, 131
political institutions   3
political regimes   209
Pollard, D.   72–96
polychronic orientation   135
Pondy, L.R.   102
Porter, M.E.   14, 23, 155, 160, 208
postal sector   186
Powell, W.W.   78, 88
power   170
  distance   143
Prahalad, C.K.   180, 193
pressure cooker assimilation   104,
     122
pressure groups   15
procedures   170
procurement   160
product development   163, 164
product-focused drivers   34, 35, 37,
     39
product/service packages   167
product/service range   40
production   111–13, 160
  and marketing costs   192
  and product technology   90
profit   111
  maximization   26
project teams   111
protectionist policies   12
publishing, printing and reproduction
     of recorded media   196
Pucik, V.   58, 213
Pugh, D.S.   142–3
pulp, paper and paper products   196

qualitative methods   108
quantitative methods   108
questionnaires   61

radio, television and motion picture
    sector   185, 196
Rafii, F.   61
railway, aircraft, spacecraft and ships
    sector   196
Rangan, U.S.   181, 183
Rasheed, A.M.A.   213
raw materials   209
reaction   117
reciprocity   137
reconfiguration   194–6
recruitment   142
refugees   106
Reger, R.K.   4, 57
regional agreements   10, 18–19
regional culture   124
regression analyses   64–7, 68
regulatory constraints   188
relationships   49, 117, 123
    building   132–4
    employee/management   114
    maintenance   161, 162
    see also interorganizational
        relationships
remuneration   140, 143, 144
reputation   36, 38
research and development   160, 161,
    164–5, 167, 171, 172, 188, 192
resource
    -based view   28
    dependence   55, 59–60
    pooling   164
    synergy   209
    transferability   28
responsiveness   155
restructuring   154, 188
retail business   195, 196
return loop   77
Reynolds   198
Ricciardelli, M.   199
rigidity   143, 169
Ring, P.S.   86, 87
risk   164, 166
    management strategies   187–91
Ritter, T.   199
Robinson, R.B.   62
role culture   113
Ronen, S.   129
Roos, J.   24, 25, 139, 160, 162

Rosensweig, P.M.   14
Roth, F.   186
Rothwell, R.   153, 155, 156, 160
Rousseau, D.M.   103, 109
Rouzies, D.   131
Rover   153
Ruber, G.L.   11
rules and regulations   3
Rumelt, R.P.   210
Ryans, J.K.   163

Salant, S.W.   60
sales   111, 163
Sales, A.L.   107
Salk, J.E.   206
Salk, S.   141
Sarayrah, Y.K.   134
Sarkar, M.   207
Sathe, V.   101, 102, 103
satisfaction   207
savings   198
scale economy   160
Schaan, J.L.   62
Schaap, A.   132
Schein, E.H.   73, 102, 103, 212
Schliesser, W.   199
Schneider, B.   102
Schneider, S.C.   58
Schoenberg, R.   142, 143, 145
Scholes, K.   153
Schumpeter, J.A.   155
scientific approaches   144
scientific instruments sector   164
Seat   153
sector of activity   183
sedentary groups   106
Segal-Horn, S.   32
segregation   105
selection   142
semiconductor sector   156
Senge, P.M.   73
separation   107, 116
services sector   3, 32–5, 46, 49,
    114–16, 185–6, 188–9, 195–6
Seyed-Mohammed, N.   136
Shaffer, G.   60
Shanklin, W.L.   163
share-ownership   11, 136
shared systems   42

shared management 210–11
Shenas, D.G. 136
Shenkar, O. 56, 58, 59
Sherman, S. 213
Sheth, J.N. 213
Shimada, J.Y. 140
Si, S. 59
Siehl, C. 102
Siemens 144, 171
silence, attitudes to 130
Silverman, B.S. 31
Simiar, F. 140
Sinclair Research 171
Singapore 88, 137
Singh, H. 208
Singh, J.V. 14
Singh, K. 72
Single Market 18–19, 185, 188
single-loop learning 78, 80
size 36, 38, 40, 44, 45, 46, 116, 185, 188
   market 39, 40
   see also interorganizational relationships and firm size
skills 4, 36–9, 44–6, 89, 90, 94, 164, 169
   technological 42
Skoda 91–2, 94
Sliwotzky, A.J. 197
Slocum, J.W. 24, 25, 169
small firms 153, 155, 159, 161–2, 164, 166–70, 172–4
Smirchich, L. 102
Snehota, I. 136
social
   capital 190
   difficulties 84
   market economy 179
Social Science Research Council 105–7, 108
socialism 12
societal level of companies 199
software sector 161, 163
Solberg, C.A. 134
Solidarity 16
Sommerlad, E. 105
Southeast Asia 13, 136
Speh, T.W. 162
Spekman, R. 24, 31

spin-out firms 157, 158
Stanworth, J. 154
steel-making 154
Stenton, G. 80
stereotypes 141, 142
Stewart, J. 199
Stiles, J. 22–49
Storey, D.J. 155
strategic
   alliances 1, 9, 196–7
   autonomy 67
   business plans 55
   business units 110
   choice/behaviour theory 26–8
   expression 192–3
   imperatives 76
   integration 83
   schemes 191
strategy and structure 210
structural autonomy 68
structure 113
sub-contracting 156
sub-cultures 119–20
success 205–7
   contributory factors 207–11
summary statistics 63–4
Sweden 137
Sweeny, G.P. 160, 161
Switzerland 167
synergy 198
systems 170
Szulanski, G. 206

Taiwan 132
take-overs 39
Takeuchi, H. 73, 74, 78, 83
Tallman, S. 14, 207, 208
Tan, J.J. 88
Tandem Computers 171–2
tandem management 92
Tarondeau, J.-C. 180
taxation 10
Tayeb, M.H. 1–5, 9–20, 82, 83, 128–45, 205–14
Teague, P. 19
technological
   assistance 42
   bleedthrough 169
   change 36

technological – *continued*
   constraints 188
   environment 46
   motives 164
   push 197
technology 45, 89, 154, 167, 171, 192
   development 38, 39
   new 154–7
   ring-fence 85, 91
   sharing 83
   transfer 46, 73, 75–6, 84–6, 89, 90–1, 93–4, 160
   see also technological; technology-based
technology-based firms and alliances 153, 163–8
   entry barriers 166
   global competition 166
   government encouragement 166–7
   market factors 167–8
   organizational restructuring 168
   research and development cycles 164–5
   technological change 164
   technological complexity 165–6
Teece, D.J. 158
telecommunications sector 41, 167, 185, 186, 188, 189, 190, 196
Teo, G. 133, 136, 137
tertiary sector 185, 195
test procedures 63
Thailand 73, 91
Thompson, A.G. 136
Thorsdottir, T. 101–25
Thory, K. 14, 145
Tidd, J. 163
time 37
   attitudes to 134–6
   horizons 76
   processing 137
timeframes 170
Ting-Toomey, S. 130
top-down pressures 191
Torrington, D. 75
Toshiba 88
Toyota 16
trade unions 15–17
traditions 92
training 41, 42, 140, 142

transaction-cost theory 27, 28
transparency 30, 40–2, 48
Transport & General Workers Union 16
Travelers Group 12
treachery 197–8
trust 41, 73, 79, 85, 86, 93, 95, 133, 197–8, 212–13
Tsang, E.W.K. 75, 82, 88
Tse, D.K. 82, 129
Tsogas, G. 18
Tung, R.L. 129, 130
Turnbull, P.W. 136

uncertainty 36, 164, 198
   avoidance 143
   environmental 41
unconscious basic assumptions 109, 110, 112, 114, 115, 118, 119
uniqueness 29–30, 37–9, 46
United Nations 195
United States 2, 4, 22, 36, 55–6, 179–80, 213–14
   context of cross-border partnerships 13, 16, 18
   national culture 128, 130, 131, 133, 134, 136, 138
   Route 128 158
   Silicon Valley 158
Urban, S. 179–200
Usunier, J.-C. 128, 133

Vahlne, J.E. 75
value 39–40, 46
   chain 160, 162, 181
   creation 26, 47
   migration 196–7
   network 197
   perceived 30
values 58, 109, 110, 112, 114, 115, 118, 119, 138
Van de Ven, A.H. 86, 87
Vendemini, S. 179, 188, 191, 198
Vickers, J. 26
Volkswagen 91–2, 153
von Hippel, E. 163

Wallace, A. 212
Weitz, B. 207

white knight acquisitions   106
Whitman, K.   58
Wilkinson, M.   171
Williamson, O.E.   24, 27, 213
Williamson, P.   27
withdrawal   105, 117–18, 122, 123
Woods, R.H.   101, 102
working conditions   114
World Bank   13
World Trade Organization   18
written agreement   133, 137

Xuan, G.-L.   57

Yan, A.   26, 27, 206
Yan, Y.   210
Yeheskel, O.   55–69
Yoshino, M.Y.   181, 183

Zegveld, W.   155
Zeira, Y.   4, 55–69
Zeng, M.   206
zero-sum game   198
Zucker, L.G.   87